ASTROLOGY FOR

ENLIGHTENMENT

ASTROLOGY FOR

ENLIGHTENMENT

MICHELLE KARÉN

M.A., D.F.Astrol.S.

ATRIA BOOKS

New York London Toronto Sydney

The information contained in this book is intended to be educational and not
for diagnosis, prescription, or treatment of any health disorder whatsoever.
This information should not replace consultation with a competent health-care
professional. The content of the book is intended to be used as an adjunct to
a rational and responsible health-care program prescribed by a health-care
practitioner. The author and publisher are in no way liable for any misuse
of the material.

ATRIA BOOKS

A Division of Simon & Schuster, Inc.
1230 Avenue of the Americas
New York, NY 10020

First Atria Books trade paperback edition November 2008

ATRIA BOOKS and colophon are trademarks of Simon & Schuster, Inc.

For information about special discounts for bulk purchases,
please contact Simon & Schuster Special Sales at
1-800-456-6798 or business@simonandschuster.com.

Designed by Jessica Shatan Heslin/Studio Shatan, Inc.

Manufactured in the United States of America

10 9 8 7 6 5 4 3 2 1

Library of Congress Cataloging-in-Publication Data

Karén, Michelle.
    Astrology for enlightenment / by Michelle Karén.—1st Atria Books trade
pbk. ed.
        p. cm.
    1. Astrology.   2. Self-actualization (Psychology)—Miscellanea.   I. Title.
BF1729.S38K37   2008
133.5—dc22   2008023807

ISBN-13: 978-1-4165-8085-0
ISBN-10:   1-4165-8085-9

To my Taurus father,

Lauri Erik Karén, 1923–2006,

who ignited my passion for astrology,

inspired my writing,

and, beyond the veil, encouraged the creation of this book . . .

To my Scorpio mother,

Solange Karén,

who believed in the power of education

and instilled in me the love of words . . .

And as the slight breeze came from the hills, stirring the leaves, the stillness, this extraordinary quality of silence was not disturbed. The house was between the hills and the sea, overlooking the sea. And as you watched the sea, so very still, you really became part of everything. You were everything. You were the light, and the beauty of love. Again, to say "you were a part of everything" is also wrong: the word "you" is not adequate, because you really weren't there. You didn't exist. There was only that stillness, the beauty, the extraordinary sense of love.

J. KRISHNAMURTI

Meditations

CONTENTS

Acknowledgments xiii

PART I: THE HOLISTIC SUN SIGNS

1. How to Use This Book 3

2. Understanding the Astrological Tools
   for Enlightenment 8

The History of the Astrological Tools for Enlightenment 9

*The Planetary Rulership of the Days of the Week
and the Hours of the Day 12*

Planetary Rulership of Each Sign 15

*Ideas for the Practical Use of the Astrological Tools
for Enlightenment 17*

3. Holistically Understanding the Zodiac 35

Aries 37

Taurus 46

Gemini 56

Cancer 66

Leo 77

Virgo 88

Libra 98

Scorpio 107

Sagittarius 120

Capricorn 130

Aquarius 143

Pisces 154

4. ENLIGHTENMENT USING THE ASTROLOGICAL TOOLS FOR
ENLIGHTENMENT OF THE OTHER SIGNS 166

PART II: STAIRWAY TO ENLIGHTENMENT
IN THE YEARS 2009–2012

5. WHY 2012? THE MAYAN CALENDAR MADE EASY AND THE
CONCRETE MEANING OF ASCENSION 193

6. THE PROPHECIES OF JOHN OF JERUSALEM (1042–1120) 207

7. 2009: DELINEATION OF THE CHART OF THE SIXTH DAY OF THE
MAYAN CALENDAR (NOVEMBER 13, 2008–NOVEMBER 7, 2009)
AND THE PLANETARY CONFIGURATIONS IN 2009 228

8. 2010: DELINEATION OF THE CHART OF THE SIXTH NIGHT OF
THE MAYAN CALENDAR (NOVEMBER 8, 2009–NOVEMBER 2, 2010)
AND THE PLANETARY CONFIGURATIONS IN 2010 237

9. 2011: DELINEATION OF THE CHART OF THE SEVENTH DAY OF
THE MAYAN CALENDAR (NOVEMBER 3, 2010–OCTOBER 28, 2011)
AND THE PLANETARY CONFIGURATIONS IN 2011 244

10. 2012: DELINEATION OF THE END OF THE MAYAN CALENDAR
(OCTOBER 29, 2011–DECEMBER 21, 2012) ASCENSION CHART
(DECEMBER 21, 2012) AND THE PLANETARY
CONFIGURATIONS IN 2012 252

11. THE MAYAN CALENDAR AND THE SIGNS 263

2009–2012 for Aries and/or Aries Rising 264

2009–2012 for Taurus and/or Taurus Rising 273

2009–2012 for Gemini and/or Gemini Rising 282

2009–2012 for Cancer and/or Cancer Rising 291

2009–2012 for Leo and/or Leo Rising 300

2009–2012 for Virgo and/or Virgo Rising 310

2009–2012 for Libra and/or Libra Rising 320

2009–2012 for Scorpio and/or Scorpio Rising 331

2009–2012 for Sagittarius and/or Sagittarius Rising 341

2009–2012 for Capricorn and/or Capricorn Rising 351

2009–2012 for Aquarius and/or Aquarius Rising 360

2009–2012 for Pisces and/or Pisces Rising 371

12. PRACTICAL STEPS TO ENLIGHTENMENT 381

Lexigrams: Ascension/Enlightenment/Master 381

Practical Checklist for Enlightenment 383

Around-the-House Checklist 393

The Survival Backpack 401

*Books, Music, Card Decks, and Web Sites
That Support Enlightenment 403*

About the Author 413

ACKNOWLEDGMENTS

A book is always a labor of love, inspiration, and magic, backed by hard yet joyful work. Many people in my life have contributed to the steps leading to the completion of this manuscript. Among many more, there are a few very special beings I particularly wish to mention here.

THE DYNAMIC ARIES:

• Genius astrologer, the late **Linda Goodman**, whose book *Sun Signs* made me realize my own vocation.

• Atria's senior editor **Johanna Castillo** for her warm understanding and her excitement over this project.

• **Jairo E. Gonzalez**, for sharing the adventure of life with me and reminding me that only love is real.

• **Isabelle von Fallois** and her husband, **Hubert Kölsch**, for reintroducing me in Hawaii to the magic of the Angels and Ho'oponopono.

THE STRONG TAURUSES WHO HAVE SEEN ME THROUGH THE FINISH LINE:

• The late **J. Krishnamurti**, whose book *Freedom from the Known* was the beginning of this whole journey.

• My friend and manager **Lee Helper**, without whose business know-how, vigilance, diligent work, and kind protection I wouldn't be where I am now.

• My literary representative **Hedda Moye**, who forced this book into being before I even knew I was writing one.

• **Carolyn Reidy** and **Peter Borland** at Simon & Schuster, whose enthusiasm fired my own.

• My friend **Jashar** and **Archangel Michael**, whom she channels, who warmly encouraged my work with transcendent insights.

THE CONSCIOUS GEMINIS:

• **Garin Gbedegbegnon**, my spiritual warrior friend who, lifetime after lifetime, has stood watch over me.

• **Karin Price Mueller** for her invaluable suggestions.

THE INTUITIVE CANCER:

• **Judith Curr** at Simon & Schuster, who believed in me the minute she met me.

THE SHINING LEOS:

• The late **Sydney Omarr**, with whom I shared many delightful evenings enthusiastically discussing our common passion.

• My very special cat, **Rafayel**, who meditated by my side every single minute of the creation of this book, in total devotion to my work, which is also his.

THE DETAILED VIRGO:

• **Dr. Todd Ovokaitys**, who for years has asked me to collaborate on his own unique work on Ascension.

THE BALANCED LIBRAS:

• **Master Keith Jones** and the whole crew at Marina Tae Kwon Do who, no matter how busy I became, saw to it that I kept progressing through my belts.

• **Gene Bua** and his talented Capricorn wife, **Toni**, for their kindness and creativity that have enhanced both my stage presence and my personal life.

THE POWERFUL SCORPIOS:

• **Jeff Levi**, who kept my computer in optimal running order and with an eagle eye made sure I backed up all my material!

• **James Thomas**, who made the technicalities sound so simple.

THE ENTHUSIASTIC SAGITTARIUSES:

• **Sira Beaumayne**, my friend, spiritual mentor, and deeply respected fellow astrologer who in my late teens, well before anyone even talked about it, introduced me to Ascension.

• **Dr. Don Trepany**, my chiropractor, for his daily adjustments, which boosted my energy and enhanced the clarity of my thoughts.

THE COMPASSIONATE PISCEAN:

• My friend **Marcela Cruz**, who literally harassed me with the Mayan calendar, convinced I would do something with it.

All my clients from all over the world and those who attended my conferences and seminars throughout the States and Europe, enriching this book with their special life stories, questions, and concerns.

To each one of you, a deeply felt thank-you.

My gratitude also goes to all the locations where this book was created: Würzburg, Germany; Helsinki, Finland; Santa Fe, New Mexico; Los Angeles, California; Phoenix and Flagstaff, Arizona; Kona, Hawaii.

May the joy, the love, and the peace of enlightenment transmute every single one of you who will hold this book. With blessings.

PART I

The Holistic

Sun Signs

1

HOW TO USE THIS BOOK

This book is not just another astrology book. Wonderful astrologer Linda Goodman, who inspired my own life's work, has already done a superb job of making astrology popular with her books *Sun Signs* and *Love Signs*. This, instead, is a book on enlightenment, a hands-on guide to using astrological tools. It is the result of over thirty years of study, thousands of readings for my clients all over the world, the observation of nature, and my own spiritual journey to enlightenment.

The *Webster's New Collegiate Dictionary* says to be enlightened is to be "free from ignorance and misinformation, based on the full comprehension of the problems involved." *Enlightenment* has within it the word *light*. Enlightenment comes when understanding and awareness dispel darkness and ignorance. As we realize that everything is connected, that what we do unto another we do unto ourselves, oneness is reached. It is a state of ultimate bliss, filled with tremendous peace, unconditional joy, and true love.

If you have thought of astrology as an entertainment column in your daily newspaper, you may wonder how it can possibly lead us to enlightenment. There are three ways:

1. Through a holistic redefinition of the planets and the signs.

The word *astrology* comes from *astro* and *logos,* literally meaning the "language of the stars." The earliest known astrological records were found in the city of Babylon in Mesopotamia in the Tigris-Euphrates Valley (present-day Iraq). They were dated back to 2000 BC. The Ancient Chaldean priests stared at the clear night skies and realized specific planetary configurations always paralleled the same world events. Their observations, backed by precise calculations, developed into the science and art known today as astrology.

Very concrete, down-to-earth, and grounded in physical reality, astrology was used to answer questions (horary astrology) or to forewarn of droughts, wars, and other calamities that would jeopardize people's security (mundane astrology). As society evolved in more complex ways, our minds took over. Psychology and the concept of dysfunctional behavior infiltrated this cosmic science. And when we started relying on mythology to explain astrological symbols, we completely lost our innocence. As we placed words between concrete reality and our experience of life, we forgot to observe nature and almost entirely stopped learning astrology firsthand.

My life changed forever when, in my early twenties, I discovered Krishnamurti's *Freedom from the Known.* To me, no other philosopher has mapped the road to enlightenment with such clarity and simplicity. Krishnamurti advocates liberation from the distortions of our memories and preconceived intellectual ideas. He reveals how our experience of "what is" could become continuously new and alive.

Astrological wisdom is based on tradition transmitted throughout the ages. But as with anything that's passed on through time, something can be lost in translation, as is the case with astrology. Over time, meanings were put together, blindly repeated, sometimes even distorted, and occasionally ended up contradicting themselves. Thus, their continuity doesn't always make logical sense. In the light of Krishnamurti's teachings, I asked myself if I could somehow clear astrology of everything that had obscured its magic and purity without having to read another book or memorizing another list.

After months of reflection, it became clear that the only way to truly learn astrology was to become as pure as the Chaldean priests who observed the seasons change, the leaves in the trees come and go, the Earth offer its harvest before returning to a barren state. I saw it was the eternal gems of nature's practical wisdom that could once again pave humanity's way to the next step of its unique and magnificent evolution.

2. Understanding John of Jerusalem's prophecy.

This very special evolution will not happen without a conscious effort from us all. John of Jerusalem, who lived over a thousand years ago, foresaw that before an incredible new world would emerge in the second millennium, a huge darkness would attempt to enslave humanity. Five hundred years before Nostradamus's *Centuries*, John of Jerusalem warned us of the great dangers already threatening our freedom.

He predicted with astounding clarity and accuracy everything that is now part of our daily existence: the discovery of America, AIDS, the creation of the European Union, the cataclysms that have recently devastated many parts of the world, the existence of a world shadow government, as well as the incredible advances of modern technology and so much more. This prophecy opens our eyes to what is surrounding us if we only care to look, making it obvious that the road to enlightenment is not an option, but an obligation.

3. Understanding how the Mayan calendar is confirmed by Western astrology.

The Mayan calendar comes to an end on December 21, 2012. That alone breeds many questions: Why 2012? What is the Mayan calendar? What is the meaning of its end? Does Western astrology confirm this? What exactly is going to happen? How can we concretely prepare?

Based on elaborate calculations, since 3114 BC—the beginning of the cycle we are still experiencing—the Mayan calendar has precisely mapped the evolution of consciousness. What makes it so important, and to some alarming, is that the calendar ends in just a few years: precisely on the winter solstice, December 21, 2012.

Those who fear the end of the calendar take it to mean the end of the world. I completely disagree with the doomsday scenarios. I feel that, far from being fearful, we should be excited. As one world ends, another one, a much more glorious and beautiful one, begins. What ends is a world based on fear. What starts is a world established on love, light, unlimited abundance, peace, and joy. We are already witnessing an incredible acceleration of evolution. To take one example, only a decade ago, the word *karma* would have meant little to people on the streets. Now it has become part of our common vocabulary, so much so that the popular television show *My Name Is Earl* is entirely based on the notion that what we sow, we reap.

All over the world, external structures are starting to crumble. The ways in which we perceive reality are changing. Our lives are being turned inside out. We are being thrust into the unknown. Although these transformations could initially feel scary, we need to look at the gifts they are bringing.

Real estate, for example, is going through a crisis, pushing many to relocate. Our economic situation is radically changing, forcing us to re-evaluate what money means to us. The divorce rate has increased alarmingly. As more and more people awaken to the lies and the lack of integrity, governments are changing all over the world. Women leaders are appearing in many countries, creating more balance by empowering the feminine.

Natural cataclysms are wiping thousands of people off the planet in a few hours. Take, for example, the May 2008 cyclone in Burma (Myanmar), where over 84,500 people died, over 53,000 are missing, and more than one million are homeless. That same month, China was devastated by an earthquake that killed nearly 70,000 people and injured more than 375,000, while 20,000 people went missing and over 4.8 million became homeless. But if we care to notice, these dramatic events are always occurring in troubled places (in Burma, ruled by the drug lords; in Thailand, a landmark for prostitution; in New Orleans, where the crime rate and the practice of black magic are very high). In this time of massive purification, we shall continue to witness the most extraordinary events ever to have occurred on planet Earth.

The only secure place in this changing world is within. Our only and ultimate security is the peace and the love achieved through enlightenment. During the next four years, not one, not two, but a mass of people will reach enlightenment. To some—or maybe to many—my predictions in this book may not make sense at first, but as we journey toward 2012 and our external reality shifts, mirroring the changes in our consciousness, I believe that everything will become absolutely clear.

Using This Book

As you read the pages that follow, away from the coldness of our computerized society, far from microwaved canned food and the fear-based consciousness we need to leave behind, I trust you will once again hear the wind blowing through the branches, smell the flowers along the way, and feel the breath of God helping us bloom into all that we already are.

2

Understanding the Astrological Tools

for Enlightenment

Ancient astrology books make a point of listing the flowers, plants, stones, metals, and other objects associated with each sign. I call them "astrological tools for enlightenment," or, more simply, "enlightenment tools." Like every student of astrology, I was familiar with those lists of enlightenment tools, but when I saw them in books, they always felt like an afterthought, something that was mentioned by obligation but might as well have been skipped. Such lists are completely omitted in most modern astrology books.

From one author to another, I'd find a lack of cohesiveness when reading about the tools. There are vast contradictions regarding which stone or plant is associated with which planet or sign. For that reason, I can understand why most authors today don't even bother with these lists and go straight into the psychological description of each sign.

But that leaves a void. The more I researched the astrological tools, the clearer it became to me that they held the ultimate keys to enlightenment. They are the means to reach bliss, pleasure, and harmony.

The History of the Astrological Tools for Enlightenment

As a young man, seventeenth-century self-taught German shoemaker Jakob Böhme had a vision that would change his life. He realized that all things on this Earth carry a specific signature. He believed the careful observation of any entity's physical characteristics gives clues to its healing properties. He shared his divine revelation in his book *De Signatura Rerum,* or *The Signature of All Things,* often referred to as the "doctrine of signatures."

Some examples:

• A sliced carrot resembles the iris of the eye, indicating that eating carrots would help improve vision. This is a fact confirmed by modern science.

• Grape clusters are reminiscent of the shape of the heart. It has since been discovered that grapes are indeed a heart-strengthening fruit.

• Walnuts look like the brain, suggesting that consuming walnuts would be good for that organ. It is now known that these nuts enhance thirty-six neuron transmitters for brain function.

The belief that we evolve in a universe where everything is in resonance with everything else is shared by many cultures. Whether among medieval alchemists, traditional herbalists, Native Americans, or Eastern cultures, we find the same understanding: affinity determines correspondences.

Astrology takes this further.

The zodiac is a division by twelve of the Earth's yearly revolution (its rotation from one point back to exactly the same point) around the Sun. Your birthday determines your Sun sign. For example, someone born June 8 has his Sun in Gemini. Each planet "rules" a specific sign, meaning that that planet "feels at home" in that sign. Think of it that each planet is an actor, or active energy, and each sign is the clothes the actor wears, or passive energy. For example, the planet Mars rules the first sign, Aries. The principles represented by Mars and Aries, such as courage, decisiveness, and leadership, are almost identical.

Beyond the planets and the signs they rule, astrology claims that everything—plants, animals, gemstones, locations, objects, and more—resonates to a specific planet and/or sign of the zodiac. Determining these associations or enlightenment tools is relatively simple.

For example, consider the following associations or tools of enlightenment and their relation to the zodiac:

- Cities, states, and countries: the date of signature of their independence or date of foundation. *Example: July 4, the United States of America's date of independence from England, indicates America is Cancer.*

- Celebrities: their date of birth. *Example: Muhammad Ali, born on January 17, is Capricorn.*

- Fictional characters: their character and specific particularities. *Example: In Gustave Flaubert's novel,* Madame Bovary, *who is a relationship-oriented, romantic, and beautiful woman, is Libra.*

- Plants, trees, spices, and foodstuffs: determined by the shape of their leaves, where they grow, their taste, their healing properties, flower color, their fragrances. *Example: Perfumed and sensual roses, the flowers of love, are associated with Venus, which rules both Taurus and Libra.*

- Gemstones: their colors, consistency, and healing properties. *Example: Milky white moonstone, which helps balance our moods, is associated with Cancer.*

- Animals: their characteristics, where they live, their habits. *Example: Small pets that need to be taken care of and are soft and comforting are associated with Virgo, the sign of service.*

- Metals: their appearance and uses. *Example: Gold, which is yellow, shiny, and expensive, is associated with royal Leo.*

• Colors: their vibration, their healing properties, how they make us feel. *Example: Red, the color of courage, blood, and war, is naturally associated with Mars and Aries.*

• Objects: their shape, their purpose, who uses them and where. *Example: Mirrors, which reflect, are popular items and were traditionally made of silver, therefore are in resonance with Cancer.*

• Locations: their appearance, how we feel in those places, and what we do in them. *Example: Kitchens, places of food and nurturing, are associated with Cancer. The immensity of the ocean, in which most things dissolve into oneness, is associated with Pisces.*

• Professions and archetypes (an archetype is a role or model that is shared by the unconscious of every individual; every other similar experience is the copy of that specific role or model; for example, "mother" is the archetype for every specific mother, whether it's our own mother, the mother superior of a convent, or the divine Mother): the objects they use, their contribution to society, the skills they require. *Example: Lovers are associated with relationship-oriented Libra, while gardeners are associated with Earth- and flower-loving Taurus.*

When the same flower, object, or archetype is found in more than one list, it simply means that it resonates to several different harmonies. For example, undertakers are associated with both Scorpio and Capricorn.

We could compare these lists (gemstones, animals, colors, and so on) to a dictionary. In this dictionary, every word is defined using other words, further refining our perception of what a particular concept means. We could also understand the meaning of these lists by likening them to what happens when we meet new people. At first we may be just attracted to their appearance and general disposition. As we get to know them better and learn their profession, their hobbies, their specific likes and dislikes, where they live, who their friends and family members are, and so on, a more precise image emerges.

The Planetary Rulership of the Days of the Week and the Hours of the Day

Each day and each hour of each day is also ruled by one of the seven planets visible to the naked eye. This means that each day is linked to a planet, which can influence what happens to you at any given time. (I'll explain the connections in greater detail later in this chapter in the section titled "Ideas for the Practical Use of the Astrological Tools for Enlightenment.")

• Monday is ruled by the Moon.

• Tuesday by Mars.

• Wednesday by Mercury.

• Thursday by Jupiter.

• Friday by Venus.

• Saturday by Saturn.

• Sunday by the Sun.

Then there are the planetary hours.

In the following diagram, the planets are ordered from the slowest revolution (Saturn) to the fastest (the Moon):

1. Saturn's revolution takes twenty-eight years. Saturn traditionally rules both Capricorn and Aquarius.

2. Jupiter's revolution takes twelve years. Jupiter traditionally rules both Sagittarius and Pisces.

3. Mars' revolution takes about two years. Mars traditionally rules both Aries and Scorpio.

4. The Sun's revolution takes about one year. The Sun rules Leo.

5. Venus' revolution takes about one year. Venus rules both Taurus and Libra.

6. Mercury's revolution takes about one year. Mercury rules both Gemini and Virgo.

7. The Moon's revolution occurs in twenty-eight days. The Moon rules Cancer.

In the diagram, you'll notice, the first hour (from midnight to one A.M.) each day starts with its own ruler (the Moon on Monday, Mars on Tuesday, Mercury on Wednesday, etc.). Each hour is also ruled by one of the seven planets, which will further influence what happens at any given time. For example, if today is Thursday, ruled by Jupiter, anything related to long-distance travel, religion, or philosophy would be favored. Between three and four P.M., the Mars hour, there would be additional positive influence on anything related to physical energy and drive, and anything having to do with desire or sexual energy, or even starting a new project. So you might choose Thursday in the Mars hour to start a training session, give a presentation in a university setting, or book an airline flight. If you wanted a pure Jupiter energy, you should choose the Jupiter hours (12–1 A.M./7–8 A.M./2–3 P.M./9–10 P.M.) on Thursday for anything related to long-distance travel, religion, philosophy, or higher education.

The great news is you only have to wait a few hours for the energy to shift, because each planet's energy will come into play four times a day. And you don't have to worry about time zones or daylight savings time. Whatever time is marked by your clock, anywhere in the world at any time of the year, is the time you use.

These lists of astrological tools help us reach enlightenment by bringing us in alignment with the universe. Each day, each hour, plant, color, location, object, and so on, is a portal, or entrance, into the energy of the specific planet and/or sign it is in resonance with.

Not everyone will feel the same connection to each of these lists.

	Monday	Tuesday	Wednesday	Thursday	Friday	Saturday	Sunday
0–1 A.M.	Moon	Mars	Mercury	Jupiter	Venus	Saturn	Sun
1–2 A.M.	Saturn	Sun	Moon	Mars	Mercury	Jupiter	Venus
2–3 A.M.	Jupiter	Venus	Saturn	Sun	Moon	Mars	Mercury
3–4 A.M.	Mars	Mercury	Jupiter	Venus	Saturn	Sun	Moon
4–5 A.M.	Sun	Moon	Mars	Mercury	Jupiter	Venus	Saturn
5–6 A.M.	Venus	Saturn	Sun	Moon	Mars	Mercury	Jupiter
6–7 A.M.	Mercury	Jupiter	Venus	Saturn	Sun	Moon	Mars
7–8 A.M.	Moon	Mars	Mercury	Jupiter	Venus	Saturn	Sun
8–9 A.M.	Saturn	Sun	Moon	Mars	Mercury	Jupiter	Venus
9–10 A.M.	Jupiter	Venus	Saturn	Sun	Moon	Mars	Mercury
10–11 A.M.	Mars	Mercury	Jupiter	Venus	Saturn	Sun	Moon
11–12 A.M.	Sun	Moon	Mars	Mercury	Jupiter	Venus	Saturn
12–1 P.M.	Venus	Saturn	Sun	Moon	Mars	Mercury	Jupiter
1–2 P.M.	Mercury	Jupiter	Venus	Saturn	Sun	Moon	Mars
2–3 P.M.	Moon	Mars	Mercury	Jupiter	Venus	Saturn	Sun
3–4 P.M.	Saturn	Sun	Moon	Mars	Mercury	Jupiter	Venus
4–5 P.M.	Jupiter	Venus	Saturn	Sun	Moon	Mars	Mercury
5–6 P.M.	Mars	Mercury	Jupiter	Venus	Saturn	Sun	Moon
6–7 P.M.	Sun	Moon	Mars	Mercury	Jupiter	Venus	Saturn
7–8 P.M.	Venus	Saturn	Sun	Moon	Mars	Mercury	Jupiter
8–9 P.M.	Mercury	Jupiter	Venus	Saturn	Sun	Moon	Mars
9–10 P.M.	Moon	Mars	Mercury	Jupiter	Venus	Saturn	Sun
10–11 P.M.	Saturn	Sun	Moon	Mars	Mercury	Jupiter	Venus
11–12 P.M.	Jupiter	Venus	Saturn	Sun	Moon	Mars	Mercury

Some of us may have a stronger affinity with plants and it is through the vegetal realm that we shall better understand a specific sign and the planet that rules it. For example, smelling or sipping some lemongrass tea, which is associated with Gemini, will help us understand the qualities of that sign.

Other people may feel more comfortable with certain objects or gemstones or colors, and still others may be particularly attracted to fictional characters. It really doesn't matter what you prefer. There is no rule. You will find your own path to enlightenment by playing with those lists, starting with the suggestions offered in the next few pages.

In Chapter 4, you will find further ideas on how to use not only the astrological tools for enlightenment for your own sign, but also for the other eleven signs.

Planetary Rulership of Each Sign

Each sign represents a specific, passive nature (remember the analogy of the clothes an actor wears). The planets are the active principles activating the signs' basic characteristics (again, remember the actor who wears the clothes). Based on our birth date, every planet can theoretically be found in any sign. Some planets—Pluto, Neptune, and Uranus—are so slow that they are generational planets. For example, every single person anywhere on the planet born between June 11, 1958, and October 4, 1971, has Pluto in Virgo, or anyone born between December 3, 1988, and January 11, 1996, has Uranus in Capricorn. Each planet feels most "at home" in one particular sign, meaning the essences of that sign and that planet blend easily. That planet and that sign share similar traits, and I go into specifics for each sign in Chapter 3. The signs are ruled as follows:

- Leo is ruled by the Sun.

- Cancer is ruled by the Moon.

- Gemini and Virgo are ruled by Mercury.

- Taurus and Libra are ruled by Venus.

- Aries (and traditionally Scorpio) are ruled by Mars.

- Sagittarius (and traditionally Pisces) are ruled by Jupiter.

- Capricorn (and traditionally Aquarius) are ruled by Saturn.

- Scorpio is ruled by Pluto.

- Aquarius is ruled by Uranus.

- Pisces is ruled by Neptune.

The following diagram explains the logic of traditional rulerships before the discovery of Uranus, Neptune, and Pluto (respectively in the eighteenth, nineteenth, and twentieth centuries).

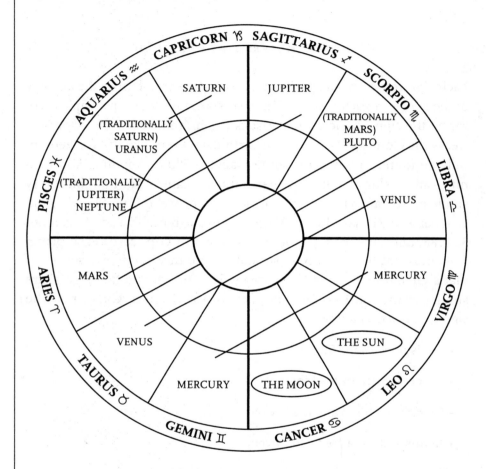

Everything in astrology is balanced and logical. The Sun and the Moon each rule only one sign, respectively Leo and Cancer. From there, we see that two signs are ruled by the same planet all the way to Aquarius and Capricorn, respectively the opposite signs of Leo and Cancer, which next to each other are both traditionally ruled by Saturn.

Ideas for the Practical Use of the Astrological Tools for Enlightenment

To reach enlightenment using the astrological tools for enlightenment, I offer some practical suggestions in the pages to come. You will enter a whole universe that will give deeper meaning to your life. You will also quickly realize that some of these ideas are already part of your daily activities.

In the next chapter, you will see what objects, colors, textures, and so on are associated with your sign. You'll be able to use these items in your daily life to enrich your world and move toward enlightenment. Following are some ideas for what you can do with the items associated with your sign.

What follows are only suggestions. Unleash your creativity. The possibilities are endless!

SYMBOL:

• Surround yourself with pictures or statues of that symbol.

• Study the habitat and customs of that animal (example: the ram for Aries), being (example: twins for Gemini), or object (example: the scales for Libra).

• Use that symbol on bedspreads, T-shirts, pendants, or coasters.

• Draw that symbol.

• Create jewelry using beads engraved with that symbol.

ELEMENT:

• Meditate on that element.

• Go in nature to a location where you can observe it, touch it, and feel it.

• For Fire, light candles or sit by a fireplace.

• For Earth, grow a plant or do pottery.

• For Air, feel the wind or imagine yourself in a plane, above the Earth.

• For Water, sit by the ocean, swim in a lake or pool, play with the water in your bathtub, acquire a water fountain, or listen to a CD with the sound of the waves in the background.

RULER:

• Surround yourself with photos of that planet.

• Study the planet's physical characteristics.

• Acquire a telescope and observe it.

• Draw the planet.

• Meditate on it.

• For the most recently discovered planets—Uranus in 1781, Neptune in 1846, and Pluto in 1930—use history books and study the changes that occurred in human consciousness (inventions, new ideas, discoveries, wars, revolutions) at the time of the planet's discovery.

AGES OF MAN:

• Study human beings at that stage of life.

• Gather pictures of people at that age.

• Spend time with beings at that age.

• Remember how you were or imagine how you will be, and write it in your diary.

NUMBER:

• Choose P.O. box numbers, street addresses, PIN numbers, telephone numbers, and other important numbers based on what you want to create:

0 (Pluto) for more power, sexuality, and passion.

1 (the Sun) for more independence and creativity.

2 (the Moon) for more intuition and sensitivity.

3 (Jupiter) for traveling, luck, philosophical or philanthropic endeavors.

4 (Uranus) for change, freedom, and rebellion.

5 (Mercury) for communication.

6 (Venus) for love.

7 (Neptune) for meditation, channeling, healing, music, art, and yoga.

8 (Saturn) for discipline, focus, and anything requiring hard work.

9 (Mars) for more energy and courage.

• Reduce the numbers that are attributed to you, such as Social Security, license plate, and passport numbers. Break them down into simple digits and see their deeper meaning. For example, a telephone number of 555-337-5672 would equal $5 + 5 + 5 + 3 + 3 + 7 + 5 + 6 + 7 + 2 = 48 = 4 + 8 = 12 = 1 + 2 = 3$, which is the number of Jupiter. This means that this particular phone number supports expansion, philosophy, and traveling.

• When meeting someone for the first time, add that person's age and yours at the time of the meeting, reduce to a simple digit, and see what planet dominates your meeting and why you came together. For example, if one person is 44 and the other is 46 at your first meeting: 4 + 4 + 4 + 6 = 18 = 1 + 8 = 9. This would be Mars, which means you came together to help develop each other's leadership abilities, courage, and personal initiative. This is likely to be a very dynamic relationship in which sexuality, if appropriate, will play an important part.

• When meeting someone for the first time, you can also add your day and month of birth with that person's day and month of birth. For example, if one was born on April 10 and the other on January 18 = 4 + 1 + 0 + 1 + 1 + 8 = 15 = 1 + 5 = 6. This is the number of Venus, so most likely this is a love relationship that will very possibly lead to marriage, peace, and harmony.

• To energize water, write a "9" (Mars) on the bottle, or to infuse it with more love, inscribe "6" (Venus).

• Wear a pendant engraved with the number associated with the planet that has the qualities you wish to emulate.

DAY OF THE WEEK:

• Schedule meetings that require feeling and imagination on Mondays (the Moon); energy on Tuesdays (Mars); communication on Wednesdays (Mercury); a broadening of horizons on Thursdays (Jupiter); romance, peace, or reconciliation on Fridays (Venus); discipline on Saturdays (Saturn); and creativity or play on Sundays (the Sun).

• Notice the day any event is scheduled to understand its deeper meaning.

• Start a project on a day of the week conducive to success.

• Note which day someone you haven't heard from in a while contacts you to understand his/her deeper motivation.

• Find out on which day of the week you were born to get a more precise sense of your personal purpose.

• See which day of the week you met someone significant to you to understand the more profound meaning of that relationship.

For examples on how to align with each day, refer to the following list regarding planetary hours.

PLANETARY HOURS:

• When someone calls you or e-mails you, note the time the message was sent and check what planet was dominant at that moment. It will give you an indication of the person's real intentions.

• When you first meet someone, note the planetary day and hour. They will give you a clue as to the meaning of the relationship that will develop between you.

• When acquiring a plant, object, gemstone, or pet, choose the planetary hour ruled by the planet associated with this plant, object, gemstone, or pet.

• When planting, choose the hour ruled by the planet associated with that plant.

• Choose the planetary hours most conducive to what you want to create in a meeting when setting the appointment time.

• When you're in a meeting that lasts more than one hour, the energy shifts. Note what new planet is ruling at that time.

• Some examples of successful planetary planning:

Matters related to glamour or success should be planned during a Sun hour or on Sunday.

Matters related to family and nurturing, requiring emotions and intuition, should be planned during a Moon hour or on Monday.

To enhance your physical stamina, repair your car, or ensure the success of endeavors requiring leadership abilities, choose a Mars hour or Tuesday. To increase the healing property of an herb ruled by Mars, ingest it during a Mars hour on any day or on Tuesday.

Literary matters or anything requiring clear, rational communication should be planned during a Mercury hour or on Wednesday.

For long-distance traveling or matters related to the law, philosophy, religion, or philanthropic matters, choose a Jupiter hour or Thursday.

To enhance a love relationship, have a romantic date, or to reconcile with someone, always choose a Venus hour or a Friday.

Plan any administrative work or labor requiring concentration, seriousness, discipline, or long hours during a Saturn hour or a Saturday.

METAL:

• Use cutlery or kitchenware in the metal associated with the planet whose qualities you want to develop. For example, decorate your kitchen with copper pans (Venus) if you want more love or to be more loving, or tin cups (Jupiter) to develop more adventurousness in your life.

• Choose jewelry, key rings, or belts made with that metal.

• Acquire a sculpture made of iron (Mars) to stimulate your courage.

• Collect copper coins (Venus) to develop a more loving disposition.

• Frame a favorite picture of yourself or someone you'd like to help with that specific quality. For example, use copper (Venus) for more love or silver (the Moon) for more receptivity and intuition.

SHAPES/TEXTURES:

• Choose the shape associated with the planet whose qualities you wish to integrate on scarves, belts, fabric patterns, mirrors, frames, furniture, art, jewelry, and more. (While all planets are spheres, you'll see the planet associated with your sign has certain shapes associated with it. For example, anything round is associated with Venus. Wearing round earrings will help you attract, feel, and express more love.)

• Draw the shape associated with the planet that has the qualities you wish to develop. For example, when you need more courage, draw the pikes or sharp angles of Mars.

FLAVORS:

• Taste the flavor associated with the planet whose qualities you wish to develop.

• Meditate on it.

• Choose it over any other flavor until you feel complete.

FOODS/HERBS/SPICES:

• To give yourself more courage before a meeting, for example, eat some of Mars' foods and herbs. For more inspiration, try the Moon's foods.

• Throughout the week, experience all the planets by creating a Jupiter meal with a table decorated with all of Jupiter's objects, colors, and music one day; the next, a Saturn feast; and so on.

• Study the healing properties of the foods, herbs, and spices associated with the planet that holds the qualities you want to develop more of in yourself.

• Whenever possible, smell the essence of that spice or place it on your pillow or in your chest of drawers.

• Make a potpourri of the herbs and spices associated with the planet whose qualities you wish to develop.

• Choose incense made of the herbs and spices associated with the planet that has the qualities you wish to develop within yourself.

TREES:

• Plant a tree associated with the planet that has qualities you want to enhance in yourself. For example, a birch tree, associated with Venus, will help you develop and attract love.

• Get photographs of that tree.

• Learn more about that tree by researching books.

• Walk in the countryside among that kind of tree.

• Get a piece of furniture or jewelry made out of the wood of that tree.

• Meditate while sitting at the foot of that tree with your back against its trunk.

PLANTS/FLOWERS:

• Look at a book on poppies (Neptune) to further develop a sense of sacredness, mysticism, and transcendent peace.

• Create a bouquet of roses (Venus) to infuse your space with love.

• Draw some tiger lilies (Mars) to develop courage and your leadership qualities.

• Wear honeysuckle (Mars) in your hair or pin it in a broach to enhance your physical stamina.

• Hang a picture of morning glories (Mercury) over your desk to enhance your communication skills.

• Place some lavender (Pisces) sachets between your sheets to enhance your dreams and come into oneness with all that is.

• Sprinkle the water of your bath with rose petals (Venus) to develop more love in your life.

• Use sunflower-decorated stationery (the Sun) or a sunflower as a business card logo to develop more self-confidence and creativity.

• Dry flowers and glue them on colored construction paper to create original cards with special messages. For example, use the flowers of Venus, love, for Valentine's Day.

GEMSTONES:

• Wear as jewelry (necklace, earrings, bracelet, broach, hairpin, ring, ankle locket, choker, pendant, or belt) the gemstone associated with the planet that has qualities you wish to develop.

• Carry it as a touchstone in your pocket, purse, or bra.

• Have it in your car.

• Place it in the face cream or body lotion you use daily.

• Place it in a bowl for decoration.

• Place it in the water of your bath to enhance its energy.

• Place it under your pillow before going to sleep at night.

• Place four gemstones with the qualities you wish to integrate around your bed or under the four corners of your mattress.

• Place that (or those) gemstone(s) in the bottle or pitcher of water from which you regularly drink.

MUSICAL NOTE:

• Play the note associated with the planet whose qualities you wish to develop on your piano or guitar.

• Sing that note.

• Listen to or dance to musical pieces in that key.

• Create harmonies around that note.

ANGEL:

• Pray to that angel.

• Have pictures of that angel.

• Create an altar for that angel.

• Draw that angel.

• Carry a little statue or card of it in your pocket or in your car.

• Name your pet with that angel's name.

OBJECTS:

• To develop, for example, more abundance in your life, place Jupiterian objects on your altar. (You can also use Jupiterian herbs, colors, animals, stones, incense, and angels.)

• Use the objects associated with the planet whose qualities you wish to develop. For example, use china to understand Venus better and your relation to love, or use a silver bowl filled with pure spring water (the Moon) to develop your intuition and sensitivity more deeply.

• Offer those objects as gifts to people you believe would benefit from developing the qualities associated with the planets to which the objects are associated.

• Create those objects. For example, in a pottery class, create vases (Venus) to attract more love.

• Collect objects associated with the planet whose qualities you wish to develop.

• Learn to play the instrument associated with the planet whose qualities you wish to develop. Listen to pieces played on that instrument and study its history.

LOCATIONS:

• Spend time in the places associated with the planet whose influence you want.

• Experience that landscape.

• Paint it.

• Go camping there.

• Meditate in those parts of your house. For example, if you wish to be more nurturing, meditate in the kitchen, which is associated with the Moon.

• Redecorate those rooms or areas.

COLORS:

• Choose cushions of the color associated with the planet whose qualities you wish to develop.

• Place a throw of that color on your sofa or bed.

• Acquire candles in that color.

• Get vases, bowls, plates, cutlery, and glasses of that color.

• Paint your walls or choose wallpaper of that color.

• Choose towels, sheets, a comforter cover, or carpets of that color.

• If possible, choose eye shadow or lipstick of that color.

• Buy shower gel, bath pearls, or soap of that color.

• Partake of foods or drinks of that color.

• Wear clothing of that color (scarves, hats, ribbons, belts, sweaters, dresses, shirts, blouses, pants, skirts, gloves, boots, and so on).

• Choose paintings predominantly of that color.

• Throw a colored piece of fabric or a sari of that color over a door.

• Create cards with construction paper of that color.

• Drink water out of a glass of that color.

• Visualize that color.

• Use lightbulbs of that color.

• Decorate your balcony with holiday lights of that color.

FRAGRANCES:

• Wear the perfume associated with the planet whose qualities you wish to develop.

• Place a few drops of that essential oil in your oil burner.

• Use body lotion, bubble bath, shampoo, or soap of that fragrance.

• Use that incense.

• Choose an air freshener, potpourri, or candles with that scent.

ANIMALS:

• If possible, adopt an animal associated with the planet or sign whose qualities you wish to develop.

• Hang posters of that animal.

• Study books on that animal.

• Take pictures of that animal.

• Whenever applicable, go on a safari or to the forest to get to know the animal in its natural habitat.

• Have a photo of that animal as a screen saver on your computer.

• Draw it.

• Acquire a little statue of it.

• Create an altar to it.

• Create stationery with its picture.

• Order checks with its image.

• Buy a stuffed-toy version of it.

• As an oracle, observe which animal you first encounter when you walk out your door in the morning. If you see, for example, a dove or a pigeon (Venus' birds), this is the message that you need to develop peace and compassion or that a new lover is soon going to enter your life.

PARTS OF THE BODY:

• Listen to the part of your body associated with the planet or sign whose influence you want and dialogue with it.

• Learn more about its function by consulting books on anatomy.

• Place the appropriate color on it. Red, the color of Mars, for example, can help heal your face, which is also associated with Mars.

• Each sign is associated with a part of the body. Whenever applicable, rub on it the essential oil associated with that sign. For example, Libra is associated with both rose and kidneys. Rub rose-scented oil on both sides of your lower back, near the kidney area.

ARCHETYPES:

• Read books on the archetype associated with the qualities of the sign you wish to develop in your life.

• Act it out.

• Write a story about it.

• Watch a film or read a novel on it.

• Explore that archetype within yourself and see how it personally relates to an aspect of your life.

• Wear that costume at Halloween.

PROFESSIONS:

• Each profession is associated with a specific sign. Choose the sign you wish to develop the qualities of and train in a profession related to it.

• Talk to or spend time with someone who is in that career.

• Read books on it. For example, if you wish to integrate the energy of Mars—courage—read about firemen.

• Watch a film in which the hero has that career. For example, choose secret agent James Bond if you wish to integrate the power and intensity of Scorpio.

HOBBIES:

• To become more communicative, try some of Gemini's hobbies, such as reading, playing tennis, writing in your diary, or just talking more on the phone.

• To develop more wisdom, try Capricorn's hobbies, such as serious research, a spiritual retreat in silence and solitude, or playing a musical instrument.

• If you wish to have more passion in your life, Scorpio's hobbies could be a good idea. Training in a martial art, bungee jumping, or reading metaphysical books will enhance a zest for life.

STATES/CITIES IN THE U.S.; COUNTRIES/CITIES AROUND THE WORLD:

• Take a trip to the location associated with the sign that has the qualities you wish to develop.

• Find a photo of that place to hang on your walls.

• Draw or paint that locality.

• Study that city/country's history and traditions.

• Learn that country's dance.

• Eat in a restaurant serving traditional food from that country.

• Wear clothes of that country.

• Acquire a doll dressed in that country's traditional costume.

• Befriend natives of that city/country.

• Move there!

CELEBRITIES:

• Read a biography of a celebrity associated with the sign whose influence you want.

• Explore that celebrity's creations. For example, choose the music of Beethoven to integrate the energy of Sagittarius, or examine the paintings of Van Gogh, an Aries, to increase your energy and courage.

• Hang that creator's art in a place where you often look.

• Acquire a reproduction of that artist's work.

- Watch the films of the actors and directors born in the signs you wish to develop the qualities of.

- Wear the clothes of the designers born in the signs you wish to develop the qualities of in your own life.

PEOPLE:

- Study the history and culture of the people associated with the sign that has the qualities you wish to develop.

- Make friends with someone of that culture.

- Attend cultural gatherings related to that people.

- Visit their country.

- Read books written by that people.

APOSTLES:

- Study the life and writings of the apostle associated with the sign that has qualities you wish to enhance in yourself.

- Get a picture or statue of him.

- Create an altar to him.

FICTIONAL CHARACTERS:

- Read the book in which he or she is the hero. For example, if you want to become more nurturing, focus on Linus in *Peanuts*, who is Cancer.

- Watch a movie with that character. For example, watching an animated film with Belgian character Tintin, who is Virgo, will help you to become more precise and detail-oriented.

• Study the character associated with the sign that has qualities you wish to develop.

• Have pictures or drawings of that character on your walls, on your cups, on your plates, as a key holder, on coasters, or as pendants.

• Wear the costume of your favorite hero for Halloween.

This is a book you will want to have handy at all times. As you meet a new person, as you plan a meeting, as you wonder what to expect in the months or years to come, and as you ponder how you can reach your full potential as a conscious human being, you will find concrete answers that you can apply immediately, bringing you joy and peace.

At the back of the book you'll find a page on which I've compiled some basic information that you might find helpful to carry around. I would recommend cutting along the dashed line so that you can always keep it on hand.

3

Holistically Understanding the Zodiac

In the pages to come, we shall redefine each sign of the zodiac holistically. *Holistic* means that each sign is explained through all its associations in every realm (plants, colors, animals, gemstones, etc.). Each plant, color, animal, gemstone, an so on, that corresponds to a given sign reflects it in its entirety, in a unique way. Every single word in the astrological dictionary related to one single energy is interchangeable.

For example, because Mars rules Aries, they are interchangeable. Thistle, one of Aries' plants, reveals something of its dynamic, aggressive basic nature. Peach and pink, the colors of Venus, give us further insight into the nature of Venus. The whole that each sign is becomes much more than the sum of its parts.

Far beyond the common abstract psychological descriptions of the signs, we start exploring a practical world of vastly alive, unlimited meaning. Once we realize, for example, that pink and white roses are associated with Venus, the planet of love and ruler of both Taurus and Libra, every time we enjoy the perfume of a rose we have the opportunity to learn a little more about Taurus and Libra. Tauruses like to take their time and smell the flowers along the way. Libras are aesthetes, attracted to the perfection of beauty. Beyond the character of Taurus and Libra, we also learn about the generosity and the magical perfume of love that fill us with a wonderful feeling of peace and happiness.

The more consciously we interact with every single aspect of our environment, our understanding of ourselves deepens, clearing the road to enlightenment in a playful manner.

An important note: If certain characteristics don't seem to match the personalities of people you know who were born under a particular sign, it may simply mean they have a stronger rising or Moon sign or many planets in another sign. For example, a very dear friend of mine was born under Aries. He certainly has the fire, impatience, courage, drive, and enthusiasm of his Sun sign—at least until you get to know him more personally. You then realize that under that strong veneer, he is shy, sensitive, spiritual, moody, devoted to his family, self-protective, intensely private, and loves cooking—none of which are typical Aries traits. His chart (the picture of the heavens when he was born) reveals that both his ascendant and his Moon are in psychic Cancer, the sign of family, nurturing, food, and the need for intimacy and security.

Remember also that if you were born prematurely, you most likely have more of the characteristics of the sign you should have been born in, rather than the ones of the sign you actually were born under. As we continue, you should check both signs to see how the enlightenment tools pertain to your life.

At one point, you may want to have a professional astrologer establish your personal chart based on your personal birth data: date (month, day, year), place (city, state, or country), and time, as precisely as possible. This will give you the blueprint of your life and it will enable you to understand yourself better. It will also help you plan your life more consciously.

I firmly believe that we have several possible futures. Contrary to a pure psychic reading, which develops the most probable future based on our past, an astrology reading, which is mathematically based, reveals the meaning behind experiences, giving precise timing for opportunities for growth. We always see the stars as influencing us. Let us not forget that this is a two-way street. We also influence the planets.

Note: In the sections to follow, the pronoun "he" is used throughout. This usage is gender-neutral and not intended to assign the male gender to any beings or items, except where specifically noted for planets and signs.

The beginning and end dates for each sign may vary from year to year. If you were born on any of these transition days, ask an astrologer to establish your chart based on your exact date, year, time, and place of birth in order to determine whether your Sun was in one sign or the next.

Aries

(MARCH 20–APRIL 20)

Symbol: The Ram

The ram is a beautiful, powerful, and proud animal with impressive curved horns. There is nothing subdued or dull about it. It covers much ground daily, thus improving the soil it gets its nourishment from. Males and females both fight against each other by violently knocking their foreheads, battling with those imposing horns. Once the frontal assault is over, they happily return to their grazing, side by side, as if nothing had happened. There is a constant alert curiosity in the ram. Moving forward dynamically, it misses nothing in its environment.

Element: Cardinal Fire

Cardinal fire is the initial spark of fire. It is pure, bright, and clear, giving light and warmth. This fire can start a huge blaze that can comfort us. But if left unattended, its giant burst of flames can destroy all that is familiar.

Ruler: Mars

The presence of rust in Mars' dust makes it look red. Its arid surface is covered with rocks, impressive canyons, and volcanoes—most of which are still active. It is frequently swept by violent winds, and there is very little water on Mars. Its polar caps are made of dry ice. Mars is about half the Earth's size, and its eccentric orbit creates unequal seasons. Despite having two Moons, Deimos (Terror) and Phobos (Fear), its moonlights are a very low-intensity. When in opposition to the Sun and seen from the Earth, Mars is one of the brightest features of the night sky.

Ages of Man
The newborn baby. Self-absorbed, he doesn't yet have consciousness of others. His needs should be attended to now!

Character
Aries bursts into this world as nature awakens in early spring. Birds chirp away in their hectic search for twigs to build their nests. The barren branches of winter disappear as they start bearing small buds. Young shoots emerge at the surface of the Earth, and bright yellow flower sprays light up the landscape, leaping forward with chaotic enthusiasm.

Similar to the newborn baby, the needs of an Aries come first. Like the ram, Aries people are brave, combative, courageous, energetic, and enterprising. Because of Aries' hope that tomorrow will be a better day, they don't always gain wisdom from experience. They act first and think later, only to forge ahead against the same wall once the wound has healed. In accordance with their fiery ruler, Mars, they are not famed for their patience or for their placid temper. Impulsive and spontaneous, they take initiatives based on their own needs of the moment without much consideration for others. But their apparent selfishness really stems from innocence. They're incapable of lying. Under their bright, positive veneer, they are actually very sensitive and more touched by rejection than anyone would suspect. Tears are usually kept inside. A belief in a happier future invariably makes them spring back into the arena of life with renewed passion and physical stamina. Aries are ingenious leaders motivated by success. They were born to overcome obstacles, solve problems, and emerge victorious.

Enlightenment Tools of Mars

Day
Tuesday.

Number
9.

Metal
Iron.

Shapes/Textures
Pikes. Sharp angles. Thin, straight, active lines. Cutting, incisive.

Flavors
Hot, spicy.

Foods
Vegetables, mostly with a strong taste: artichoke, carrot, caper, chive, garden cress, garlic, horseradish, leek, mustard, nettle, onion, chili pepper, radish, rhubarb, spinach.
Seeds: flaxseed.
Oil: safflower.
Edible flower: nasturtium.

Herbs/Spices
Often with a strong, acid taste, creating heat in the body, mostly curing the head: allspice, curry, feverfew, galangal, hound's-tongue, masterwort, myrtle, white mustard, pepper (black, cayenne, cubeb, red, white), tarragon, tobacco.

Trees/Shrubs
Mostly thorn-bearing: holly, red barberry.
With red bark: arbutus.

Plants
Bearing red berries, with thorns, spiky leaves, or poisonous: cacti, Madagascar dragon plant, madder, thistle.

Flowers
Anemone, bachelor's button, red clover, crocus, cuckoo flower, forsythia, gentian, gorse, honeysuckle, narcissus, stonecrop, tiger lily.

Musical Note
G.

Planetary Dominion
War, aggression, courage, leadership, pioneering spirit, fire, enthusiasm, virility, danger, lust, energy, drive.

Angel
Camael or Samael.

Enlightenment Tools of Mars and Aries

Objects
Iron and steel instruments: sharp and cutting tools, cutlery, scissors, hair or laundry dryers, darts.
War weapons: armor, shields, swords, sabers, knives, rifles, military medals, acid chemicals, explosives, fires.
Laboratory instruments: the dentist's drill.
Clothes: cowboy hat, red sweater, red leather jacket, motorcycle jacket, pirate, gladiator or Superman costume, tap shoes, sheepskins.
Items used by sportsmen: helmets, caps, fencing equipment, hiking boots, tennis racket, ice skates, punching bag, stopwatch, toboggan.
Anything red: red jewels, red Ferrari.
Percussion instruments: castanets, cymbals, drums, gongs, triangles, vibes, xylophones.

Locations
Outdoors: arid, eroded, or sandy land. Newly cultivated soil, land devastated by fire, places visited infrequently, hideouts, uncharted territories, low hills.
Places where there is fire, blood, sharp metal instruments, and/or places where athletic skills are required: gyms, butcher shops, tool stores, garages, forges, furnaces, open fires, places where metal is cut, laboratories.
In and around the house: ovens, chimneys, barbecues, high ceilings, fancy plasterwork, walls facing east, dog kennels.

Weather
Hot, with red clouds.
Also: forest fires.

Colors
Fiery red, scarlet.

Fragrances
Galangal, honeysuckle.

Gemstones
Mostly red in color: diamond, red agate, red aventurine, bloodstone, orange celestite, firestone, garnet, hematite, red jasper, lodestone, fire opal, magnetite, ocher, iron pyrite, ruby, ruby zoisite, red topaz.

Animals
Biting insects: horsefly, wasp.
Innocent: ostrich, ram, sheep.
Prey animals: fox, shark.
Some animals actually born in April under Aries: bobcat, striped skunk, American marten, fisher, long-tailed weasel, American mink, wolverine, northern river otter, sea otter, northern raccoon, harbor seal, coyote, red fox, island gray fox, squirrel, mountain beaver, pygmy rabbit, Townsend's mole, coast mole.

Parts of the Body
Head (skull, bones of face, head arteries), nose, sinews, sense of smell, adrenals, bile, gallbladder, left ear, the body's heat (perspiration), metals, muscular system.

Archetypes
Young men. Men who use energy and force in an assertive and positive way.

Professions
The steel and building industries.
Related to building: engineers, carpenters, insurance agents.

Metalworkers: railway workers, smiths, mechanics.

Related to new territories: adventurers, pioneers, reporters.

Employments using sharp objects: bakers, barbers, butchers, hairdressers, tailors, chemists, dentists, pharmacists, doctors, surgeons, alchemists, firemen, law enforcers.

Military men: generals, soldiers, gunners.

Athletes in sports requiring courage, dexterity, and strength.

Hobbies

Competitive and hazardous: cycling, rally driving, martial arts, wood carving, grafting, metalwork.

Social mixers: gallery openings, sporting events, triathlon races.

Enlightenment Tools of Aries

State
None.

Cities in the States
Homer (AK), Berkeley (CA), San Francisco (CA), Greeley (CO), Pueblo (CO), Stamford (CT), Newark (DE), Fort Lauderdale (FL), Twin Falls (ID), Springfield (IL), Danville (IL), Wichita (KS), Ann Arbor (MI), Grand Rapids (MI), Kalamazoo (MI), Mankato (MN), Joplin (MO), Great Falls (MT), Henderson (NV), Elizabeth (NJ), Paterson (NJ), Albuquerque (NM), Binghamton (NY), Ithaca (NY), Poughkeepsie (NY), Syracuse (NY), Utica (NY), Portland (OR), Harrisburg (PA), Erie (PA), Oshkosh (WI), Wausau (WI).

Countries
Cambodia, Ethiopia, Guatemala, Ireland, Luxembourg, Spain, Zimbabwe.

World Cities
Ancient Athens (Greece), Birmingham (U.K.), Capua (Italy), Florence (Italy), Galatia (Turkey), Krakow (Poland), Leicester (U.K.), Marseilles

(France), Naples (Italy), Padua (Italy), Saragossa (Spain), Sparta (Ancient Greece), Utrecht (the Netherlands), Verona (Italy).

Famous Personalities

Johann Sebastian Bach, Béla Bartók, Charles Baudelaire, Warren Beatty, Jean-Paul Belmondo, Jacques Brel, Otto von Bismarck, Marlon Brando, Matthew Broderick, Mariah Carey, Casanova, Charlemagne, Charlie Chaplin, Julie Christie, Francis Ford Coppola, Russell Crowe, Bette Davis, Céline Dion, Max Ernst, Serge Gainsbourg, Jennifer Garner, Linda Goodman, Alec Guinness, Harry Houdini, Elton John, Keira Knightley, David Letterman, Steve McQueen, Diana Ross, Omar Sharif, Simone Signoret, Arturo Toscanini, Vangelis, Vincent Van Gogh, Paul Verlaine, Tennessee Williams, Reese Witherspoon.

People

The Jews and the Muslims.

Apostle

Simon Peter, founder of Christ's church.

Cartoon/Film Characters

Asterix the Gaul, Popeye, Superman, Little My (of the Moomins series), Scarlett O'Hara (of *Gone with the Wind*), Pinocchio (whose nose grew when he told a lie!), Tarzan, Tristan (of *Tristan and Isolde*), Sir Gawain (of the Arthurian legends).

The Aries Woman

If you're looking for an old-fashioned woman who will wait on you hand and foot, bat her feminine eyelashes, and drink your every word, run! Quite capable of opening her own doors, earning her own money, and making up her own bright mind, the Aries woman is exciting, positive, and forceful. She is an equal to any man she knows and proud of her independence. Life with her is never boring. She is always on the go, and as soon as she gets somewhere, she's already on the lookout for the next adventure. Cherish her, listen to her, give her the first place in your heart and in your life. You'll have a devoted mate who will challenge you but when the world is getting you down, she will invariably bring up your spirits.

Impulsive, she is very spontaneous in love and has a sexual appetite likely to match your own. She's fun, never wallows in self-pity, and always wants to remain in charge of her own life, no matter how good a provider you are to her. Her style may be a little rash. She can lack patience with household obligations or children who are a little too sensitive or weak, but her dynamic energy toughens everybody up and creates a home life that never falls into a rut.

Quite a romantic at heart, she sees you as no less than her knight in shining armor, someone of whom she's proud. Be totally there for her when she needs you, absolutely admire her without any reservation, but don't ever, ever smother her with constant adoring declarations of devotion or she'll get bored and lose interest. She will ultimately respect you and be validated by your strength of character when she realizes that you can totally embrace and nurture all that she is without ever curbing her enthusiasm for life.

Don't lie to her. Her anger at having been betrayed could be more devastating than you may be ready to handle. She is direct and she demands straight answers. Her temper can simmer down as quickly as it erupted, and fortunately, unless she was cut very deeply, she is incapable of holding a grudge. However self-absorbed she may seem at times, remember that it is a mark of her purity and innocence. Never forget that her heart is very real and much more sensitive than she'd like anyone to know.

The Aries Man

Expect your life to be blown apart by a whirlwind of energy if you are in love with an Aries man. You will need to master the subtle balance of being completely present to his needs without giving up your own life. Be engaged by him when he's around, and happily go about your own business when he's not. This will give you plenty to share with him when he returns from his own battles, keeping him interested in you.

Life is far too exciting for him to miss a beat. As a result, he may find it challenging to be on time when something new has distracted him.

With a disarming smile, he will turn around and make everything good again, illuminating your world with his positive charm.

A passionate lover, he is not necessarily versed in the art of subtle seduction. He likes to win. Your happiness makes him feel good about himself. He can be the Prince Charming you read about as a little girl, a man in every sense of the word, but also a little boy in many other ways. He needs to play and feel free, but he is scrupulously honest when it comes to his true commitments. He also is a romantic idealist who needs you to be his princess, feminine, bright, beautiful, smiling, and a positive mate. It's worth the effort. Never allow intimacy with him to make you settle in a comfort zone where you are willing to accept the ordinary rather than the extraordinary. The extraordinary is what makes him thrive. Storybook romance is what he's after, where beautiful princesses are saved from their dungeons and for whom dragons should be slain. Life will certainly never be boring with an Aries man by your side.

He treats his children more like his friends and he won't be taken aback if they are rebellious. He might even encourage their fighting spirit, never having lost it himself. Having a family means extra support, a nest to come back to. His battles should be your battles and his enemies, yours also. It doesn't mean you should agree with everything he does, but when you don't, make sure you tell him tactfully and without ever watering down his dynamism. He will listen, and as quickly as he went in one direction, realize he might head a different way. Don't cling. Don't pursue him. Let him conquer you on a daily basis while creating the heaven of peace and harmony he desperately needs. It will help him to not feel lonely and to continue to have a reason to fight.

The Aries Child

Warmhearted and kind, he is nonetheless more than a little self-absorbed. From day one, he will make his likes and dislikes crystal clear. There is nothing subtle about this energetic child who, if you're not careful, will happily rule the household. His needs should be yours at exactly the time he's feeling them, even if they arise in the middle of the night when you most need your beauty sleep.

From the time he is playing in the sandbox, he could get into quite a few battles with playmates who don't understand that he's the boss.

Then he could burst into temper tantrums that explode like fireworks, only to dissolve almost as fast as they came on. When unchallenged, he will gladly share his toys and he will be very generous with his possessions.

He needs to be involved in a lot of activities. The discipline and intense physical demands of martial arts could provide one of the best structures for his young energy to unfold harmoniously. Thriving on challenges, he will never let one go by without grabbing it. That could be the best way for you to make him successful in school. Because he is less than excited by homework, you will need to stimulate his pride to help him reveal the best he has to offer. Set up high stakes and he will rise to the occasion and meet them, zooming through his books and achieving the best grades—which he knows he deserves. His intelligence is keen and should be constantly stimulated. His ability to absorb new knowledge is directly related to how exciting it is to him.

As an adolescent, he could be prone to fast driving and impulsive behavior. Patience is not his strong suit. Surprises will be lost on him. He'll tear through gift wrapping at the speed of light to get to what's inside the box without delay.

He could also be a spendthrift and may need to learn how to balance his weekly allowances. Very early on, he will want to earn his own money, as this will give him the sense of the freedom he needs to feel fully himself.

Despite his bravado, he has a very tender heart and needs much admiration and love to unfold into his own light. Never spare your hugs or compliments, keep his little body and his mind active, and he'll grow into a very balanced adult you will be proud of.

TAURUS

(APRIL 20–MAY 21)

Symbol: The Bull

When left to its own devices, the bull is a powerful yet placid and sensual animal. Peacefully grazing among the flowers, its movements are slow and deliberate. Undisturbed by birds perching on its back and flies hanging around its eyes, it lives in good harmony with all living beings, ruminating grass over and over until fully digested. When provoked, however, it charges forward with blind passion and can be most dangerous to whomever is standing in its way. Uncomplicated and forceful, the bull is an animal of great physical strength—difficult to stir but equally impossible to stop once angered.

Element: Fixed Earth

Fixed earth is the fertile, heavy earth of freshly plowed soil. It gives strength to flowers and gardens, in full bloom, filling the air with perfumes. It helps luscious green grass flourish. Fixed earth is most rampant in the middle of spring, when bird nests are full of tiny, demanding, hungry baby birds, with parents busily flying back and forth to provide food for their offspring. Fixed earth is found at this very sensual time of year, when the world is filled with beauty.

Ruler: Venus

Never farther than sixty degrees from the Sun, Venus reacts the strongest to the Sun's intense light. Venus is the shiniest planet in the sky. The Greeks, thinking that they were seeing two planets, gave her two names: Phosphoros at dawn and Hesperos at twilight. Similar to the Moon, Venus has phases. However, because of the presence of white clouds shrouding her surface, she mostly remains a mystery to us.

Ages of Man

Early childhood, when the baby realizes that its smile and charming ways are its most valuable possessions.

Character

Taureans are affectionate, amorous beings, deeply appreciative of beauty and elegance. Charming, they also are grounded, practical, reliable, and steadfast. Taurus people are usually very good with money, which affords them the comforts of life that they find so pleasurable. To Taureans, only that which is concrete and can be touched is real, making them very solid and trustworthy. They are slow to set into motion, but unstoppable once on a given path. Often accused of stubbornness, they are really particularly persistent and stable. Excellent planners, they are composed and productive, firm in their beliefs and sound in their decisions.

They enjoy the good things in life, particularly food as well as comfortable and soft clothes of great quality. They are acutely sensitive to perfumes of all sorts. I personally know a Taurean who literally spends hours every day happily smelling the roses in his garden. Taurus people are very protective of their possessions, have a great aesthetic sense, and are usually tasteful decorators. They are lovers of beauty and art, and they are likely to have an impressive musical collection. The luxurious and expensive objects they surround themselves with are, to them, the measure of their worldly success.

Their patience is legendary. Peaceful, they are extremely sensual and tremendously enjoy touching and being touched. Yet beneath their placid exterior, anger can build up slowly and gradually, often over years. When it does reach the point of no return, the explosion is formidable enough to destroy everything in sight. Thankfully, this kind of anger will only strike once or twice in a lifetime. Just make sure you stay out of the line of fire, and hope that you did nothing to provoke it.

Taureans are normally caring, warmhearted beings who thrive on peace and harmony. Generous with what they choose to share of their possessions, composed and calm, they are among the most loyal and charming people around.

Enlightenment Tools of Venus

Day
Friday.

Number
6.

Metals
Copper, bronze, brass.

Shapes/Textures
Rhythmical curves, full and sensual. Warm and soft (marshmallow-style).

Flavors
Fragrant, aromatic, warm, pleasant, and sweet.

Foods
Most fruits: apples, apricots, bananas, blackberries, red cherries, gooseberries, grapes, huckleberries, peaches, pears, persimmons, plantains, plums, pomegranates, strawberries, tomatoes.
Vegetables: alfalfa, asparagus, burdock, dandelions, green peas, sorrel.
Legumes: chickpeas, lentils, navy beans.
Delicacies: tonka beans, dessert wines, liqueurs (mirto, arrack), sweets (stevia), candy, fine chocolates (particularly cherry brandy chocolates).

Herbs/Spices
Fragrant and sweet, soothing to the throat: bishop's weed, cardamom, carom seeds, marshmallow root, myrtle, sanicle, green tea, jasmine tea, thyme, valerian, vervain.

Trees/Shrubs
Most fruit trees: apple, apricot, cherry, peach, plum, vine.
Also ash, birch, butterfly bush (buddleia), crab apple, elder, poplar.

Plants
Delicate, with tender leaves: lycopodium.

Flowers
Fragrant, beautiful in bouquets, mostly pink and/or found growing wild in the fields: pink azalea, apple blossom, pink aster, cherry blossom, cowslip, cyclamen, daisy, elecampane, freesia, pink gerbera, white hydrangea, larkspur, white lilac, peace lily, pink mallow hibiscus, golden marguerite, meadowsweet, large pink or white rose, *Silene caroliniana* variants.

Musical Note
A.

Planetary Dominion
Luxury, fine art, courtship, love, marriage, pleasure, harmony, peace, balance, beauty.

Angel
Hagiel or Anael.

Enlightenment Tools of Venus and Taurus

Objects
Related to beauty: bath pearls, perfumes, makeup, perfumed soap, scented oils, massage tables.
Objects related to finances: purses, safes, coins, banknotes, piggy banks, money belts or clips, jewel boxes.
Decoration of the home and garden: copper ornaments, children's toys, potted flowers, bouquets, herb garden, sundial, music CDs, reclining chairs, framed paintings, modeling clay, heavy sculptures.
In the garden: plows.
Nice and comfortable clothes: comfortable yet fine clothes (especially women's), soft fabrics (flannel, chamois skin, suede), silk scarves, heavy jewelry.
Musical instruments: clarinet, guitar, harp.

Locations
Outdoors: flower and vegetable gardens (the Garden of Eden), fertile meadows, dimly forested and farming land, rolling hills, fields of wild-flowers, farmers' markets.
Stores: banks, furniture stores.
Houses: one-story country houses, cowsheds, stables, warm and cozy inns with excellent wholesome home cooking.
Indoors: quiet, warm, dimly lit rooms with low ceilings. Wine cellars. Tile roofs.

Weather
Pleasant.

Colors
All pastel colors: pale blue, pink, soft green.
Red-orange, creamy white.

Fragrances
Calming, expensive, and connecting us to Mother Earth: spikenard.

Gemstones
White stones: alabaster, white coral, white topaz.
Green stones: green agate, chrysocolla (a stone of peace, used to attract love), chrysoprase, dioptase, emerald, green garnet, green sapphire.
And pink: rose quartz, pink tourmaline.

Animals
Bull and cattle.
Small, silky, warm, and soft animals: hamsters, rabbits.
A few animals born in May, under Taurus: American bison, bobcat, western spotted skunk, striped skunk, long-tailed weasel, American badger, sea otter, ringtail, northern raccoon, harbor seal, Guadalupe fur seal, red fox, island gray fox, North American porcupine, American beaver, rock squirrel, western gray squirrel, pygmy rabbit, desert cottontail rabbit, California bat.

Parts of the Body
Throat and neck (carotid artery, jugular vein, larynx, thyroid, tonsils, vocal cords).

Archetypes
Young women. Lovers.

Professions
Related to wealth and property or land ownership: architects, art dealers, artists, bankers, builders, cowboys, farmers, financiers, gardeners, insurance brokers, moneylenders, land owners.

Artistic and sensual: cooks, dancers, entertainers (with a solid and grounded sense of humor), massage therapists, models, musicians, painters, sculptors, singers, vocalists. All the professions related to making women more beautiful: dressmakers, embroiderers, aestheticians, florists, hairdressers, linen drapers, milliners, needle workers, perfumers, tailors.

Hobbies

Cooking, decorating, dining out, dancing, arranging flowers, embroidering, gardening, golfing, knitting, landscaping, meditating, playing or listening to music, painting, sculpting, smelling the roses, doing tapestry, strolling in the countryside, giving or receiving a massage, exploring aromatherapy.

Enlightenment Tools of Taurus

States
Louisiana, Maryland, Minnesota.

Cities in the States
Oakland (CA), Wallingford (CT), Honolulu (HI), Pocatello (ID), Champaign (IL), Lexington (KY), Pittsfield (ME), Duluth (MN), Hastings (NE), Buffalo (NY), Long Island City (NY), New Rochelle (NY), Rochester (NY), Greensboro (NC), Winston-Salem (NC), Pittsburgh (PA), El Paso (TX).

Countries
Austria, Ecuador, Israel, Japan, Paraguay, Sierra Leone, Tanzania, Togo.

World Cities
Dublin (Ireland), Leipzig (Germany), Mantua (Italy), Lucerne (Switzerland), Palermo (Italy), Parma (Italy).

Famous Personalities
Andre Agassi, Anouk Aimée, Karen Bishop, Johannes Brahms, Charlotte Brontë, Pierce Brosnan, Cher, George Clooney, Bing Crosby, the

band Coldplay, Salvador Dalí, Donovan, Kirsten Dunst, Duke Ellington, Enya, Henry Fonda, Audrey Hepburn, Billy Joel, Krishnamurti, Jay Leno, Shirley MacLaine, Mâ Ananda Moyî, Michelle Pfeiffer, Prokofiev, Sugar Ray Robinson, Shakespeare, Tchaïkovsky, Rudolph Valentino, Doreen Virtue, Orson Welles.

People
The Druids, the ancient Egyptians.

Apostle
Simon the Cananaean, who was preoccupied with land and finances.

Cartoon/Film Characters
Daisy the Cow, Obelix (of *Asterix & Obelix*), Ferdinand the Bull, Falstaff (of Shakespeare's *Henry V*).

The Taurus Woman
Don't tell her lies. She is a very grounded, practical woman who wants hard facts and does not thrive on romantic illusions. She is solid, deliberate in all that she does, and quite a realist. A superb cook, she entertains her friends in style, creating some very memorable and pleasurable evenings.

She loves everything soft and surrounds herself with silk, velvet, and mohair. Her sense of smell is so well developed that she cringes at distasteful scents and naturally gravitates toward very earthy or exotic fragrances. Flowers adorn her home and even if her garden is only a tiny balcony, it overflows with natural plants.

The sensuality of a Taurus woman is a dimension into which she flows easily and with relish. She needs to touch those she loves and be touched in return. Her massages are out of this world and she certainly owns more than one book on the art of tantric lovemaking. When without a partner, she soaks in her bathtub for hours with all sorts of essential oils, incense, music, and candlelight.

She is a master at the art of doing nothing, but she cannot be accused of being lazy. She works very hard to reach her goals. She likes the comfort of money, which gives her a sense of her own value. She is unlikely to wait around for a man to provide her with what she needs. Creating her own prosperity is never at the expense of her femininity. She is good to her children and she won't shut her door to strangers or strays, as long as they don't take undue advantage of her generosity.

The Taurus woman creates relationships for the long run. Extremely loyal, she is shocked if the same loyalty is not given back to her. She expects the same solidity she offers, but she never allows disappointment to get the best of her. She has too much common sense and is too practical to wallow in self-pity. She just counts her losses and, without looking back, she deliberately moves on.

She exudes grace and has a very earthy beauty. She probably gravitates toward heavy jewelry made of real gemstones and comfortable yet elegant clothes. Romance is never far from her. She naturally relates sensually to everything in her world, from peeling potatoes to watering her plants to petting her dog, or to taking tender care of her friends.

The Taurus Man

Being in love with a Taurus man will feel very warm and cozy. This man is truly a man in every sense of the word. Honest, trustworthy, and hardworking, he will never deny any luxury to his family. But he needs to be the man. He won't put up with someone telling him what to do or how to do it, and he has great distaste for masculine vulgarity or frivolousness. He needs his woman to be feminine, peaceful, and graceful. Very determined, he keeps his own counsel and may not be the most talkative type on the planet, but his words are worth their weight in gold. Deliberate, he rethinks his thoughts many times before expressing them and doesn't change his mind once he's come to a definite conclusion. That may include deciding whether you are the one of his dreams. He will be slow in declaring himself, but once he does, he will be a loyal and sensual lover. This man plays for keeps and is a builder.

He takes his responsibilities very seriously and makes sure that his family is well provided for. He is very devoted to his children—particularly his little girls—and insists that they get the solid education that will enable them to create stability for themselves.

He probably takes pride in his body and is involved in some athletic activity that enables him to enjoy the fresh air of the countryside that he so loves. He needs trees and flowers to soothe his soul and he's not immune to the magic of poetry and music.

The Taurus Child

I know a beautiful little Taurus girl who once was very excited at the thought of drinking a sip of my tea. She was used to tea with tons of milk and sugar. When she found out that mine was plain, she looked at me in horror before spitting the contents of her mouth back into my cup.

A Taurus child knows exactly what he wants and what he doesn't. And there is no use in trying to coax him into something he has decided he won't have. No matter how small this child is, you will have a determined little bull on your hands who will not budge one inch. This child is so tuned in to his senses that if his sweater feels funny, his food doesn't taste good, or the soap doesn't smell right, he will simply not use them. You might as well get used to that and be the one who adapts, because he won't. Firmly planting his feet into the ground, he will cross his tiny arms over his chest, with a frown on his face.

Schoolwork can be painfully slow, as this child will not learn something that doesn't make sense to him. He will need to ruminate over his lessons until they are digested. But once his, that knowledge will never leave him.

He will delight in learning an instrument, playing team sports, and should be given plenty to read to stimulate his imagination. He may ask some very grounded questions and will not easily buy into fantasy. He needs hard facts and figures and should not be told phony stories.

He will take his piggy bank very seriously and will start saving his cents and quarters like a pro, very aware of the security it gives him. He will share his toys generously and will deliberately choose which ones he is ready to part with. Once he decides to give something away, it is really a gift with no strings attached.

The Taurus child is kind and nurturing to his siblings, especially his younger brothers and sisters. He spends hours in the bathroom grooming himself and he loves the kitchen. Cooking is second nature to him. Craft-making or creating jewelry are also very enjoyable pastimes. He delights in making his own cards and little girls will happily knit away scarves for the whole family. It is a good idea to give him a little piece of land to plant some flowers and he will take pleasure in watching them grow. He is also good with pets and very responsible for their well-being.

This child should be given tons of hugs. Touch is a powerful form of communication for him. He may be slow in deciding what he wants to do with his life, but once he chooses, he will never give up. He is quite capable of creating an empire, real and solid.

GEMINI

(MAY 21–JUNE 21)

Symbol: The Twins
Gemini is the first of only three human characters in the whole zodiac. Light and playful, as well as difficult to differentiate from one another, human twins usually have their own shared language and are extremely telepathic with each other.

Element: Mutable Air
Mutable air is primarily our breath, as well as drafts, quickly moving breezes, the soft winds of spring. Mutable air is light and elusive.

Ruler: Mercury
Because Mercury only shines briefly at sunrise and sunset, the ancients, believing that they were in the presence of two different planets, gave it two names. Small and fast, Mercury has no moon, an almost non-existent atmosphere, and is covered with shallow craters and fine dust. Despite being the planet closest to the Sun, Mercury only reflects six percent of the Sun's light. Because it always exposes the same side to the Sun, making one half torrid, while the other is forever ice-cold and plunged in darkness, this planet is almost impossible to study.

Ages of Man

Adolescence, when we are curious are full of life and insatiable in our need to explore the world.

Character

Gemini is the stage in nature when seeds thrive on the wealth of their environment to develop their full potential. The leaves and flowers are pure, young, and bright. A new cycle of life has begun.

I feel blessed to be surrounded by many good Gemini friends. Their elusiveness makes them disappear, sometimes for months at a time. That might make one believe they are flighty, yet the opposite is true (as often with this dual sign). Geminis are actually surprisingly loyal and constant. Just don't wait for them when they're not around. Go about your own business. Every time they come back, it will then be a pleasant surprise. With a Gemini, you will feel that you are with two distinct people, if not more. One of my dear Gemini friends always writes me two letters back to back, one composed by each of the twins within him. The letters usually have completely different yet complementary views.

Communicative, Geminis make great counselors and are fun conversationalists. They are either prolific writers or they avoid committing their thoughts to paper altogether, for fear of being tied by their words.

Change is the essence of life for Geminis. Excitable, curious, inquisitive, and intelligent, they have an excellent memory. They are mentally sharp with a witty sense of humor and an uncanny ability for imitation of others' idiosyncrasies.

They are usually tall and lean. But even those who are a little more plump move at the speed of light, making you swear you are seeing double. (Wasn't your Gemini friend, now happily chatting on the phone at the other side of the room, just sitting next to you a moment ago?)

Versatile and agile, Geminis are good in business, with an eloquence that can make them wrap anyone around their little finger. They enjoy moving rapidly from one thing to another, shuffling concepts and discovering what people around them think. All this while avoiding all forms of imprisonment for themselves. Like adolescents, they may not be entirely clear as to what lifestyle suits them the best. And like Mercury, their planet, which eternally reveals only one side, they may be inclined to hide their deeper motivations. They have an ever-irresistible need to try something new. Out of curiosity, they are likely to try many different masks, all which expand their awareness of themselves and the world around them.

The minds of Geminis are very finely tuned to higher spheres of consciousness and will be even more so as we progress through the years to come.

Enlightenment Tools of Mercury

Day
Wednesday.

Number
5.

Metal
Quicksilver (mercury).

Shapes/Textures
Short, incisive lines, and thin, flexible curves. Sandy, crumbling.

Flavors
Cool, slightly astringent.

Foods
Bittersweet: molasses, bayberry, mulberry, beer.
Nuts: almonds, Brazil nuts, filberts, hazels, pecans, walnuts.
Vegetables grown above the ground: celery, endive, green beans.

Herbs/Spices
Small, with blue or yellow flowers, insect repellent, easing stress, enhancing to the brain, and good for the circulation: white balsam, butcher's broom, calamint, catnip, caraway, greater celandine, comfrey, costmary, dill, echinacea, hops, *Ginkgo biloba*, white horehound, hyssop, lemon balm, lemongrass, lemon verbena, marjoram, mint, monks-

hood, peppermint, skullcap, spearmint, Saint-John's-wort, tabasheer (bamboo sap).

Trees/Shrubs
Most nut-bearing trees: almond, hazel, walnut.
Bamboo, eucalyptus, mulberry, rowan.

Plants
Budding shrubs, perennials growing fast on sandy and arid ground with small flowers as well as discreet or no fragrance, small plants that help the brain and memory: fern, Jacob's ladder, spider plant, spotted spurge, Texas sage, false red yucca, ground-cherry, vetiver.

Flowers
Mostly blue, yellow, or orange, or with two colors: blanket flower, butterfly milkweed, strawberry cinquefoil, clematis, cornflower, fireweed, pink lady gaura, morning glory, blue honeywort, wild indigo, iris, Jacob's ladder, knapweed, leadwort (or plumbago), day lily, leopard lily, snapdragon, bird's-foot trefoil.

Musical Note
E.

Planetary Dominion
The mind, commuter travel, communication, knowledge, logic, reasoning, flexibility, curiosity, ideas, messages, literary affairs, the signing of documents, immediate neighborhood, close relatives.

Angel
Raphael.

Enlightenment Tools of Mercury and Gemini

Objects
Everything connected with communication, education, and learning: books, newspapers, periodicals, magazines, dictionaries, language CDs,

letters of the alphabet, computers, electronics, correspondence, legal documents, e-mails, faxes, DHL, FedEx, Internet, iPods, pictures, postcards, contracts, letters, manuscripts, messages, phones, phone cards, radios, gadgets, files, receipts, bills, banknotes.

Art supplies: acrylic paints, finger paints, spray guns, colored ink, writing material, paper, pencils.

In the house: wicker baskets, basket chairs, knickknacks, ceiling fans.

Clothes: lamés, printed calicos, disguises, razzle-dazzle clothes, cheap jewelry gloves, reversible jackets, bicolored sweaters.

Shoes: rollerblades, ice skates.

Hand-operated machines: looms, sewing machines.

Games: cards, chess, dominoes, marbles, puzzles, Scrabble.

Means of transportation: cars, bicycles, sleighs, strollers, buses, taxis, small airplanes, hang gliders.

Related to traveling: driving directions, navigation systems, road signs, traffic lights, car keys.

Precise instruments: compasses, thermometers, barometers, watches, stopwatches, crystal prisms, kaleidoscopes.

Musical instruments: flutes, harmonicas, trumpets.

Also any keys, such as for the office or home.

Locations

Outdoors: deforested and vented hills, open and well-irrigated lands swept by winds, higher locations accessible on foot.

Where people go in passing: suburbs, streets, fairs, markets, playgrounds.

Places of exercise and/or entertainment: tennis courts, bowling alleys, seats in theaters.

Communication hubs: telephone booths, offices, communication and information centers, post offices, schools, railway stations, bus stops.

Stores: notions stores, grocery stores, department stores.

In the home: bookshelves (also shelves used for tapes, CDs, and DVDs), filing cabinets, desks.

Weather

Cold, dry, windy.

Colors
Multicolored, striped, shifting nuances: pale yellow, sky blue, slate gray.

Fragrances
Lemongrass, peppermint, patchouli.

Gemstones
Mostly yellow, promoting mental clarity: banded agate, tree agate, alexandrite, ametrine, citrine, lemon chrysoprase, leopardskin jasper, golden brown zircon.

Animals
Most birds: sparrows, whooping cranes, carrier pigeons, magpies (who steal shiny objects), parrots (talkative), barn swallows.
Volatile animals: hyenas, monkeys (mischievous), weasels.
Jumping, annoying, or transmuting insects: fleas, mosquitoes, grasshoppers, beetles, butterflies.
A few animals actually born in June under Gemini: bighorn sheep, pronghorn antelope, elk, mule deer, western spotted skunk, American badger, ringtail, northern fur seal, Guadalupe fur seal, North American porcupine, American beaver, yellow-bellied marmot, rock squirrel, pygmy rabbit, Brazilian free-tailed bat, fringed bat, California bat, western small-footed bat.

Parts of the Body
Arms (clavicle, fingers, hands, shoulders), humerus, brain, nervous system, respiratory system (bronchial tubes, lungs, speech, trachea), upper ribs, thymus, ulna.

Archetypes
Intellectuals, itinerants, teenagers, thieves.

Professions
News anchors, accountants, acousticians, agents (particularly literary or travel agents), architects, astronomers, bookkeepers, chiropractors, filing clerks, stand-up comics, computer specialists, bus or taxi drivers, disc jockeys, educators, mental healers, essayists, grocers, journalists,

librarians, linguists, mathematicians, merchants, messengers, mimes, telephone operators, street performers, postmen (or mail carriers), printers, publishers, radio hosts, reporters, secretaries, stationers, statisticians, stenographers, storekeepers, storytellers, schoolteachers, tennis players, translators, commercial travelers, quizmasters, writers.

Hobbies

Varied, mentally challenging activities involving play and communication: talking on the phone, meeting with friends, writing stories, calligraphy, stand-up comedy, open microphone night, karaoke, acrylic painting, reading magazines, going to movies, doing crossword puzzles, partying, playing tennis, Internet surfing, hang gliding, sailing, learning languages, listening to the radio, driving fast.

Enlightenment Tools of Gemini

States

Arkansas, Kentucky, Rhode Island, South Carolina, Tennessee, West Virginia, Wisconsin.

Cities in the States

Flagstaff (AZ), Hot Springs (AR), Santa Ana (CA), Hartford (CT), Bridgeport (CT), Waterbury (CT), Dover (DE), South Bend (IN), Des Moines (IA), Springfield (MA), Worcester (MA), Kansas City (MO), Las Vegas (NV), Vineland (NJ), Scranton (PA), Cranston (RI), Newport (RI), Houston (TX), Burlington (VT), Milton (VT), Tacoma (WA).

Countries

Denmark, Egypt, Germany, Guyana, Iceland, Italy, Jordan, Kuwait, Norway, Sweden, Tonga.

World Cities

Cardiff (U.K.), London (U.K.), Louvain (Belgium), Melbourne (Australia), Nuremberg (Germany), Plymouth (U.K.), Tripoli (Lebanon), Versailles (France).

Famous Personalities

Anastasia, the Automobile Association, Confucius, Jacques Cousteau, Johnny Depp, Sir Arthur Conan Doyle, Olympia Dukakis, Isodora Duncan, Albrecht Dürer, Bob Dylan, Ian Fleming, Anne Frank, Errol Flynn, Hergé, Elizabeth Hurley, Angelina Jolie, John F. Kennedy, Nicole Kidman, Henry Kissinger, Stan Laurel, Thomas Mann, Paul McCartney, Marilyn Monroe, Prince Rainier of Monaco, Mike Myers, Lionel Richie, Robert Schumann, Brooke Shields, Richard Strauss, Igor Stravinsky, Donald Trump, Queen Victoria, the Volkswagen, Richard Wagner, Mark Wahlberg, Walt Whitman, William Butler Yeats.

People

Afrikaners.

Apostle

James, who, a little slow in accepting Christ's authenticity, eventually became a very active and talkative evangelist.

Cartoon/Film Characters

Don Juan, Dr. Jekyll and Mr. Hyde, Hobbes (of *Calvin and Hobbes*), Peter Pan, Professor McGonagall (of the Harry Potter series), Thomson and Thompson (of *The Adventures of Tintin*).

The Gemini Woman

If you're looking for variety, search no further. This is a woman who is every woman you've ever met, and every woman you ever hoped and dreaded to meet. Her inner winds change fast, modifying both her appearance and her interests. She can be serious, funny, hard, creative, homey, cutting, outgoing—all in one day and sometimes all at once. As a Gemini friend of mine puts it, referring to the twins living within her: "If you don't like me, don't worry, stick around for another five minutes and you will!"

The Gemini woman's mind is bright and she is a great conversationalist who knows something about pretty much everything under the Sun. She can also make a great sounding board for your own ideas and will give you penetrating feedback.

She moves fast, thinks fast, and speaks fast. Always active, she loves traveling and relishes change. Loyal when she so chooses, she nonetheless remains an incorrigible flirt. Only really faithful to herself, she can easily love several men at once while mastering the art of betraying none. Less physical than she is mental, for her the real fusion is a fusion of the minds rather than a sexual one.

She loves to read and certainly subscribes to many magazines that keep her informed. You will often catch her doing several things at once.

Good with children, rather than acting in a purely motherly way, she treats them more like friends, training their minds at the same time she trains their little bodies. She will always lend a fascinated ear to their stories and she will stimulate their fantasies. Neither marriage nor motherhood should ever curb her freedom. A jailed Gemini is a very sad Gemini indeed. Trapped air quickly becomes stale. She needs to expand her wings, explore life, and make new friends.

If she is typical of her sign, she will spend hours on the phone and will love writing e-mails. She's more prone to short, informative messages than lengthy, heart-pouring ones. She will find a way to get the whole story from the person she's communicating with—whether he wants to share or not—while remaining pretty discreet about her own. She likes to remain free, and, being so many people at once, it is hard at times for her to share all that she is. There is always a special brand of magic in a Gemini woman, a deep, elusive mystery that never quite reveals itself no matter how hard it tries.

The Gemini Man

Love is an exploration for the Gemini man—a light and tender game. Like the spring air, he could twirl around, led by his changing impulses and lacking a unifying principle, never settling down. He is always fascinated by mystery—the pursuit of something elusive that never quite allows itself to be captured.

Ambivalent, impatient, penetrating, his feelings are still full of changing nuances that may be a well-kept secret—even from himself. His sincerity in the moment is undeniable, but in the next instant he may be projected into the unknown of what remains to be explored.

He will mainly be attracted to you because of your mind. The more lively and bright, the bigger the attraction. He will be drawn to your interest in the world and in people, as well as your ability to quickly adapt and constantly change. It is best to remain light and playful. Heavy, passionate, romantic love declarations are not his cup of tea. Present and charming one day, he may be gone the next. Like the two sides of his planet, when he reappears, it could be his twin self, dark, cold, and unfeeling. The shock could crash any sensitive woman. But this too shall pass. Enjoy him when he's on his good side and don't allow his more obscure side to wound you. Take him in stride and keep busy when he's not around.

Love with a Gemini man could feel like a very special friendship. His lively conversation will captivate you. It could be fun to keep up with his varied interests while adding some of your own to the mix. Just don't make plans for the future. Allow the changing winds that guide his course to take you into the unknown. Married, Gemini men should never be taken for granted. Even they don't know what tomorrow will bring. Stay alert and dynamically present in the now, renewing your love every day, and all will be well.

The Gemini Child

If your Gemini child is trying to convince you that he can watch television, listen to music, browse the Internet, and play with a football while doing his homework, you should believe him. He can. Doing one thing at a time doesn't come naturally to him, but being everywhere at once does. He may get easily bored in school, but at the very last minute he will know all the information he needs for his exams, seemingly out of thin air. There is no denying that his mind is bright. He has the extraordinary ability to tap into knowledge through invisible antennae. He needs a lot of activities to maintain the pace he enjoys.

He has a gift with words and will treasure the dictionary. Encyclopedias of every kind are great gift ideas for this child, whose alert and inquisitive mind soaks up information like a sponge. On a rainy day, memory games could be fun to play with him—and he will probably win every time. He thinks fast and speaks fast, but his attention span can be shockingly short. Sometimes you might wish he would just shut up, but because he is constantly sorting information, if you listen carefully, you will invariably discover gems of deep perception in the way he views the world. Gemini's intuition stems from pure intellectual logic.

He is gifted when it comes to languages, and he is also drawn to traveling. As he grows into his teens, he will enjoy his freedom and is likely to try all sorts of different jobs, just for the fun of wearing multiple hats. Gathering information here and there, he knows just enough about a large number of topics.

He's likely to spend lots of time on the phone, so it could be a good idea to get him on a solid calling plan with conference call and call waiting so he can happily chat away with his numerous friends. He'll talk to many of them simultaneously about all sorts of subjects.

Living with a Gemini child will certainly keep you on your toes. There is something very magical about him, bordering on genius. One assurance is that around him you won't feel you are growing old and you will never be alone.

CANCER

(JUNE 21–JULY 22)

Symbol: The Crab

The crab is a protective little creature armed with a powerful set of claws and a matching will. His thick carapace makes up for the fact that he has no backbone. His hard shell hides a very soft inside. When scared, he protects himself by running backward and vanishing into a burrow built in the sand. Impossible to evict from this fortress, he carefully tucks his legs beneath him and, hidden under his shell, cautiously waits for the danger to pass. Although capable of locomotion in all directions, he tends to move sideways, carefully strategizing while never losing sight of his prey. If that which he covets shows signs of moving away, he throws caution to the wind, running directly to it, then hanging on for dear life. His reduced abdomen is entirely hidden under his thorax, making it look like his stomach stems right out of his mouth. He is omnivorous, but mostly feeds off algae. Although his natural habitat is the ocean, he can also spend long periods of time on dry land.

Element: Cardinal Water

The cardinal water of Cancer is spring water, as it first emerges from the ground, untouched by man. It is joyous and pure, full of minerals and sweet beauty.

Ruler: The Moon

The Moon initially was symbolic of the child. The Greeks changed it to symbolize the mother. The Moon is also the soul. To us on Earth, the Sun and the Moon seem to be exactly the same size, but this is an optical illusion. In reality, the Moon is much smaller. She has no light and warmth of her own. As she rapidly circles around the Sun (her full revolution occurs in twenty-eight days), her various phases reflect the Sun. The dance of the Moon with the Sun is much like the exchange of power between a woman and a man. A man surrenders his power to his woman, who honors his trust by giving his power back to him, enriched.

Ages of Man

Babyhood and early childhood. Ideally, this is the time when we have a nurturing mother who lovingly takes care of us, meals we don't have to worry about, and our own room full of toys.

Character

Cancers bring us back to our true divine roots. Fascinated by history, archaeology, and past lives, Cancers are the guardians of our lineage and where we really come from. Their sharp memories ensure that we do not forget our way to our divine truth.

Home is central to Cancers. It is the place where they protect their vulnerability by "mothering" and entertaining the people they cherish. Extraordinary cooks, they are nurturing and caring. They make perfect hosts and will always be touched by an invitation to a home-cooked meal. Because they never lost their connection to the purity of their own innocence, they are also wonderful with children—their own and those they adopt. One Cancer friend of mine for five consecutive weeks, day and night, every two hours, spoon-fed a baby bird, minuscule (the size of half of a finger), still featherless, and blind, who had been rejected by his own mother.

Visionary artists with psychic abilities, Cancers have a special talent for drawing and photography. Their humor is warm, with an occasional touch of craziness. They are more observant of their surroundings than they may appear to be, and their immense capacity to reflect the world around them tremendously enriches their natural creativity. Many famous novelists and painters are born under this sign. They feel more than they think.

You can trust your deepest secrets to Cancers. They are sympathetic listeners who will never betray what has been confided in them. Yet they keep their innermost thoughts to themselves, only revealing their inner treasures to those who have earned their confidence over time. Easily touched by emotions, they tend to be self-protective.

Impressionable, they are also magnetic leaders, who instinctively know how to motivate others. Because money spells security to Cancers, they are very good at earning it and making it multiply.

Quite romantic and somewhat old-fashioned when it comes to style, they are also tenacious, refined, discreet, patient, and peaceful. Loyal and faithful to their true affections, they have as many shimmering moods as their ruling planet, the Moon, has phases. The secret alchemical mystery of Cancer is that these shifts are only an illusion. Beneath their various changes, they remain identical to themselves.

Enlightenment Tools of the Moon

Day
Monday.

Number
2.

Metal
Silver.

Shapes/Textures
Crooked lines, irregular curves, liquid.

Flavors
Insipid, odorless.

Foods
Vegetables with a high water content and little flavor: cabbage, cucumber, lettuce, squash, pumpkin, samphire, zucchini, watercress.
Watery fruit: melon, papaya, watermelon.
Fungus: mushroom
Seafood: shellfish.
Milk: coconut, cow, or goat milk.
Also: mesquite flour, sesame seeds.

Herbs/Spices
Those good for the stomach, PMS, or babies, promoting sleep and/or helping cure lunacy: asafoetida, borage, dittany of Crete, mayweed, purslane, sea salt, saxifrage, smooth bedstraw.

Trees/Shrubs
With round and spread-out leaves, rich in sap: alder, camphor, weeping willow, white willow.

Plants
Soft, with juicy, thick leaves: aloe vera, duckweed, moonwort. '

Flowers
Delicate and mostly white: white camellia, night-blooming cereus, white convolvulus, cotton, dog rose, white gardenia, jasmine, arum lily, madonna lily, water lily, white plumeria, ocean pearl, white lily of the Nile, white aster, arctic queen clematis, white peony, stephanotis.

Musical Note
F.

Planetary Dominion

Agriculture, plant growth, birth, domestic life, the feminine, fertility, nurturing, motherly love, security, home (place of residence), changes, sea travel, divination, dreams, visions, the subconscious, memory, magic, fantasy, imagination, intuition, emotions, empathy, journeys for pleasure, popularity, public life, worldly affairs.

Angel

Gabriel.

Enlightenment Tools of the Moon and Cancer

Objects

Those used every day, particularly in the kitchen: boxes, fine glassware, vases, bowls, gourds, kitchen utensils, cookbooks, framed photos, ordinary furniture, simple clothes, vintage clothes, furnaces, salt lamps, Walkman, earplugs, comforters.

All things associated with washing and laundry: washing powder, laundry baskets.

Bathroom accessories: bath pearls, scented soap, candles, rubber ducks.

Things related to the past, or that are of financial and/or emotional value: genealogical trees, antiques, ancestors' biographies, old music records, collections of stamps, coins, or plants, silver jewelry, old sheet music.

Homes (even if only temporary): aquariums, cradles, fish tanks, sailboats, rafts, sleighs, stalls.

Objects of reflection: scrapbooks, ink, paint, pastels, charcoal and pencils, mirrors, photographic plates, silver plates, lunar calendars, silver-plated articles, and water-filled silver bowls (in which the future can be read).

Wind instruments: trumpet, harmonica, Pan flute.

Locations

Related to the ocean and/or water: lakes, rivers, fish ponds, seasides, beaches, landing stages, docks, harbors, fountains, springs, ditches, baths, wells, lake or beach houses, Jacuzzis.

Places related to nurturing and protection: hotels, caravans, apartments, spas, family houses, the baby's bedroom, laundry rooms.

Places related to food: cellars, restaurants, dairies, grocery stores.

Weather

Wet and chilly.

Colors

Cream, light gray, silver and silvery hues, pearl, shimmering white.

Fragrances

Camellia, camphor, gardenia, jasmine, lily, onycha, sandalwood.

Gemstones

Mostly white: chalk, white opal, moonstone, mother of pearl, selenite, snow quartz, white topaz.

Also: blue amber, bowenite, blue calcite, blue chalcedony, pink chalcedony, geode, rainbow obsidian, clear quartz (scrying ball in which the past and the future can be read), phantom quartz.

Animals

Living on the farm: poultry, goose, lamb.

Filling the night with harmonics: frog.

From aquatic habitats: otters, crabs, oysters, eels, lobsters, shellfish.

Those that carry their home on their backs: snails, turtles.

Those who squat in others' nests, expecting their hosts to feed them: cuckoos.

Some animals actually born in July under the sign of Cancer: ringtail, northern fur seal, Guadalupe fur seal, western jumping mouse, American beaver, alpine chipmunk, golden-mantled ground squirrel, pygmy rabbit, pocketed free-tailed bat, fringed bat, long-eared bat, little brown bat, Yuma bat, long-legged bat.

Parts of the Body

Female body parts: breasts, nipples, female reproductive organs, ovaries, the womb.

Alimentary/digestive system: abdomen, esophagus, stomach.

Diaphragm, ribs, sternum.

Pancreas.

The right eye in men, the left eye in women.

Body fluids in general: lymphatic system, perspiration, gastric and intestinal juices, salivary glands.

Archetypes

Ancestors. The masses. Women in general: mothers, grandmothers, housewives, female officials such as a countess or a princess. Babies and small children. Homeless people. Pilgrims and travelers.

Professions

Domestic staff: cleaning lady, governess, housekeeper, janitor, laundryman, maid, relief commissioner, valet, waiter, washwoman.

Caretakers: employment agent, hotel manager, instrument tuner, medium, naturopath, nurse, welfare worker.

Connected to food and/or money/silver: baker, brewer, businessman, caterer, chef, cook, dairy farmer, milkman, silversmith, winemaker.

Connected to oceans/water: boatman, fisherman, fishmonger, marine, merchant marine, naval officer, oceanographer, plumbers, sailor.

Connected to history: collector, museum curator, antiques dealer, historian.

Wanderers: coachman, door-to-door salesman.

Children or related to children: obstetrician, midwife, nursery or primary school teacher, social worker.

Businesses operated from the home or related to homes: real estate agent, interior designer.

Artists: novelist, painter, photographer.

Hobbies

Cooking, baking pastries, designing silver jewelry, interior decoration, creating beautiful tables, doing crafts with children, collecting perfume bottles, establishing the family tree, antiques shopping, swimming, sailing, painting, photography.

Enlightenment Tools of Cancer

States
Idaho, New Hampshire, Virginia, Wyoming.

Cities in the States
Stockton (CA), Orlando (FL), Pensacola (FL), Peoria (IL), Gary (IN), Baton Rouge (LA), Portland (ME), Muskegon (MI), Greenville (MS), Concord (NH), Portsmouth (NH), Santa Fe (NM), Niagara Falls (NY), Oklahoma City (OK), Norman (OK), Watertown (SD), Wichita Falls (TX), Richmond (VA), Casper (WY), Sheridan (WY).

Countries
Afghanistan, Algeria, Argentina, the Bahamas, Burundi, Canada, Cape Verde, Czechoslovakia, Djibouti, Iraq, Madagascar, Malawi, Mozambique, New Zealand, Oman, the Philippines, Rwanda, Scotland, Solomon Islands, Somalia, Thailand, the United States of America (home to immigrants from all over the world), the Seychelles Islands, Vietnam.

World Cities
Algiers (Algeria), Amsterdam (the Netherlands), Berne (Switzerland), Cádiz (Spain), Genoa (Italy), Istanbul/Constantinople (Turkey), Lübeck (Germany), Manchester (U.K.), Milan (Italy), Stockholm (Sweden), Tokyo (Japan), Tunis (Tunisia), Venice (Italy), Wellington (New Zealand).

Famous Personalities
Victoria Abril, Isabelle Adjani, Pamela Anderson, Richard Bach, Mary Baker Eddy, Kathy Bates, Nathalie Baye, Julius Caesar, Pierre Cardin, Barbara Cartland, Marc Chagall, Tom Cruise, John Cusack, the 14th Dalai Lama, Lady Diana, Will Ferrell, the Food Channel, Garibaldi, Tom Hanks, David Hasselhoff, Ernest Hemingway, Hermann Hesse, Frida Kahlo, Helen Keller, Elisabeth Kübler-Ross, Michelle Kwan, Mary Magdalene, Tobey Maguire, Nelson Mandela, Amadeo Modigliani, Pablo

Neruda, George Orwell, Marcel Proust, Rubens, Antoine de Saint-Exupéry, Carlos Santana, Neil Simon, Jessica Simpson, Ringo Starr, Cat Stevens, Meryl Streep, Nikola Tesla, Robin Williams, Marianne Williamson.

People
Black Africans.

Apostle
Andrew, the first apostle to be summoned by Jesus into service. Initially a disciple of John the Baptist, Andrew's first reaction when discovering the Messiah was to run and tell his brother Peter to come and meet Christ.

Cartoon/Film/Novel Characters
Calvin (of *Calvin and Hobbes*), Linus (of *Peanuts*), Madame Butterfly, the Little Prince, Kermit the Frog, Wendy (of *Peter Pan*), the pure and gallant Sir Galahad (of the Arthurian legends) who discovered the Grail, Captain Haddock (of *The Adventures of Tintin*), Hagrid (of the Harry Potter series), Olive Oyl (of *Popeye*).

The Cancer Woman
She is a woman of many moods. Touched by great love stories of the past, under the right Moon phase, a Cancer woman can strike you as flirtatious, funny, and even outrageous, but normally she's reserved and a little shy. Her secret emotions run deep. Imaginative, she is also very romantic and loves poetry.

Her love of children leads her to either raise her own family or take care of abandoned or abused children. She most certainly has a pet or two. She will take care of them with understanding and sensitivity. Very in tune with their deeper needs, she knows how to bring out the best in her offspring and how to nurture their souls.

Happy to stay home, she will no doubt choose a profession that won't force her to wander too far away from it. She is an amazing cook who loves to take care of those she cherishes. Focused on security, she has food (as well as money) stashed in the most unlikely places.

She has secret dreams and is powerfully loyal to her true ties. Her rich humor is contagious. She can light up a room with her jokes and crazy laughter.

There is something very enchanting and warm about this woman. She will play all the feminine roles of nurturer, wife, confidante, lover, mother, caretaker, friend, and leader. From her heart alone, she is capable of making a huge difference in the world.

The Cancer Man

It is a rare Cancer man who isn't a fabulous cook, a great photographer, an amazing painter, and a sensitive parent. And yet, his obvious nurturing and feminine attributes do not make him effeminate in any way. He is compassionate, but he is also very much a man who needs security. He will work very hard to create the financial stability that makes him comfortable and enables him to afford the luxuries he wants his loved ones also to enjoy.

Most of the time he keeps his thoughts to himself. His receptivity to his environment is intense. He reflects his external circumstances almost as if he were a living photographic plate. Imaginative, he is highly intuitive and very much in tune with the more enlightened dimensions of consciousness. Yet he loves to laugh and has his own very special brand of humor.

Very attached to his home, his mother, his family, and his roots, this is a man who will always nurture the vulnerable until they bloom into their own magic.

Slightly shy, reserved, and old-fashioned, he may not pursue you aggressively and he certainly won't rush into a romantic situation but will take his time to know you. Once he's made his decision, he will be determined and tenacious in winning you over. He will fill your mailbox with romantic messages and send you a rose a day until you can no longer resist his advances. For a Cancer man, there is no letting go once he's made up his mind that you are the one who will mother him and his children.

Because he is a man of many facets, the magic of his planet, the Moon, casts silver spells on his moods, triggering his imagination and inspiring his soul to create a more nurturing world.

The Cancer Child

Give a Cancer child tons of crayons and construction paper and you will be amazed at his creative genius. One of the abused Cancer children I took care of would always and for the longest time study a model craft I had made. When he would finally get to work, the results were absolutely unique and brilliant.

The Cancer child needs tons of hugs and a stable home with lots of familiar toys. He will play with them over and over again until they're almost unrecognizable. That they are battered and dirty won't matter to him. Old toys make him feel safe. Paint white clouds on the walls of his room to trigger his imagination and get him books of fairy tales that you can read to him until he can read them himself. Any pet he takes care of will also become his best friend. When he grows older, he'll happily nurture his younger brothers and sisters.

He is likely to resort a lot to crying when his feelings are hurt. You will want to take him in your arms and protect his heart from the world, as it's not always a sensitive place. Gifts may not be received enthusiastically. Cancer children need to make what is given to them theirs with the help of time.

This child venerates traditions. I once stayed at a friend's place, and the day I left to move into the apartment I had found, her little Cancer boy told me he was expecting a card from me. It took me a while to understand that he was referring to a formal invitation to come and visit, a nice, written message sent by mail.

He will love to journal, but make sure you offer him a diary with a lock so that no one can pry into his secrets. Swimming should also be part of his early education, as should playing a musical instrument.

He will carefully place his weekly allowance in a piggy bank and at a shockingly early age he will find ways to earn his own money. When he was a mere six years old, my late Cancer husband invented a complicated device for selling candy to his little brother and sister. They had to place a penny in a box for the coveted sweets to land into their cupped hands. He made a small fortune.

The Cancer child is one who will never wander far from home, no matter where life takes him. Very attached to his mother, he will always find ways to connect with his family, making his parents and siblings feel loved.

LEO

(JULY 22–AUGUST 23)

Symbol: The Lion
Indisputably the ruler of all animals, the lion in nature is a very sociable, powerful creature with an impressive, glorious mane. His natural state is to rest on a low branch in the savanna, lazily meditating in the sunset. While males sleep about twenty-one hours a day, females do most of the hunting. When it's time to eat, the male lions serve themselves first, followed by the lionesses. Cubs get the remains of the feast. Their little ones' wildest fantasies are tolerated without reprimand. Whether it is climbing on their parents' backs, swinging from their manes, biting their tails, or scratching their necks, their placid and liberal parents watch them with pride, supporting their offsprings' growing egos.

Element: Fixed Fire
Fixed fire is the bonfire that radiates both light and warmth. It is the happy fire of evening campsites in the middle of summer.

Ruler: The Sun
The Sun is the Earth's nearest star, a million times larger than our planet. Its most amazing feature is that it generates the entirety of its light from within. We can only stare at about one-millionth of its radiance. It is so bright that during daytime, it rules the sky, eclipsing all the other stars and planets. At high noon, there are no shadows, only light, explaining why philosophers born in sunny countries are less tormented than those coming from the north, where darkness prevails. The enormous power of the Sun's electromagnetic field is the unifying force that keeps the entire solar system together, all the way out to Pluto.

Ages of Man

Young adulthood, before responsibilities settle in.

Character

Leo represents the time of the year when we lazily lie on the beach, enjoying the sun and the warmth of leisurely summer days. For a moment, we forget about responsibilities and obligations and just live our lives to the fullest with a more carefree attitude. The terraces of cafés are full and tourists invade the streets, looking for exotic objects to adorn the homes they will soon return to.

Leos are natural leaders. They are generous and unquestionably glamorous and dramatic. Magnetized by the limelight, they are attracted by fame and wealth. Even shy Leos still rule from behind the scenes. Take Danielle Steel, for example, who rarely grants interviews. In her own quiet way, with over five hundred million copies of her novels sold internationally, she is one of the world's most famous female writers.

Cheerful, commanding, and creative, Leos are dignified and proud. Their known weakness to flattery comes from a need to be reassured that they are as beautiful, powerful, and royal as they'd like to be. Secretly, they are not always confident and they thrive on external admiration to support a positive self-image. Once reassured that they are ultimately fascinating, the most beautiful, and, without a doubt, the best, they generously shine their glory on their court. Idealism rules Leo's big heart. Never selfish, Leos lavishly shower rich and abundant gifts on those they love.

Leo's kindhearted happiness, sunny disposition, and life energy are deeply healing and highly contagious. They are delightful, enthusiastic, and exuberant. While they are liberal, they also may be quite organized, loyal, faithful, trustworthy, and courageous. In the same way that their ambitions are fueled by their need to be in center stage, money is enjoyed mostly for the luxuries it affords them and the bounty it enables them to generously share.

Leos, like their ruler, the Sun, are the light of a room. In their dazzling presence, everybody feels just that much better. As a Sagittarius friend of mine enthusiastically puts it, "Leos are stars, man. They rock!"

Enlightenment Tools of the Sun

Day
Sunday.

Number
1.

Metal
Gold.

Shapes/Textures
Circles, full curves, spirals, solid.

Flavors
Aromatic, bittersweet, and slightly acidic.

Foods
Vegetables: burdock, fennel.
Citrus and slightly acidic fruit in general: bergamot orange, grapefruit, kumquat, lime, orange, pineapple, mango.
Red meat in general.
Elegant and expensive foods: rare oils, caviar, lobster, special wines, champagne, liqueurs, candied angelica.
Also olives, almond butter.

Herbs/Spices
Those that strengthen the heart, enhance eyesight, neutralize poisons, or dissolve the effects of negative magic: garden angelica, common bearberry, calamus root, calendula, chamomile, cinnamon, eyebright, foxglove, English hawthorn, orange blossom, parsley, rosemary, saffron, heart trefoil.

Trees
Citrus trees in general: grapefruit, lemon, orange.
Also ash, acacia, cedar, laurel, oak, palm, copal from tropical trees.

Plants
Elegant: New Zealand flax, red fountain grass, holly fern, restios.

Flowers
Those that smell nice, require a lot of sun, with majestic yellow or orange flowers: dahlias, yellow or orange gerbera, gladiola, Indian heliotrope, yellow hibiscus, yellow jessamine, white lily flower (fleur-de-lys), yellow lily, marigold, sunflower, sunburst, yellow orchid, zinnia.

Musical Note
C.

Planetary Dominion
Glamour, elegance, class, leadership, entertainment, speculation, wealth, fame, vitality.

Angel
Archangel Michael.

Enlightenment Tools of the Sun and Leo

Objects
Valuable, rare, and expensive, handmade, created by renowned artists, in numbered editions, gold-leaf-gilded, or encrusted with diamonds: crowns, emblems, golden frames, precious ornaments, scepters, impressive lamps, toys or furniture in wood, valuable art, rare antique Easter or Christmas decorations, perfume bottles, opera seats, merry-go-rounds, theater or concert tickets, jewelry boxes, cosmetic cases, hatboxes.
Glamorous clothes: fur coats, precious fabrics such as cashmere, expensive jewelry particularly in gold, elegant accessories (silk scarves, feather boas, showy hats), high-heeled shoes or boots, designer clothes, glamorous film costumes, fine leather jackets, tiaras, wedding dresses, elegant evening gowns, hair accessories.
Personal adornment: tanning spray, elegant perfumes.

Exclusive vehicles: Rolls-Royces, Porsches, Ferraris, Jaguars, presidential or VIP cars, yachts.

Musical instruments: saxophone, grand piano.

Locations

Places constructed with magnificence. Glamorous, they inspire happiness while awakening pride and admiration: castles, palaces, exclusive spas, solariums, tanning salons, elegant sports clubs, mansions, minarets, opera houses, theaters, towers, impressive villas, casinos, fortresses, ancient houses turned into museums, luxury hotels.

Outdoor locations: sundecks, golf or tennis courses, parks planted with centenary trees, parking lots decorated with flower beds.

Wild, hot, rocky, and difficult-to-reach natural locations: precipitous rock faces, deserts, cliffs, natural sites that create fortresses.

Areas abounding in game: forests, jungles, wild animal reservations, safaris.

Indoors: entrance halls (the more showy the better), elegant dining and living rooms, rooms where cards and music are being played, fireplaces, stages, thrones.

Weather

Light, soft spring rains, summer heat, fall fog, winter drizzle.

Colors

Gold, orange, purple, deep yellow.

Fragrances

Arabic gum, bay, cedarwood, cinnamon, copal, neroli, orange blossom, petitgrain, saffron, eau de Cologne.

Gemstones

Yellow amber, orange calcite, carnelian, cat's-eye, yellow diamond, gold jacinth, Herkimer diamond, peridot, white sapphire, sunstone, tiger's-eye, golden topaz, white topaz, rutilated quartz.

Animals

Felines: cats, lions, tigers, panthers, cougars.

Noble animals: thoroughbred horses, racehorses, peacocks, swans, pedigreed dogs.

Insects: honeybee, glowworm.

Those whose fur is precious: ermine, chinchilla.

Mythical: sphinx.

A few animals actually born in August under Leo: rock squirrel, pygmy rabbit, long-legged bat.

Parts of the Body

Heart (aorta), back (spine, spinal cord), circulatory system, the spleen.

The left eye in men, the right eye in women.

The vital forces, equilibrium.

Archetypes

Men in positions of authority: fathers, leaders.

Noblemen: dukes, emperors, kings, monarchs, princes.

People of independent means: heirs, shareholders.

Professions

Related to businesses where huge sums of money are handled: the stock market, big investors, treasurers, fundraisers.

Related to gold and precious gems: goldsmiths, gold dealers, jewelers, gilders.

Rich and famous entertainers: film or rock stars, circus artists, professional dancers.

Connected to glamour: supermodels, fashion designers.

Game professionals: golf, poker, tennis.

Government leaders and leaders in positions of prominence: ambassadors, CEOs, chairmen, commissioners, directors, executives, generals, lieutenants, magistrates, managers, presidents, high sheriffs, superintendents, employers, organizers, overseers.

Connected with bees: beekeepers.

Related to the heart: cardiologists, heart surgeons.

Hobbies

Cheerful games, creative activities: acting, directing, writing for the theater, oil painting.

Leisurely activities: sunbathing, entertaining friends, dancing and ice-skating for fun, attending a play.

Glamorous activities: dressing up, spending time at a luxurious spa, getting a fancy manicure, going on a shopping spree, buying expensive jewelry.

Enlightenment Tools of Leo

States

Colorado, Hawaii, Missouri, New York.

Cities in the States

Hollywood (CA), Miami (FL), Chicago (IL), Hutchinson (KS), Baltimore (MD), Boston (MA), Rochester (MN), St. Joseph (MO), Albany (NY), Lawton (OK), Warwick (RI), Charleston (SC), Montpelier (VT).

Countries

Bahrain, Benin, Bhutan, Bolivia, Central African Republic, Chad, Colombia, Congo, Cyprus, Gabon, Hungary, India, Ivory Coast, Jamaica, South Korea, Liberia, Maldives, Niger, Pakistan, Peru, Senegal, Singapore, Tunisia, Upper Volta, Vanuatu, the south of France.

World Cities

Bath (U.K.), Bombay (India), Bristol (U.K.), Damascus (Syria), Madrid (Spain), Portsmouth (U.K.), Prague (Czech Republic), Rome (Italy).

Famous Personalities

Ben Affleck, Neil Armstrong, Sri Aurobindo, James Baldwin, Lucille Ball, Halle Berry, Helena Blavatsky, Napoleon Bonaparte, Emily Brontë, Sandra Bullock, Steven Carell, Coco Chanel, Jim Davis, Claude Debussy, Alfred Hitchcock, Aldous Huxley, Mick Jagger, Tove Jansson, Magic Johnson, Carl Gustav Jung, Jacqueline Kennedy, Gene Kelly, Jennifer Lopez, Sydney Omarr, Madonna, Sean Penn, Roman Polanski, Robert

Redford, J. K. Rowling, Arnold Schwarzenegger, Yves Saint-Laurent, George Bernard Shaw, Danielle Steel, Hilary Swank, Charlize Theron, Mae West.

People
Ancient Atlanteans.

Apostle

John, the favorite disciple.

Cartoon/Film Characters
El Cid, Garfield, Swee'Pea (of *Popeye*), the King (of *The King and I*), the Lion King, Moomintroll (of *The Moomins*), Sir Lancelot (of the Arthurian legends), Vitalstatistix (chief of the tribe in *Asterix & Obelix*), Harry Potter.

The Leo Woman

It is hard to ignore the Leo woman. She behaves like a queen and expects to be treated as one. Beautiful, elegant, and charming, she can also be very funny and display a wonderful sense of humor in moments of egoless simplicity.

She is drawn to expensive furniture or designer clothes, but that does not make her a snob. She just has a taste for luxury and sees it as her divine right. She was born to rule and does it in style. A Leo Rising friend of mine owns the most impressive collection of tiaras. She believes it is a must-have for every woman.

Generous to a fault, the Leo woman is also warm, kind, and attractive to both men and women. Men may see her as a challenge but a great prize to win. Women envy her grace and have even more respect for her when they realize that she is willing to generously share her secrets.

She never quite lost her connection to her inner child and she knows how to relate to little ones with playfulness. They adore her.

She needs to be creative in her life or her dazzle will tarnish. She is great with crafts and naturally drawn to the limelight, and will want at some point to get onstage. Gifted for drama, she also has a wonderful comedic timing. When she's not taking herself too seriously, she can be the funniest actress you've ever met.

Stylish gifts are a must, and she likes to be wined and dined. Vulgarity and cheapness are depressing to her grandiose soul. It is not necessarily the amount of money you spend on her, but how much elegance and admiration you lavish her with. She is very sensitive to appreciation, and compliments should never be spared. Admire her and treat her like the queen she is, and your rewards will be out of this world.

The Leo Man

The Leo man needs to rule. King of your heart, he also wants to feel he is a role model for his children and admired by his neighbors and colleagues. He loves to be needed and he is a romantic at heart. Nothing will be too expensive when he takes you out. He wishes to shine and make his woman feel loved and cherished. Only a queen or an admiring servant will attract this special man. He will be at your feet if you dress well, be feminine and sensitive, yet bright and independent, without completely allowing yourself to be tamed. He will woo you with lavish bouquets of flowers, champagne, and caviar.

A Leo man has a big ego and needs a lot of reassurance that he is sexy and magnificent in every sense of the word, which, of course, he is. There is more uncertainty under this man's surface than he outwardly shows, and this makes him vulnerable to flattery. Don't ever in a million years dictate to him or humiliate him in any way, least of all in public. When you suggest change, do so with respect. Don't negate yourself, but don't outshine him either. You will need to find a delicate balance of allowing him to radiate his light without letting yourself be eclipsed by his brilliance.

Lavish with his affections, a Leo man is grandiose. Literally born breathing romance, he could put any Prince Charming to shame. A Leo man without love in his life is as miserable as a lion in captivity, pacing his cage. Love is second nature to the Leo man and if his mate neglects it, he will roar. In a display of his divine right, he may be possessive (you are his woman, don't you forget that) and harmlessly flirtatious (his gift of himself to his court). No matter what the appearances are, this man is loyal to true love that's kept alive and vibrant. It is too much trouble to chase after princesses when he has found his queen.

He will love going out, attending gallery openings, seeing plays, going to the movies, and having guests at home. Because he is a born entertainer, there will always be an admiring crowd around him. His heart is as large as his light is bright. He will never leave you without protection. Adulating him is really a small price to pay, and the happiness you give him will be returned to you a millionfold. A Leo man is never selfish.

The Leo Child

The Leo child is full of positive energy ready to burn. Cheerful and bright, he needs to measure himself up against his little companions and come out number one. Yet because he always practices good sportsmanship, the other kids won't resent his natural radiance and they're even likely to adore him. Secretly not so sure of himself, he still assumes the position of leadership and soaks up all the compliments that come his way, fishing for more. Far from making him arrogant, admiration helps him build a healthy sense of self. When his royal blood is acknowledged, it makes him more generous to others.

He excels in sports, loves drama, and is likely to be the life of every party. Don't even think about getting him anything at a thrift store. He is drawn to the latest fashion and designer clothes. The little girls love shiny shoes, purses, princess dresses, and all sorts of accessories and jewelry, the more scintillating the better. Crowns and tiaras are an absolute must. The little boys will walk around proudly with a velvet cape, an impressive crown, and a golden scepter.

One of my little nephews in Finland is a Leo. He may be just peacefully sitting in his seat in the back of his parents' car, but I see him on a throne, holding a scepter in his left hand, quietly ruling his kingdom, as his father and I—respectively his chauffeur and bodyguard—humbly serve him. His older sister is also a Leo. She silently glows whenever complimented on her beautiful hair and great sense of style. Those two children always try to outshine each other, the little boy by pulling out all the largest sheets of paper he can put his hands on to draw big, impressive buildings, and the little girl by decorating the table with elegance, folding napkins with mastered artfulness.

Leo children will blind you with their charm. Their happy disposition makes them a delight to have around. But should they be expected to do menial jobs such as taking out the garbage or cleaning the dishes, they will let out a loud roar as if saying, "These are commoners' tasks! Please! Remember whose court you're in!"

Your Leo child takes class seriously. There may be spells of wanting to enjoy beauty naps or, when in his teens, partying. But when he springs into activity, his beautiful energy raises a storm of sparkles. Fired by the need to be the very best, he'll master his lessons in no time at all.

Leos naturally attract the limelight. As a Leo Rising child, I was the perfect example. I was about five years old. One hot summer day, my mother was nervously driving with me through Paris, where we lived at the time. The heat was excruciating, and with the amount of traffic on the Champs-Élysées, it would be a challenge to get to the Finnish Embassy in time to obtain my father's new passport. My mother was getting more anxious by the minute when she noticed everybody around her pointing at the backseat, laughing. Intrigued, she turned around to find me, stark naked except for my little sun hat, my smiling mouth covered with melted chocolate, cheerfully waving at the neighboring cars.

When left in charge of other kids, the Leo child is a good disciplinarian—at least until his natural playfulness surfaces. His instinct is to allow others to simply be. The whirlwind of happy exuberance that ends up occurring validates his ego. One of the young instructors at the Tae Kwon Do studio where I train is a beautiful Leo, always smiling and positive. In the way he welcomes the students, you would swear that he owns the place. He proudly sports an impressive mane and is the leader of the demonstration team. Every year he comes up with new creative scenarios to showcase his flying side kicks and show off his brick-breaking skills. Besides the minor details of some last-minute unplanned chaos, his shows are always much enjoyed by the crowd that enthusiastically applauds while he beams with pride.

It may be no small feat to raise a king or a queen, but the light that will shine upon your life will feel like a thousand golden sunrises.

Virgo

Symbol: The Virgin

This is the second sign symbolized by a human being: a young girl, a virgin. Pure and beautiful, she is shielded by her innocence. Full of hopes and dreams for the future, she still needs to find her way. Her attentive awareness of her environment is what helps her ward off danger.

Element: Mutable Earth

Mutable earth is the beautiful, fertile earth, which yields its abundance for our sustenance before becoming barren again. This is nature's last gesture of generosity. All the fruits of our labors are rewarded and need to be organized and protected for us to survive the approaching hardship of winter.

Ruler: Mercury

Because Mercury only shines briefly at sunrise and sunset, the ancients, believing that they were in the presence of two different planets, gave it two names. Small and fast, Mercury has no moon, an almost nonexistent atmosphere, and is covered with shallow craters and fine dust. Despite being the planet closest to the Sun, Mercury only reflects six percent of the Sun's light. Because it always exposes the same side to the Sun, making one half torrid, while the other is forever ice-cold and plunged in darkness, this planet is almost impossible to study.

Ages of Man

Adulthood, when we start facing our responsibilities, such as getting a job, renting a first apartment, handling our own finances, and paying taxes.

Character

When the Sun enters Virgo, nature becomes markedly softer. Despite the warm days, morning mists tend to linger, taking longer to dissipate, and they shroud the horizon with mystery. The morning fogs dissolve, leaving the air crisp and clear, glossing the shining leaves with a very special purity. As summer comes to an end, it is time for harvesting and storing food in diligent preparation for the cold and dark days to come.

Virgos are very capable, intelligent, and industrious beings. Attentive to detail, they are meticulously hardworking perfectionists whose high standards can at times make them seem a little critical. Busy, practical, organized, and precise, they are particularly reliable and productive. Order and cleanliness are essential to their well-being, and because of their sensitive digestive systems, they are health- and diet-conscious. It is likely many have studied homeopathy, naturopathy, and acupuncture in-depth, and they doubtlessly know every property of every supplement and are active vegans or organic raw foodists.

They can be very talkative, yet don't always trust themselves to be as clever as they are. Their admiration for those who seem more knowledgeable is boundless.

The cool, unemotional makeup of Virgos does not make them insensitive. Quite the opposite is true. Their unassuming and modest ways imbue them with a very haunting and special kind of charm. Extremely kind, and modest yet precise observers of human nature, they serve others in a mostly shy and modest manner. They appear to be dreamers, but that does not mean they are. Their no-nonsense devotion is practical and sensible. While waiting in line, they are very likely to fumble through their purses to come up with the exact change.

We occasionally bump into a scattered and disorderly Virgo who seems completely to contradict the description I've just given. This is because of the dual side of this sign's ruler, Mercury. If we look again, we discover that behind that apparent chaos is a very orderly mind, with neatly stored data in constant use by an efficient and bright intelligence. There is no escaping the Virgo's need for order, whether it is within or without. As we progress through the coming years, Virgos will become increasingly liberated from worry, restlessness, and the incessant mental activity that binds them, thus freeing their hopes and wishes into even purer dimensions.

Enlightenment Tools of Mercury

Day
Wednesday.

Number
5.

Metal
Quicksilver (mercury).

Shapes/Textures
Short, incisive lines, and thin, flexible curves. Sandy, crumbling.

Flavors
Cool, slightly astringent.

Foods
Bittersweet: molasses, bayberry, mulberry.
Nuts: almond, brazil nut, filbert, hazel, pecan, walnut.
Vegetables grown above the ground: celery, endive, green beans.
Freshly squeezed vegetable and fruit juices.
All edible sprouts: wheatgrass, mustard, wheat, mung beans, chickpeas, alfalfa, barley.
Cereals: oat, wheat, rye, rice, barley, millet, buckwheat.
Vitamins and herb supplements.
Caffeine-free herb teas.
Also pollen.

Herbs/Spices
Small, with blue or yellow flowers, good for digestion, as a laxative, or to relieve anxiety: calamint, caraway, chickweed, comfrey root, echinacea, hyssop, lovage, senna, Saint-John's-wort, tabasheer.

Trees/Shrubs
Most nut-bearing trees: almond, hazel, walnut.
Bamboo, eucalyptus, mulberry, rowan, umbrella, ponytail palm.

Plants

Office plants: arrowhead vine, Boston fern, Chinese fan palm, ficus, Lady Jane, "Jade" pothos, triumph, dwarf *Schefflera*, silver queen, warneckei.

Flowers

Baby's breath, bouncing bet, cornflower, fireweed, morning glory, blue honeywort, iris, lady's slipper orchid, plumbago, lily of the valley, purple heart, sweet William, Queen Anne's lace, pimpernel, Peruvian lily, adder's tongue, lantana, heartsease, butter orchid, periwinkle, sweet cicely.

Musical Note

E.

Planetary Dominion

The mind, commuter travel, communication, knowledge, logic, reasoning, flexibility, curiosity, ideas, messages, literary affairs, the signing of documents, immediate neighborhood, close relatives.

Angel

Raphael.

Enlightenment Tools of Mercury and Virgo

Objects

Useful, related to office work: desks, typewriters, computers, dictionaries, atlases, accounting books, bookcases, filing cabinets, Swiss watches, catalogs, documentaries, reference books, almanacs, calendars, calculators, paper presses, containers, organizers, dividers, boxes, labels, notebooks, staples, staplers, hole punchers.

Related to health and sports: hand sanitizer, rubber gloves, organic foodstuffs, nutrition and recipe books, medication, vitamins and supplements, homeopathic remedies, flower remedies, essential oils, traveling drugstore, tennis racket, golf equipment, whistle, compass, Ping-Pong table.

Machines maneuverable by hand: looms, sewing machines, toasters, juicer, hourglass.

Related to nature: watering cans, window boxes, gardening tools, thermometer.

Practical clothes: made from cotton, jersey, flannel, or linen, work clothes, stockings (especially compression stockings), gloves, and detailed accessories such as belts and broaches.

Practical items requiring precision: pins and needles, sewing kits, accessories related to crocheting and knitting, such as yarn.

Craft-making items: glue, construction paper, glitter, crayons, special scissors, thread, papier-mâché, toothpicks, pipe cleaners.

Also worry dolls.

Locations

Outdoors: pasturelands, fields where cereals are grown, furrows ready for sowing, ricks (stacks of hay or straw), forages, arable land (especially if it is a little dry), fertilizable flat enriched soil, private gardens.

Stores: bookstores, drugstores, warehouses.

Related to work and learning: offices, libraries.

Related to health and service: health spas and resorts, free health clinics, foster care, animal hospitals, charitable societies.

On the farm: dairy farms, grain elevators, malt houses.

Indoors: quarters reserved for staff, private practices, home offices, apartments, houses or rooms rented or for rent, food storage rooms, locked rooms, pantries, toilets, pharmaceutical cupboards.

Weather
Cool, dry, windy.

Colors
Speckled or spotted patterns. Beige, navy blue, soft brown, slate gray, dark green, pure white.

Fragrances
Orris, fern, African violet, vetiver.

Gemstones

Moss agate, amazonite, yellow aragonite, green calcite, white howlite, jasper (dalmatian, green, mookaite), prehenite, blue sapphire, fade quartz, variscite, verdite.

Animals

All domestic pets, anchorites, solitaries, and small animals: hamsters, canaries, goldfish.
Service dogs for the blind.
Animal actually born in September, under Virgo: rock squirrel.

Parts of the Body

Abdominal organs, organs related to digestion, bowels (peristaltic action), duodenum, large and small intestine. Nervous system (lower dorsal nerves), pylorus, spleen.

Archetypes

Single people, virgins.

Professions

Related to health and nutrition: acupuncturists, dieticians, doctors, nurses, crop growers, masseurs, naturopaths, health officers, botanists, yoga teachers.
Requiring attention to detail: accountants, agents, personal assistants, astronomers, inspectors, data processors, high-technology technicians, secretaries, consultants, scientists, researchers, craftsmen, blacksmiths, watchmakers, manicurists.
Related to the sharing of information: critics, freelance journalists, librarians, teachers, linguists, writers.
Also experts in any field.

Hobbies

Useful, detailed, intelligent, and varied: activities in clubs or societies meeting for study, careful collection and arrangement of data (stamp collections, creating an herbarium), memory games, playing chess, doing crossword puzzles, Scrabble, detailed construction work, crafting, wood carving, origami, ikebana, embroidery, gardening, taking long walks in the countryside, bicycle rides, harvesting, literary criticism, putting things in order, cleaning and scrubbing, quiet reading, the study of diet and nutrition (veganism, raw food, holistic healing), diary writing, yoga.

Enlightenment Tools of Virgo

State
California.

Cities in the States
Kodiak (AK), Fayetteville (AR), Los Angeles (CA), Colorado Springs (CO), Manchester (NH), Minot (ND), Reading (PA), Rutland (VT), Norfolk (VA).

Countries
Belize, Bulgaria, Chile, Guinea-Bissau, North Korea, Malaysia, Mali, Malta, Mexico, Papua New Guinea, Qatar, St. Christopher-Nevis, Swaziland, Switzerland, Trinidad and Tobago, Uruguay, Venda.

World Cities
Athens (Greece), Baghdad (Iraq), Basel (Switzerland), Cheltenham (U.K.), Corinth (Ancient Greece), Georgetown (Guyana), Heidelberg (Germany), Jerusalem (Israel), Lyons (France), Paris (France), Reading (U.K.), Strasbourg (France), Toulouse (France).

Famous Personalities
Marc Antony, Anne Bancroft, Leonard Bernstein, Beyoncé, Robert Blake, Andrea Bocelli, Maurice Chevalier, Agatha Christie, James Coburn, Sean Connery, David Copperfield, Queen Elizabeth I, Peter Falk, Greta Garbo, Richard Gere, Sir Paul Getty, Hugh Grant, Jeremy Irons, Elia Kazan, Tommy Lee Jones, Stephen King, Arthur Koestler, Goethe, Jean-Michel Jarre, Sophia Loren, D. H. Lawrence, Maria Montessori, River Phoenix, Keanu Reeves, Nicole Richie, Adam Sandler, Claudia Schiffer, Peter Sellers, Oliver Stone, Mother Teresa, Tolstoy, Raquel Welch, H. G. Wells.

People
Sami.

Apostle
Philip, who had a servant's heart.

Cartoon/Film Characters
Alice (in Wonderland, who carefully read every label of every beverage she absorbed), Fillyjonk (of *the Moomins*), Queen Guinevere (of the Arthurian legends), Tintin.

The Virgo Woman

Slow to give her heart, it is equally hard for the Virgo woman to take it back. Although symbolized by the virgin, hers is a quiet, earthy, yet profound sensuality. It takes a very special man to awaken passion in her, but once aroused, it cannot be eliminated and it will forever haunt her soul.

Profoundly devoted to her husband, she is also a caring mother who insists on education and giving her children all the practical tools they need to be efficient in the world. She could spend a lot of time picking up after everybody and cleaning the kitchen after her whole family has been long asleep. She needs order to think straight and needs to fully complete one day before being able to start the next. Waking up in a messy house is not her idea of bliss or a healthy start to her morning.

She is likely to read carefully every label and know exactly what she is serving her loved ones for dinner, what vitamins should be taken, and which plants will calm a persistent cough. She might have her own herb garden and even grow some vegetables.

She is an avid reader and is not mentally lazy. Dictionary games or Scrabble can be favorites of hers. She is also likely to stay physically fit and dress impeccably with perfectly matching colors. You will wonder how she can stay so neat when everybody around her is sweating and messing up their clothes. A Virgo friend of mine always wears stockings, no matter how hot it gets, even when she knows she won't have any company. Very aware of germs, the Virgo woman probably takes more showers than anybody you know.

A special purity shines through her clear eyes. No matter how much of a woman she is, there is a part of her that remains untouched by life and love, eternally pure and chaste.

The Virgo Man

The Virgo man could have faraway, transparent eyes and a soft look to him, but he is not a dreamer. He is a very hard worker and very much a worrier, seeking perfection in everything he does. He will also demand that the woman he falls in love with meets his high standards. She should be clean in mind, body, soul, and spirit, intelligent and solid.

Manipulation and games send him running in the opposite direction. His basic instinct is celibacy, and he can live a very long time without feeling the burning need for a mate. After much inner deliberation during which you will have to be spotlessly patient, once he finds the perfect princess whose foot fits the glass slipper, he will declare himself with simplicity. His flame will never dim.

His devotion to you and his children will be admirable. He will deny you nothing, will be hardworking, neat, and orderly. He is likely to insist on organic foods and will be very specific about what he will eat and what he won't. Chances are he is a good cook. Committed to repairing his house, he will learn all the jobs he can to keep everything in his world functioning properly.

He may be a bit of a jack-of-all-trades, changing careers as soon as he has mastered and reorganized his profession. He will eventually find what makes him happy and give himself fully to it. His ambition is to serve, not to become head of the company. His selflessness and humility command respect from his employees, bosses, and colleagues.

This is not a man who needs to outshine his mate. He will be happy to take the backseat when it is your time to be in the limelight, silently supporting you with his quiet strength. Completely monogamous, he expects the absolute same loyalty on your part. Should you stray, you will find yourself without a husband anymore. He marries for life, but when his trust is betrayed, his apparent ability to cut you out of his heart will make it seem like he has none. This is not true. He just holds no illusion and knows for a fact that a shattered vase cannot be fixed back to its initial perfection.

He will at times feel too good to be true, but he is very real and grounded. He will be totally by your side as long as you journey with him in joined perfection.

The Virgo Child

The Virgo child could have some interesting habits. He may not like his laundry to be washed with the rest of the family's clothes. He may sort out his food. He may wash his plate twice and decide that from now on he will only eat pineapple. It is unlikely that you will have to beg him to tidy his room. That is a given with this child, who probably also plans ahead and chooses the outfit he will wear the next day, neatly folding it on a chair next to his bed.

Bright in class, he loves learning and will need no help to complete his homework. An encyclopedia or a chemistry or magic kit will bring a big smile to his face. From an early age, you will notice his need to serve. He'll happily set the table and clean the dishes, and is likely to offer to help with garden work. He will gladly take care of all the needs of his own pet, who in turn will give him the warm comfort of having a little furry friend.

When it comes time to start dating, he may be a little shy and could need some encouragement. Although beautiful, tidy, and smart, he can feel less attractive than his classmates. His slight insecurity stems from his need for perfection and his tendency to compare himself to others who are bolder or louder than he.

Quiet, more solitary pastimes are his favorites, and he especially loves to spend time making objects that will prove useful. The Virgo child is a delight to have around. Curious and interested in his environment, he will ask all sorts of intelligent questions and demand equally sound answers. He is highly sensitive to his surroundings and could develop illnesses as a way to protect himself from disharmonies. Although he is naturally talkative, it is not always so easy for him to express deep, intimate emotions. For the sake of peace, he tends to keep most of his feelings buried inside. It may be a good idea to support diary writing and make sure that no one pries into his most secret thoughts until he decides he'd like to share his secret moods.

Greatly observant, he can make the whole family laugh with his astute imitations of people's quirks. He has the gift of recreating accents and mannerisms.

This is a bright child whose contribution to humanity is likely to be very special.

LIBRA

Symbol: The Scales
This is the only sign of the zodiac to be symbolized by an inanimate object. Observing an old-fashioned scale will give you much insight into Libra's character. Designed to weigh through counterforce, the loaded side dips down while the other rises. When weights are placed on the side that is in the air, it lowers. Reversing roles back and forth many times, through trial and error, the two sides eventually reach that rare moment of perfect equilibrium. And even then, it only takes the slightest movement to shift the weight and once again upset the balance. The scales are also symbolic of justice and the weighing of the soul after death. According to Plato, at the beginning of Creation we were androgynous. When the separation into female and male came, Virgo and Scorpio, which had until then been one sign, separated into two. Libra appeared in the middle as a representation of marriage, the unification of opposites.

Element: Cardinal Air
Cardinal air is moving air, the soft and cooler wind of fall.

Ruler: Venus
Never farther than sixty degrees from the Sun, Venus reacts the strongest to the Sun's intense light. Venus is the shiniest planet in the sky. The Greeks, thinking that they were seeing two planets, gave her two names: Phosphoros at dawn and Hesperos at twilight. Similar to the Moon, Venus has phases. However, because of the presence of white clouds shrouding her surface, she mostly remains a mystery to us.

Ages of Man

Marriage. When in adulthood we strive to join our life with another.

Character

In Virgo, the harvest was carefully stored away. As the Sun enters Libra at the fall equinox, the days and nights are of the same length. Nature reaches a fragile balance. It is the special point where darkness gradually starts increasing every day. The trees explode in a display of bright colors, heralding the death that will take place in Scorpio. An almost tangible silence pervades the atmosphere. Imbued with peace and softness, it inspires meditative contemplation.

This sign has many contradictions. Libras like people but hate crowds. They are very active, but they go through phases of complete lethargy. While they are talkative, they are also very good listeners.

Affectionate, Libras prefer companionship to solitude. Lovers of beauty, peace, and harmony, to them marriage is a more natural state than remaining single. They are very good at bringing people together, and they know how to create interesting social mixers. Tactful and diplomatic, they are also charming, even-tempered, and attractive. Anger and impatience distress them, as do loud noises and clashing colors. A slightly tilted framed photograph could upset their sense of order. Their innate respect for culture, art, and education draws them to beautifully illustrated books and objects that are pleasing to the senses. Fond of ease and comfort, they relish in creating elegant atmospheres.

Justice is paramount to them and they will do anything that's fair. But because of their ability to always see both sides of an issue, they often find it difficult to make decisions. Libras are highly objective and they analyze every situation rationally. Their intense distaste in hurting anyone can lead them at times to side with people of completely opposing views. While they are weighing the pros and the cons, they cannot be rushed. It is at their own pace, through the seemingly endless comparison of one thing to another, that they reach that elusive point of balance where all falls magically into place. Soft music, pastel colors, and gentle words are soothing to their soul, which is forever in search of peace.

Enlightenment Tools of Venus

Day
Friday.

Number
6.

Metals
Copper, bronze, brass.

Shapes/Textures
Rhythmical curves, full and sensual. Warm and soft (marshmallow-style).

Flavors
Fragrant, aromatic, warm, pleasant, and sweet.

Foods
Most fruits and berries: apples, apricots, bananas, blackberries, red cherries, cranberries, gooseberries, grapes, huckleberries, peaches, pears, persimmons, plantains, plums, pomegranates, strawberries, tomatoes, fruit preserves.
Vegetables: alfalfa, asparagus, burdock, dandelion, green peas, sorrel.
Legumes: chickpeas, lentils, navy beans.
Delicacies: chocolate, tonka beans, macaroons, marzipan, royal jelly, dessert wines, liqueurs (mirto, arrack), sweets (stevia, honey, candy in general, cotton candy).

Herbs/Spices
Fragrant and sweet and/or good for the complexion and/or the kidneys: bearberry, Chinese boxthorn, centaury, Chinese dodder, Mormon tea, sarsaparilla root, spotted cranesbill, green tea, jasmine tea, parsley, yarrow.

Trees/Shrubs
Most fruit trees: apple, apricot, cherry, peach, plum, vine.
Also ash, birch, butterfly bush (buddleia), crab apple, elder, poplar.

Plants
Delicate, with tender leaves: lycopodium.

Flowers
Fragrant, mostly pink or peach, beautiful in bouquets: anemone, apple blossom, pink aster, azalea, cherry blossom, cyclamen, freesia, gladiolas, heartsease, hydrangea, larkspur, white lilac, lily, peace lily, pink mallow, meadowsweet, *Silene caroliniana* variants, roses.

Musical Note
A.

Planetary Dominion
Luxury, fine art, courtship, love, marriage, pleasure, harmony, peace, balance, beauty.

Angel
Hagiel or Anael.

Enlightenment Tools of Venus and Libra

Objects
Expensive, elegant, and refined: vases, Persian rugs, soft and warm carpets, linen or silk sheets and cushions, sculptures, masters' paintings, etchings, Oriental prints, rare furniture, beautifully illustrated books, wallets, money, cherrywood or rosewood music or jewelry boxes.
Enhancing beauty: silk or embroidered clothes, lace, ribbons, gloves, evening gowns, silk underwear, jewelry, perfumes, makeup, perfume bottles, flower bouquets, napkin rings, bath salts, candles.
Toys: juggling balls, airplane models, Barbie dolls.

Also gifts in general, organza gift bags, scales, concert tickets, love poems.

Locations
Outdoors: hillsides, locations where the air is fresh and pure, sandy fields, neat gardens with a profusion of flowers, public gardens.
Also windmills.
Places where people gather to entertain themselves or improve their beauty: social centers, dancing halls, concert halls, hair salons, elegant restaurants, art schools, public baths, coffee shops with terraces.
Indoors: baths, bedrooms, living rooms, attics.

Weather
Moderate and nice.

Colors
Shades of blue from pale to ultramarine, pastel green, peach, soft rose.

Fragrances
Apple blossom, galbanum, ginger, myrtle, rose.

Gemstones
Green chrysoberyl, emerald, fuchsite, white jade, lapis lazuli, white marble, opal, prehnite, Chinese turquoise.

Animals
Beautiful insect: butterfly.
Beautiful birds: dove, hen, nightingale, swallow, song thrush.

Parts of the Body
Features: dimples, hair, complexion.
Also kidneys, lumbar nerves, adrenal glands, vasomotor and venous systems.

Archetypes
Beauties, lovers, pleasant people full of grace and harmony, people in love, playboys, seducers, sweethearts, wives, young women.

Professions

Artists: actors, models, jugglers, poets, singers, dancers, engravers, illustrators, fashion designers.
Beauticians: decorators, florists, gardeners, jewelers, perfumers.
Peacemakers: diplomats, staff officers.

Hobbies

Lazy and peaceful: reading quietly, picking flowers to create a bouquet, decorating, painting, receiving a facial, getting a manicure, having tea with a friend.

Enlightenment Tools of Libra

States
None.

Cities in the States
Riverside (CA), St. Augustine (FL), Rock Island (IL), Roswell (NM), Chapel Hill (NC), Eugene (OR), Rapid City (SD), Knoxville (TN), Waco (TX), Alexandria (VA).

Countries
Botswana, China, Fiji, France, Guinea, Lesotho, Nicaragua, Nigeria, Portugal, Saudi Arabia, Syria, Tuvalu, Uganda, Yemen Arab Republic.

World Cities
Antwerp (the Netherlands), Copenhagen (Denmark), Frankfurt (Germany), Johannesburg (South Africa), Leeds (U.K.), Lisbon (Portugal), Nottingham (U.K.), Vienna (Austria), Zürich (Switzerland).

Famous Personalities
Julie Andrews, Brigitte Bardot, Neve Campbell, Jimmy Carter, Montgomery Clift, Matt Damon, Catherine Deneuve, Michael Douglas, William Faulkner, Sarah Ferguson, Gandhi, George Gershwin, Rita Hayworth, Vladimir Horowitz, Deborah Kerr, Ralph Lauren, Franz Liszt, John Lennon, Marcello Mastroianni, Arthur Miller, Yves Montand,

Viggo Mortensen, Olivia Newton-John, Friedrich Nietzsche, Eugene O'Neill, Clive Owen, Gwyneth Paltrow, Christopher Reeve, Tim Robbins, Nora Roberts, Susan Sarandon, Bruce Springsteen, Oscar Wilde, Kate Winslet, the band U2.

People
Tibetans.

Apostle
Nathanael or Bartholomew, the first disciple of Christ.

Cartoon/Film Characters
Madame Bovary, Charlie Brown (of *Peanuts*), Don Quixote, the Lady of the Lake (of the Arthurian legends), the Heartbreak Kid, Mary Poppins.

The Libra Woman
It is a rare Libra woman who will not marry at least once. Capable and independent, she is quite equipped to deal with life's demands on her own, yet her need to share her life with a good man makes her feel incomplete without that companionship.

Her social graces are impeccable. She is one of the best hostesses of the zodiac. Her friends will feel very welcome at her place. The taste with which she decorates her house could make a home designer look like an amateur. She will most certainly serve tea with her best china and have matching napkins, artfully folded. Chocolates, delicate cookies, and sweets will also be featured at her elegant gatherings.

No matter how feminine she looks, she is more than just her appearance. She has a very bright mind and takes an active interest in world affairs, but remains fair. There is no sense in asking her to blindly side with you. She will want to know what the other person's motivations are and why you attracted such a situation to yourself. After going back and forth, she may end up deciding that both you and the other party were right. Her opinions will invariably be offered in a calm voice and be as balanced as can be. She is a master negotiator and a fabulous mediator. In conflicts, she is consistently the bringer of peace.

Money is only important to her because it can afford her the beautiful clothes and jewelry she likes. She doesn't necessarily have expensive taste, but she seeks harmony in all things. She would never dream of wearing a blouse that would not flatter her hair color or consider leaving her nails undone.

She will treat her children as equals and will give them each the same amount of attention. Screaming and yelling will be discouraged very early on. Around her, they will learn balance and harmony and will be taught peace and justice.

A Libra woman is the epitome of womanhood. She is quiet and intelligent, with the exact perfect measure of masculine and feminine energy and features that are both beautiful and balanced.

The Libra Man

This man is charm incarnate. His smile will sweep you off your feet. He is a great lover of beauty in life in general, and in women in particular. A perfect body or a stunning face will make his head turn. Yet his need to always reach balanced decisions may lead to much indecisiveness: What if she is the right woman for me? What if she isn't? Should I move forward? Or not? He is just doing his best to be fair.

He can seem at times detached from the realities of life. Remember that his element is air. Seen from a plane, the fields are all neat, colorful, and well defined, almost abstract. Like the Libra woman, his deeply ingrained sense of justice could make him side with someone you feel has wronged you. The more passionate you are, the colder he can seem. It's his way of keeping things in balance. He is a great lover, yet his inability to dwell on the intricacies of the human heart can make him seem a little short on empathy. His logic alone is not very helpful in understanding the deeper meanders of the heart.

Despite his intense dislike of hurting anyone's feelings, vulgarity, as well as anything loud or disharmonious, will send him running to the hills. Aesthetics, elegance, refinement, calm, and equilibrium are musts for this man. Without those requisites, he feels very out of balance and might not even be aware of why. He was born to take things at face value and not to explore the deeper recesses of the human soul. His sense of justice is his most developed skill. He believes that women and men should be given equal opportunities and in his marriage he will do his fair share of work. The peace that emanates from him is almost tangible and will protect you like a halo of light.

The Libra Child

I am blessed with the friendship of a beautiful little Libra girl. One day she shook my sleeve and urgently whispered into my ear, "Come with me." I followed her outside. The landscape was shrouded in fog. In sheer delight, she looked up at me and with a radiant smile, extended her arms in a gesture of embrace. "God's breath," she simply said.

She is also the one who insisted on sharing her favorite musical collection with me, making sure that I listened to each CD so I could tell her what I thought. For Halloween, she dressed as a princess and bore her tiara with grace and charm. Faced with the more bully demeanor of her sister, a grounded Taurus, my little Libra friend just smiles philosophically.

It is also she who, one day, showed up very pensive, with her fingers each in turn resting on the tip of her thumb in meditative posture. "This is a great mystery," she whispered in a soft voice. "What is?" I asked. "It is a great mystery," she slowly repeated, "that I can dream when I'm awake and be awake when I dream." Indeed, uniting opposites is Libra's special magical skill.

Never underestimate the power of seduction of Libra children's smiles. They will drown you in their charm and wrap you around their little fingers. Do not dream of making them wear clashing colors or rough fabrics. To remain in balance, they need comfort, harmony, and beauty. And avoid giving them a choice. That could lead to paralyzing anxieties.

To this child, justice is a big issue. If you want everyone to get an equal slice, ask him to cut the cake. If he is offered two pieces of candy, he'll make sure to bring one back for his sibling. Be careful, though, with this child's sweet tooth. It could lead to dental and weight complications.

The Libra child seeks companionship and makes friends easily. Sharing is the spice of life to a Libra and should be supported. He may request a little night-light in his bedroom so he doesn't feel alone. He also needs tons of bright, matching colors and beautiful harmonies to keep his soul peaceful. The rewards later will be a sweet, balanced human being with poetry in his heart.

SCORPIO

(OCTOBER 23–NOVEMBER 22)

Symbols: The Scorpion, the Eagle, the Phoenix
All three symbols relate to Scorpio.

The scorpion symbolizes less-evolved Scorpios. In nature, scorpions have hardly evolved at all, either because they were created perfect or because they resisted evolution. Scorpions are nocturnal, solitary animals that prefer hot climates. Depending on the threat, their sting can paralyze or kill. In some cases, after mating, the female devours the male. Scorpions are equipped to survive extreme conditions, such as high levels of radiation.

The eagle represents Scorpio's higher level of evolution. This majestic bird rules the sky. Its piercing eyes can detect prey miles away. The first-hatched chick usually destroys its younger sibling still in the egg. Only the most powerful will survive.

The phoenix represents Scorpios who have reached total mastery of life and of themselves. This mythical bird, with beautiful red and gold feathers, was said to be immortal. He cyclically built a nest with cinnamon twigs and set it, as well as himself, on fire. From the ashes that remained emerged a gloriously powerful and stunning new phoenix.

Element: Fixed Water
Fixed water is the impenetrable water of lakes. Still, silent, dark, and cold, without revealing anything of the mysteries lying below its surface, it mysteriously mirrors the trees on its bank.

Ruler: Pluto
When the general assembly of the Astronomical Union decreed that Pluto no longer was a planet, many people wrote to me in a panic. But

you may be reassured. The three criteria necessary for a planet to be accepted by the general assembly of the Astronomical Union are:

1. It is a body orbiting the Sun.

2. It is massive enough to support its own gravity.

3. It is clear of small planets or asteroids.

If this definition were to be applied strictly, Earth, Mars, Jupiter, and Neptune, who all share their orbits with asteroids, would not be planets, either. To me, the decision to say Pluto is not a planet is like arbitrarily deciding one day that from now on we shall call the color red, green. Does this change of name alter in any way the actual nature or vibration of red?

Pluto was discovered on March 1930, between the two world wars, as Nazism was a mounting power. Pluto may have at one point been a satellite of Neptune. Its icy and rocky surface gives it the appearance of a convex mirror. Despite its distance from the Sun, it reflects more than fifty percent of its light. As the last planet of our solar system, it heralds our entrance into interstellar space. It is what is called a "transpersonal" planet, meaning that because of its extremely slow revolution around the Sun (about 250 years), it affects whole generations.

Ages of Man
Maturity, when we start thinking about the mysteries of life, and may begin investigating the occult, researching death and the afterlife.

Character
When the Sun enters Scorpio, nature is close to dying. In a passionate last surge of life, it displays its brightest and richest colors. The leaves turn bright red while other trees seem to be covered with gold. The colder days are upon us and the nights are longer. Halloween and All Saints' Day, both centered on the dead, are Scorpio celebrations.

I think Scorpios are among the most fascinating and magnetic people around. The emotional wounds their sharp perceptions can inflict will either destroy the most vulnerable, or help those who have the courage, to grow much stronger.

You will recognize Scorpios by their intense stares. When needing to remain anonymous, aware that the intensity of their eyes gives them away, they often wear sunglasses. They despise weakness in others as much as they do in themselves. Never victims, Scorpios choose their own destiny, sometimes in convoluted ways.

I admire Scorpios for their phenomenal capacity to transmute difficult circumstances into power. One of the many Scorpios I am privileged to know has an extraordinary story. He was abused by his parents as a child. As a teenager, when his parents were passed out drunk, he raised his brother and his sister on his own, making sure they had food to eat and that they did their homework. Knowing no better, following his parents' example, he soon became a drug and alcohol addict himself. In his early twenties, he passionately desired a child. With the birth of his daughter, his self-destruction dawned on him. Without any help, almost overnight, he broke his habits. His girlfriend, also an addict, chose not to. To protect his little girl, he left her mother. In the same way he had taken care of his siblings, he educated his daughter single-handedly. After two years of intense training, he earned a black belt in Tae Kwon Do. Today, in addition to being a respected martial artist, he is studying to become a nurse.

This man's journey exemplifies the willpower of Scorpio, who has to experience extremes of behavior to feel alive. In one lifetime, he has the ability to rise from being a scorpion residing in the darkest places to the highest heavens dominated by the eagle, his truest symbol.

Deep, devoted, driven, Scorpios are superior beings with intense feelings. They are drawn to the metaphysical and the mysterious. A Chinese proverb recommends, "In darkness, give yourself to the darkest." Scorpios live by that rule. "Within darkness shines the light," says the Bible. "It is only because darkness did not recognize it, that it remained dark." Scorpios are beyond intuition. They know, and it is their knowingness that makes them find what was hidden.

While living in Switzerland, I once had a Scorpio cleaning lady. She had a knack for finding places to clean that I never even would have thought of. She was so thorough that she would pull the fridge out every week to get to whatever was behind it. She worked efficiently, without a pause, without a word. She never listened to the radio, nor answered her own phone while she was working. She was being paid to clean and she honored that commitment, leaving my apartment invariably spotless.

Passionate, powerful, reserved, and fiercely private, Scorpios are a law unto themselves. Because they are fascinated by sexuality, death, and the afterlife, their intense stare probes beneath the surface, bringing to light what was buried and in need of transformation. Scorpios are among the most loyal people there are. Betrayal by others leaves deep wounds. They may forgive, but they will never forget. Scorpios are demanding people, but the rewards are many. Your courage to live up to their intensity will unleash your own power to manifest your wildest dreams.

Enlightenment Tools of Pluto
Note: You may also want to look into the associations of Mars (Aries), as this was the traditional ruler of Scorpio before Pluto was discovered. Pluto is the higher octave of Mars, meaning that Pluto expands the associations of Mars.

Day
None.

Number
0 (0 added to any number increases its power. You will agree that $1,000,000 is a lot more than just $1!).

Metals
Plutonium, steel, tungsten.

Shapes/Textures
Bold, straight lines. Sharp angles. Complex, alterable combinations. The void.

Flavors
Extremely attractive or repulsive, liberating sensuous aromas.

Foods
Aphrodisiacs: arugula, avocados, caviar, bitter dark chocolate, liqueur-filled chocolates, coffee, garlic, ginger, licorice, oysters, pine nuts, raspberries, truffles, vanilla, wine.
Alcohol: absinthe, pastis.

Herbs/Spices
Mostly aphrodisiac or abortive: wormwood, bistort, yerba maté, turmeric, tribulus, yohimbe, woodruff, saw palmetto, southernwood, winter savory, pennyroyal, guarana, guggul, palmarosa, tormentil, coriander, common rue.

Trees/Shrubs
Areca catechu, blackthorn (tree of magic), bramble, ebony, mahogany, mimosa (the leaves of which react to touch), sandalwood, styrax.

Plants
In decomposition: fall leaves.
Primitive: liverwort.
Needing very little water: cactus.
Persisting well into the winter: devil's shoestring.
Parasites: dodder.
Carnivorous: pitcher plant.

Flowers
Related to the dead: chrysanthemum, tuberose (called bone flower by the Aztecs), purple heather, calla lily.
Dramatic-looking: black poppy, Baccara rose, barkarole rose, black beauty rose, black magic rose, torch ginger, red ginger, pineapple ginger, *Nicolaia elatior,* deadly nightshade.
Carnivorous: sundew.
Also desert rose, edelweiss, geranium, rhododendron.

Musical Note
None.

Planetary Dominion

Shared financial resources: inheritances, pensions, taxes, indemnities, Social Security funds, debts, financial empires.

Planetary resources/changes: global warming, the recycling of energy, nuclear energy, nuclear fission, the Earth's mineral wealth.

The metaphysical: occultism, white magic, atheism, agnosticism, life after death, iridology.

Related to power: secret contracts, radical reforms, street combat, secret weapons, martial arts.

Also sexuality.

On the darker side: black magic, conjuring, the CIA, the FBI, the Mafia, terrorism, organized crime gangs, religious fanaticism (the Inquisition), rackets, totalitarian regimes, underground organizations, dictatorships, anarchy, corruption, torture, rape.

Angel

Azrael.

Enlightenment Tools of Pluto and Scorpio

Objects

Related to power, enhancing wealth, or bringing luck and protection: safes, buried or sunken treasures, secret caches, time bombs, logic bombs, spy equipment, security locks, ancient swords, amulets, touchstones.

Around the house: enamel or ceramic objects, dried flower arrangements, silk sheets, erotic art, magnifying glass, ecosphere, terrarium, bonsai, ultraviolet lamp.

Books and music: magic books, books on the great mysteries of this world, magic wand, classical music CDs.

Furniture: mahogany furniture.

Vehicles: motorcycles, race cars.

Clothes: black leather clothes, black leggings, bodysuit, slinky gowns, masquerade eye masks, dominatrix accoutrements, sexy lingerie (especially in black or red silk), black leather stiletto thigh boots, chaps, heavy studded belts, chain earrings, snakeskin bags and shoes, bustiers.

Accessories: black leather attaché case or wallet.

Also synthetic substances obtained by disintegration and recondensation.

Locations

Outdoors: places where insects proliferate or reptiles thrive, quicksand, stagnant and polluted waters, muddy locations, everglades, marshlands, swamps, bogs, poorly drained soil, flat and windy land in danger of flooding, foul places of decomposition and putrefaction, rivers, ponds, orchards, grottos excavated with explosives, petrified forests, fossil quarries, oil wells, mines (particularly if unused), graves, ruins.

Dangerous locations: underground or underwater military bases, places destroyed by revolutions or terrorist activities (Ground Zero in New York City), locations where a murder or a rape occurred, rooms where secret societies congregate.

In cities: ghettos, the slums, poor neighborhoods, slaughterhouses, brothels, vandalized or abandoned villas, isolated and difficult-to-reach dwellings especially if in need of much repair, mausoleums, haunted houses.

Indoors: kitchens, bathrooms, toilets, basement, garage, humid and locked rooms, secret caches, sewage disposal, piping, sinks, atomic shelters.

Weather

Stormy, cool, wet.

Also volcanic eruptions and natural catastrophes involving water (tsunamis, floods).

Colors

Black, blue-green, dark brown, deep gray, burgundy, dark red (the color of blood), maroon.

Fragrances

Siamese benzoin, coriander, sandalwood, vanilla.

Gemstones

Apache tear, boji stone, red coral, kunzite, labradorite, lava, malachite, nebula, mahogany obsidian, obsidian, desert rose, black pearl, tourmalated quartz, serpentine, snakestone, staurolite, green turquoise, unakite.

Animals

Those that transform: caterpillars into butterflies, snakes (who shed their skins), tadpoles into frogs.
Prey birds: eagles, vultures.
Most insects and poisonous spiders: mygale spider, brown recluse.
Vermin: rats, termites.
Reptiles: alligators, lizards, iguanas, crocodiles, geckos.
Also scorpions, wolves, dinosaurs, dragons, fossils.

Parts of the Body

Bladder, cervix, coccyx, descending colon, genito-urinary system (sexual organs: penis, scrotum, vagina, uterus, ovules, prostate, spermatozoa), nasal bones, rectum, sphincter, the enzymes enabling proper metabolic functioning, the balance between an organism's anabolic and catabolic phases.
Also personal magnetism, piercings, tattoos.

Archetypes

Gothic or heavy-metal teenagers, people of extraordinary courage who risk their lives to save others, survivors of extreme conditions, vampires.

Professions

Requiring courage: martial artists, fire eaters, firemen, military men (especially those in the navy).
Piercing secrets: private detectives, spies, magicians, metaphysicians, occultists.
Related to sexuality: prostitutes, porn stars, gynecologists, sex therapists.

Related to healing: surgeons, healers, hypnotherapists, psychiatrists, pathologists, past-life regressionists, pharmacists.
Related to research: nuclear scientists, researchers.
Related to death: coroners, undertakers.
Also sanitary inspectors, tax collectors, public analysts, archaeologists, pirates, butchers.
And negatively: terrorists, suicide bombers, hard-core criminals (gangsters, murderers, serial killers).

Hobbies

Investigating secrets, the most fascinating of which being anything related to birth, death, and sexuality (reading books on tantra and, better yet, making love), sports that test one's limits, mystery games, Monopoly, chess, watching a thriller, scavenger hunts, dancing the flamenco, tango dancing, learning and performing magic tricks.

Enlightenment Tools of Scorpio

States
Montana, Nevada, North Carolina, North Dakota, South Dakota, Oklahoma, Washington.

Cities in the States
Fairbanks (AK), Little Rock (AR), Fresno (CA), Denver (CO), New Haven (CT), West Palm Beach (FL), Boise (ID), Decatur (IL), Salina (KS), Rockville (MD), St. Paul (MN), Jefferson City (MO), St. Louis (MO), Trenton (NJ), Newark (NJ), Schenectady (NY), Charlotte (NC), Fayetteville (NC), Johnstown (PA), Philadelphia (PA), Providence (RI), Aberdeen (SD), Barre (VT), Rock Springs (WY).

Countries
Angola, Antigua and Barbuda, Belgium, Brazil, Dominican Republic, Equatorial Guinea, Honduras, Lebanon, Panama, St. Vincent and the Grenadines, South Africa, the old Soviet Union, Transkei, Turkey, Zambia.

World Cities

Dover (U.K.), Fez (Morocco), Ghent (Belgium), Liverpool (U.K.), Messina (Italy), Valencia (Spain).

Famous Personalities

Christiaan Barnard, Richard Burton, Albert Camus, Prince Charles, Marie Curie, Alexandra David-Néel, Charles de Gaulle, Alain Delon, Bo Derek, Leonardo DiCaprio, Dostoyevsky, Sally Field, Jodie Foster, Indira Gandhi, Art Garfunkel, André Gide, Whoopi Goldberg, Princess Grace of Monaco, Billy Graham, Jon Heder, Robert Kennedy, Martin Luther, the comic strip *Mickey Mouse*, Claude Monet, Demi Moore, Mike Nichols, Georgia O'Keeffe, Madame Pele (the Hawaiian goddess of volcanoes), Pablo Picasso, Winona Ryder, Julia Roberts, Auguste Rodin, Meg Ryan, Carl Sagan, Martin Scorsese, Sam Shepard, Alfred Sisley, Henry Winkler, Yanni, Neil Young.

People

Arab people, Native Americans.

Apostle

Thomas, the courageous skeptic, and St. John, who wrote the Apocalypse.

Cartoon/Film Characters

The invisibility cloak (of the Harry Potter series), James Bond, the Cheshire Cat (of *Alice's Adventures in Wonderland*), the Gypsy (of D. H. Lawrence's novel *The Virgin and the Gypsy*), Lady Chatterley's lover (of D. H. Lawrence's novel *Lady Chatterley's Lover*), Sir Mordred and Morgan le Fay (of the Arthurian legends), Harold (of *Harold and Maude*), Siddhartha (of Hermann Hesse's novel *Siddhartha*), Spiderman, Voldemort (of the Harry Potter series).

The Scorpio Woman

Devotion is the Scorpio woman's middle name. She is passionate, sexy, powerful, and psychic. Her loyalty is intense and unless you have wronged her terribly—in which case you would have to be a very brave man indeed—she will never let you down. She will protect her children fiercely and spare them nothing that will make them strong, healthy, and smart. She may be a little stern at times and will not give in to their whining, but that's because of her lack of respect for any form of weakness.

If she is truly in love, there is no discomfort she won't endure to stand by her man. She marries for passion and stays committed through thick and thin. She respects strength and power. She offers both in abundance, and she needs the same from you in return.

She will not tolerate disloyalty. She has the courage of her own integrity and expects the same from you. Living with her will definitely toughen you up. She has passionate opinions on everything and it is useless to ask her to water down her ideas. Things to her are either black or white. She despises gray zones.

Her home is likely to be decorated lavishly with rich, sensual colors, creating the feeling of a cozy, private space to retreat from the world. She knows everything about everybody but rarely reveals her own secrets. No matter what she is going through in her personal life, none of her friends or neighbors will ever suspect anything is wrong.

The Scorpio woman is dutiful and respectful of her engagements. Her word is gold. Her heart is all at once on fire, mysterious, and cool. She will help you to see new things about yourself, and if you are courageous enough to walk with her, you will discover landscapes you never knew existed.

The Scorpio Man

The depths of this man's darkness equal the heights of his light. His life will exemplify both. In order to reach the summit of his own nature, he needs to plunge to the bottom of the abyss.

The Scorpio man's love is intense. If there is a good reason for him not to declare his passion—for example, if he has a socially unacceptable love, such as for a married woman—it can burn for years in the secrecy of his heart. There can be a streak of cruelty in this man's love, a secret weapon he uses to protect his deep sensitivity by attacking first, even when there is no threat. Extra cautious, he doesn't take anything or anyone at face value. Betray him once and you may never see him again.

There is no denying that a Scorpio is strong and will never be vanquished. He needs to win. It's in his soul.

He probes and unravels every secret that comes his way. Before admitting to being taken with you, he will scrutinize you intensely. He takes love very seriously and is a romantic at heart. To him, sex devoid of love has no appeal. He wants to be able to give himself fully. Many women will be fascinated and under the charm of his powerful magnetism, but only a very strong, confident, intelligent, sensitive, and feminine woman can handle his power. You will be tested many times. Your ability to go through the rings of fire he lights without succumbing to the lethal heat will determine whether you are worthy of his loyal devotion. Admire him, respect him, even fear him, but don't ever play with his feelings. His heart is very real and very sacred to him. If his fire is dangerous, his ice is a lot worse and, if directed against you, could leave an indelible mark.

In a constant need to test his own limits, he regularly needs to be reborn from his ashes. As he gradually purifies his soul of all its lesser instincts, he is able to express the most sacred dimensions of his soul. Reading the unknowable is to him the ultimate goal of sex. And having a lifelong partner to share this journey with, someone who will cherish him without ever losing her own power or challenging his, is his secret desire.

The Scorpio Child

A beautiful little four-year-old Scorpio boy I lived with for many years was so hurt one day that he threatened to go to the middle of the lake and drown himself. I knew better than to jokingly tell him to do it. This would have proven fatal. Scorpio children feel things intensely. Love and sexuality will be on their minds at a shockingly early age, so it is a good idea to openly discuss with them the facts of life. Prone to doing everything with passion, they will fall in love before they can even walk.

There could be a fascination with darkness, but it never stems from being influenced by friends. A Scorpio makes his own choices and is capable of stepping out of abysses at will. He will most likely be attracted to dangerous sports that force him to outdo himself and he will always reach for new heights. A martial art would be a great idea, as it will train his body, his mind, and his spirit while giving him the discipline he needs. It will also offer role models he can both respect and admire.

Scorpio children may go a little overboard in everything they do, whether it's food, play, or scaring themselves to death. My Scorpio mother, when she was a little girl, had discovered an old illustrated medicine book describing all the deformities that could plague the human body. For hours every day, she would absorb the contents of its pages in fascinated horror, enjoying every moment of her self-inflicted mental pain with pure relish.

These children are wise and mature beyond their years. They are likely to develop their adult handwriting in their early teens. They need to relate emotionally to everything they learn and to be given a loving hand as they grow into powerful adults.

Never allow yourself to be fooled by their ability to take enormous amounts of pain without flinching. If every child needs love, young Scorpios need maybe a little bit more. Beware, however, of a tendency to manipulate. They will most likely tell a detailed tale to lure you into bringing them a cup of hot chocolate because it simply never occurred to them just to ask.

One little Scorpio boy I know, when he was not invited to the party of someone he considered his friend, stoically swallowed his pain and told his mother that the other little boy had just forgotten. Scorpio children are intensely loyal to their friends, but they won't tolerate the kid who, unaware, steps on their toes. The retaliation will be at least double the harm caused. They want to make sure that the lesson is drilled into that intruder's head, so that he won't tread on the Scorpio's territory without having been invited.

These children keep their own feelings secret, yet they are intensely aware of every one of your moods and concerns. With their eagle eye, your young Scorpios will know exactly what you need. The generosity of their intense souls and their own special brand of personal magic will soothe your pain and heal your heart.

SAGITTARIUS

Symbol: The Arrow

Remember playing darts? Aimed at a goal, be it the bull's-eye, also called the cork, or at a specific number on the board, the dart shoots through the air, covers some distance, and lands. The idea of focusing on a destination and having to travel to it are all contained within the arrow: the archer's symbol.

Element: Mutable Fire

Mutable fire is the remains of the fire—the ashes that will be dispersed by the wind.

Ruler: Jupiter

Aptly called the king of the planets, Jupiter revolves around the Sun in twelve years, a macrocosm of the twelve months it takes the Earth to complete her own revolution. The largest of all the planets, Jupiter is a massive ball of gas with a gigantic magnetic field and more than sixty moons. On his four satellites are valleys, mountains, and even erupting volcanoes. His rings, weaker than Saturn's, are mostly made of dust. Jupiter's atmosphere is turbulent, with high-velocity winds caused by the planet's internal heat.

Ages of Man

Mature age, when we philosophically reflect on life and travel the world.

Character

With Sagittarius comes the end of fall. The terseness of winter is right around the corner. Yet, nature promises that the fallen leaves covering the ground will, in a few months, turn into new life again when spring returns.

Sagittarians may not be the most diplomatic souls on the planet, but that's because they are the most sincere. Incapable of lying or keeping a secret, they tell things as they are, in total innocence. In trying to make good, they may end up adding insult to injury, in the most naïve and well-meaning manner. Truth to them is paramount. Children at heart, they will genuinely be brokenhearted when their honest intentions are misunderstood.

Traveling is another one of their passions. They make ardent explorers who are fascinated by foreign cultures. You'll never have to beg a Sagittarian to hop on a plane to a distant country. Should adventure luckily and unexpectedly knock on their door, most of them have their suitcase already packed. They are lovers of nature. They will be as happy sleeping in a forest under a tent as they are in a palace.

Sagittarians' high intelligence leads them to an active involvement in world affairs, the law, religion, philosophy, publishing, and/or higher education. Natural rebels against authority, they support all sorts of causes and they vehemently fight injustice in the world. Sagittarians can always be found at the latest fashionable place and on the battlefield, passionately ranting on their soapboxes. They also enjoy lecturing, writing, and sports.

"God," claim the Bedouins in Arabia, "took a handful of winds of the south, and blowing His breath upon them, created the horse." Like the horse, the Sagittarian animal, they need total freedom. Fast as the wind, they move quickly and in their enthusiasm often trip and spill the contents of their attaché case. But no matter the state of chaos their papers are in, all the facts remain clear in their bright minds. They are attracted to danger and many own a motorcycle or are drawn to climbing.

Gambling comes naturally to them and with their inordinate trust in luck, they usually attract good fortune. Sagittarians are born optimists. No matter how bad things may look, they only focus on the silver lining of every cloud. And because they walk around with their heads in the clouds, trusting in the bounty of life, life is invariably generous to them.

They are very lavish with their own possessions. Should someone genuinely need their help, they will never keep the strings of their purse tightly shut. They could even at times be completely extravagant and spend more than they earn. With their beautiful belief that tomorrow will bring more abundance, life always does.

Sagittarians often make clowns of themselves, but in the king's court, wasn't the fool the wisest of all?

Enlightenment Tools of Jupiter

Day
Thursday.

Number
3.

Metal
Tin.

Shapes/Textures
Large, expanding into generous curves. Elastic rubber bands that spring back.

Flavors
Sweet, soft, and aromatic. They are balanced and pleasing to the senses.

Foods
Dried fruits in general: currants, figs, sultanas, prunes, apricots, apples, pears, pineapples, mangos, candied ginger, papayas, bananas.
Vegetables and edible flowers: dandelion leaves and flowers.
Nuts: roasted chestnuts.
Sweets: nutmeg sweets (Indonesia), marrons glacés, maple syrup, sugar syrup, fruit nectars, jams and marmalade, fruit preserves.
Alcoholic beverages: dandelion wine, ouzo, eggnog, mulled cider, Chartreuse liqueur, Augsburg ale, pastis.

Herbs/Spices
Tonics or herbs good for the liver, aiding digestion, and/or bringing luck and prosperity: agrimony, anise seed, avens, balm of Gilead, borage,

wood betony, chervil, clove, coolwort, hart's-tongue fern, juniper berries, milk thistle, nutmeg, sage.

Trees/Shrubs

With large trunks and/or leaves, or healing: banyan, baobab, bodhi, juniper, maple, white oak, magnolia, red sycamore, sassafras, balsam poplar.

Plants

Acanthus, blue heliotrope.

Flowers

Mostly with large, purple flowers or offered on special occasions: purple lilac, magnolia, poinsettias, purple bearded iris, blue hydrangea, allium, purple dahlia.

Musical Note

B.

Planetary Dominion

All matters of a positive nature: happiness, freedom, joviality, benevolence, mercy, generosity, loyalty, noble-spiritedness, success, luck, a positive attitude, enthusiasm, honesty, adventurousness, faith, trust.

Angel

Zadkiel or Sachiel.

Enlightenment Tools of Jupiter and Sagittarius

Objects

Objects related to luck: lottery wheels, the Green Card Lottery.
Religious items: altars, scepters, Bibles, rosaries, crosses, ankhs, Tibetan bells, dorjes, prayer books, incense burners, dream catchers.
Clothes: particularly men's underwear, clothes made out of velvet or brushed velour or covered with sequins, sports clothes (shorts, T-shirts,

polar fleece jackets, parkas, jogging pants), prom dresses; woolen, suede, and fur coats.

Uniforms: judges' robes, academic dresses (for a graduation ceremony), ecclesiastical garments (great cape), leotards.

Objects symbolizing power: judge's staff, medals, diplomas, crowns, impressive furniture, chalices.

Impressive vehicles: trains, buses, limousines, merchant fleet.

Related to travel and adventure: backpacks, suitcases, travel bags, tents, hiking shoes, carry-on luggage, computer bags, skis, ice skates, skateboards, surfboards, racing bicycle, scooters, travel books, trampoline.

Also gold goblets, lazy Susan tabletops, beanbags, a feather quill pen with purple ink, Oriental rugs.

Locations

Outdoors: the open sea, mountain summits, elevations from which the horizon can be seen, open prairies where horses gallop in freedom, forest fires, safaris.

Related to traveling: high bridges, horse tracks, horse stables, foreign countries.

Homes: large mansions surrounded by lots of land, skyscrapers, open houses.

Athletic places: gyms, running tracks.

For leisure: theaters, merry-go-rounds, health resorts.

Related to wealth: banks.

Places of worship: cathedrals, chapels, churches, minarets, monasteries, synagogues, temples.

Related to justice: tribunals, magistrates' courts.

Dedicated to learning: universities, publishing houses, libraries.

Indoors: clean, pleasant, and spacious rooms. Rooms situated on upper floors. The largest room in a house. Balconies with a view. Locations close to the ceiling. Wardrobes, cupboards.

Also charitable and philanthropic institutions.

Weather

Nice and serene. Warm and breezy. Winds from the northeast.

Colors
Deep royal blue, purple.

Fragrances
Clove, juniper, nutmeg, sage.

Gemstones
Apatite, azurite, carbuncle, celestite, falcon's eye, blue howlite, iolite, jacinth, kyanite, pietersite, rhodochrosite, blue topaz, watermelon tourmaline, blue turquoise.

Animals
Large and kind, great helpers of humanity: horse, elephant, deer.
Beautiful birds bringing happy messages: stork, snipe, golden pheasant, skylark, turkey.
Mythical: centaur.
Animal actually born in December under Sagittarius: eastern gray squirrel.

Parts of the Body
Arterial system (iliac arteries), pelvis, blood, circulation, liver (hepatic system), hips and thighs (femur, gluteus, and sartorius muscles, sciatic nerve, coccygeal and sacral bones), pituitary gland.
Also growth.

Archetypes
Moral and mental superiors, men in the prime of life, gamblers, positive people, foreigners.

Professions
In the financial world: bankers, cashiers, investors, speculators.
In the law: lawyers, judges.
In organized religion: clergymen, priests, ministers, bishops.
Businesses connected with woolen clothing: clothiers.
Professions connected with horses: hunters, horse jockeys, ranchers, horse trainers.

Careers connected with foreign countries: travel agents, foreign language instructors, flight attendants, ambassadors, interpreters, tour guides.

In higher education: university teachers, professors, publishers, philosophers, lecturers, orators, politicians.

Sportsmen: athletes, archers.

Entertainers: actors, clowns.

Also grocers.

Hobbies

Mental and physical games, sports: archery, hiking, horseback riding, jogging, rock climbing, camping, learning languages, studying the law, attending lectures, philosophy, religion, traveling.

Enlightenment Tools of Sagittarius

States

Alabama, Delaware, Illinois, Mississippi, New Jersey, Pennsylvania.

Cities in the States

Birmingham (AL), Tuscaloosa (AL), Montgomery (AL), Anchorage (AK), Long Beach (CA), San Diego (CA), San Jose (CA), Wilmington (DE), Tampa (FL), Columbus (GA), Macon (GA), Valdosta (GA), Annapolis (MD), Grand Island (NE), Youngstown (OH), Lancaster (PA), Columbia (SC), Greenville (SC), Spartanburg (SC), Chattanooga (TN), Jackson (TN), Memphis (TN), Beaumont (TX), Spokane (WA), Cheyenne (WY).

Countries

Bangladesh, Barbados, Bophuthatswana, Ciskei, Finland, Kenya, Laos, Mauritania, Mongolia, Suriname, United Arab Emirates, Venezuela, Yemen.

World Cities

Acapulco (Mexico), Avignon (city of the Palace of the Popes, France), Budapest (Hungary), Cologne (Germany), Rotterdam (the Netherlands),

Sheffield (U.K.), Stuttgart (Germany), Sydney (Australia), Toledo (Spain), Toronto (Canada), York (U.K.).

Famous Personalities
Louisa May Alcott, Woody Allen, Ludwig van Beethoven, Hector Berlioz, William Blake, Maria Callas, Dale Carnegie, Sir Winston Churchill, Miley Ray Cyrus (Hannah Montana), Emily Dickinson, Joe DiMaggio, Walt Disney, Kirk Douglas, Jane Fonda, Jimmy Hendrix, Billy the Kid, John Milton, Frankie Muniz, Brad Pitt, Charles Schulz, Frank Sinatra, Socrates, Steven Spielberg, Benedict de Spinoza, Ben Stiller, Marisa Tomei, Toulouse-Lautrec, Tina Turner, Mark Twain, Dick Van Dyke, Gianni Versace.

People
Nomadic: Bedouins, Inuit, native Australians. Also Esperanto speakers.

Apostle
James of Alphaeus, who along with Peter (Aries) and John (Leo)—all Fire signs—were the three founders of Christ's church.

Cartoon/Film Characters
King Arthur (of the Arthurian legends), Henry Higgins (of George Bernard Shaw's *Pygmalion*), Lucy (of *Peanuts*), Mowgli (of *The Jungle Book*), Gaston Lagaffe, Pippi Longstocking, the Ghost of Christmas Past (of Charles Dickens's *A Christmas Carol*), the Wardrobe (of *The Chronicles of Narnia*), Robinson Crusoe.

The Sagittarius Woman
The Sagittarius woman has the most incredible heart. She is generous—sometimes to a fault. She is funny and bright, and an eternal optimist. Because she is addicted to adventure, things are never dull around her. She loves people and attracts all sorts of varied and interesting characters in her circle. The more fashionable, spiritual, and intellectual they are, the better. She is very gifted and creative. The expression of her

opinions is always direct. She only tells the truth, and she does it in such a candid way that even though it may hurt, no one can hold it against her. She never means any harm. When she realizes she has stirred trouble, in her best attempt to make everything right again she will shower you with the generosity of heartfelt gifts and kind words.

She is as open-minded as can be and loves children and animals alike. Seeing herself as her children's big sister rather than just their mother, she excitedly explores life with them. Her home can feel at times like a circus, with something new happening all the time.

She is a warm and loving friend. She will happily loan you money—without any interest—if she has the cash, and she'll offer you a meal if you're hungry. No matter how grim things may look in her own life, she always keeps her eyes fixed on brighter horizons. After all, tomorrow is another day, and who knows what magic it will bring?

She is an exuberant and loyal partner. However, she cannot survive without her freedom—freedom to meet new people, freedom to ride her horses, freedom to fight against injustice, and freedom to travel. Her smile shines as bright as the sun. The Sagittarius woman makes all things better just by her presence. Her heart is pure and full of magic. Her faith is so strong that she has the ability to make happen anything she focuses on. She visualizes something positive that she wants and it becomes true. There is something of an angel in her, the power of having never forgotten that we are all one and that what she gives to another, she really is giving to herself.

The Sagittarius Man

I once met a Sagittarius man who was raving about his marriage. When I asked him what made it so wonderful, he answered with a bright smile, "My wife is always positive. She is open-minded, has a great sense of humor, and loves camping." I didn't get a chance to further the conversation, but I'm sure she was a Sagittarius, too.

Sagittarius men are a lot of fun. They are bright, positive, and full of adventurous ideas. Exploring the world is one of their passions. They are likely to speak several languages, and at one point or another he will try living abroad. Marriage is unlikely to be a priority. The Sagittarius man is already wed to his freedom and that is one commitment he will not relinquish easily. But once he does say yes to a woman, his profound sense of integrity will make him truthful and loyal to his ties.

Sagittarius men love the outdoors, and a hiking trip, for example, is very romantic to them. Their minds will fascinate you. Well read, they have the knowledge of an encyclopedia. They love movies and are Web enthusiasts. They love attending seminars and conferences, where their bright personalities attract all sorts of people to them. The more, the merrier.

They love parties and social mixers and they have an ability to relate to everyone from the janitor to the CEO of any top company. They know something about everything and they can hold their own in fascinating conversations.

When unattached, they may not be the most monogamous souls on the planet. They are passionate and full of energy to burn. Sexual contact is a highly enjoyable experience to them, so they generously share themselves with many partners for the love of variety and exploration.

Their hearts are kind and childlike. One Sagittarius friend of mine writes songs for children. His performances are joyful and fun. His young, cheering audiences adore him, seeing him as their adopted big brother. There is something very sweet in his clownlike act—a beautiful, enthusiastic innocence.

The Sagittarius man does not do too well with heavy, emotional scenes. The fastest way to his heart is through play, positive energy, and happiness. If he truly loves you for you, he will go to the Moon and back again, drawing a bright rainbow of eternal hope on the walls of your heart.

The Sagittarius Child

One of my dearest friends is a beautiful little five-year-old Sagittarius girl. The first time I met her, I couldn't help but make an admiring comment about her princess dress. She turned around and squarely stared at me. "Actually," she slowly and almost pompously explained, "this is not a princess dress. I am the Empress of the Universes." Oh, excuse me! Immediately forgiving my ignorance, she gave me a mischievous, bright smile that shone like a thousand suns.

Sagittarius children always ask a lot of questions, and no superficial or vague answer will satisfy their insatiable curiosity. Those little philosophers and judges really want to understand the workings of the universe. They will be ecstatic to receive a telescope or an encyclopedia for their birthday.

Sagittarius children also need a lot of exercise and an abundance of sun and fresh air. Team sports are highly enjoyable to them, as is theater, ballet, or horseback riding. For their spirit to bloom into all that it can be, they need to be surrounded by freedom and positive energy.

Keen observers of human nature, they are little clowns who will make you bend over in laughter at their imitations of people. Being the victims of an injustice can totally crush their innocent hearts. They will vehemently defend the underdogs and exclude no one from their games.

As soon as your Sagittarius child is capable of traveling on his own, he will grab a backpack, kiss you good-bye, and cheerfully head for new, unknown horizons. Fascination with foreign cultures and languages is an intrinsic part of his soul. He needs to explore ever-expanding spaces to truly discover his innermost truth. And once he does, he will know the universality of all that is within his own self, tirelessly sharing his spiritual wisdom with the world.

CAPRICORN

(DECEMBER 21–JANUARY 20)

Symbols: The Domestic Goat, the Mountain Goat, and the Sea Goat
These three symbolize the three levels of consciousness associated with Capricorn.

The domesticated goat is one of the earliest species to have been employed by man. It is inquisitive and curious, and its extensive explorations are done by nibbling all sorts of inedible things with its tongue and upper lip. This animal is both affectionate and social.

The mountain goat sports beautifully curved horns. An avid climber, the size of its hooves makes it easy for it to climb rocks with speed and dexterity, never sliding. Going down is more arduous. Although its digestive system allows the breaking down of almost any organic substance, it is usually fastidious in its eating habits. On summer afternoons, it can be seen enjoying the heat of the sun before retiring into the forest at night.

The sea goat is wise beyond its years. It is the sage who has completed his cycle of incarnations—he has cleared his karma. As he is about to leave the wheel of karma forever, he looks back, seeing humanity's suffering. Although he doesn't need to, he returns as the master he has become, with the goal of teaching the rest of humanity how to follow his example.

Element: Cardinal Earth

Cardinal earth is the cold earth of winter. Despite its apparent sternness, the soil, hardened by frost, covered with ice or snow, protects seeds due to germinate in the spring with its inner warmth.

Ruler: Saturn

Saturn is probably the most beautiful planet to grace the night sky. His rings most likely result from the disintegration of a Moon that came too close (Capricorns can be quite private people.) Saturn, whose warmth is generated from the inside, is made of captive iridescent dust, extremely fine, solid ice crystals, and gases. It is the farthest planet of our solar system to be visible to the naked eye.

Ages of Man

Old age and retirement, when we can enjoy the wisdom we have acquired throughout our life and can leisurely focus on quiet activities.

Character

As the Sun enters Capricorn, the trees are barren. Devoid of leaves, flowers, and fruit, stripped of all distraction, nature is down to its essential structure. The landscape is silent and peaceful, yet death is only surface-deep. Underground, seeds are patiently waiting for spring.

Capricorn's natural instinct is sobriety. He always prefers the most direct path, rather than a convoluted one. Capricorns have both simplicity and staying power. They are builders. Nothing ruffles their patience. No matter how demanding the efforts required are, once on specific tracks, they rarely give up.

They have a very keen awareness of time. To them, time is energy and should not be wasted. Time is valued more than anything else in their lives.

To feel comfortable, similarly to the mountain goat climbing rocks, Capricorns need to reach the highest point of the social ladder and be at the top of their chosen field. They are ambitious, extremely hardworking, and capable of enduring much sacrifice to attain their chosen goals. Their methodical concentration, practical organization, and persistence make them born autocrats.

Deliberate, dutiful, prudent, penetrating, and highly responsible, they can seem hard-hearted or, worse, boring to more exuberant people. The truth is Capricorns can be a little shy and insecure, hence their need to rise to positions of authority.

Capricorns appear to be masters at self-control, but they can be much more passionate and funny than they seem to be from their more rigid and frozen surface. Once emotionally involved and on secure ground, Capricorns reveal a completely different side of themselves: freer, lighter, and happier. They become noticeably younger with the passing of time. As children, they often look like little old men and dignified elderly ladies, but they display the vibrancy of adolescence in maturity.

Capricorns are natural leaders with an ageless wisdom. Their ability to discern between what is essential and what is not imbues them with a respectability and a seriousness that is not easily topped. Dignified and concerned with appearances, Capricorns tend to be rather conventional dressers. They are usually impressive to others and even slightly feared. Yet, however self-effacing they may appear, like the fabled tortoise in her race against the hare, they should never be overlooked. With her slow movements, the tortoise seemed doomed, but that impression didn't consider her persistence. Her single-minded focus saw her through the finish line—first.

Enlightenment Tools of Saturn

Day
Saturday.

Number
8.

Metal
Lead.

Shapes/Textures
Short, straight, hard lines, ornament-free but well drawn. Cold, hard, and heavy.

Flavors
Bitter, acid, sour, acrid, pungent, astringent.

Foods
Canned and/or pickled vegetables: red beets, pickles, sauerkraut.
Vegetables: eggplant, parsnips, turnips, potatoes.
Starchy foods: whole-grain bread, pasta.
Winter fruits: medlar, quince.
Sweets: sour fruit balls, candy.
Alcoholic beverages: dry wines.
Also sour cream, balsamic vinegar, amaranth, malt.

Herbs/Spices
Those that have a grounding quality, relieve melancholia, and alleviate rheumatism: pellitory, henbane, star anise, boneset, mandrake.
Those that are good for joints, bones, teeth, and skin: bloodroot, knotted figwort, belladonna, Solomon's seal, pepperwort, common starwort, nailwort.

Trees/Shrubs
Mostly wintergreen and/or coniferous: cypress, spruce, *Boswellia* tree, pine, Chinese red pine, Fortingall yew (the oldest tree in Europe). Also aspen, beech, cypress, elm, medlar, spurge olive, tamarind.

Plants
Spurge, ivy, dogbane mistletoe, mosses.

Flowers
Purple rock cress, desert rose, hyacinth, black and purple orchid, dark blue pansies, tulips, clivias.

Musical Note
D.

Planetary Dominion
Discipline, ambition, karma, efficiency, organization, leadership, duties, responsibilities, seriousness, wisdom, patience, old age, growing younger with time.

Angel
Cassiel.

Enlightenment Tools of Saturn and Capricorn

Objects
Of the Earth: manure, compost, Earth minerals, rocks, charcoal, the atomic condition of matter.

Garden or home improvement tools: ropes, hooks, chains, shovels, hammers, weights, clubs, plumb lines, ice picks, metal bars, padlocks, shackles, door locks.

Sports and entertainment: golf clubs and balls, dominoes.

Time-measuring devices: sundials, watches, wristwatches, timers, stopwatches, hourglasses, mantel clocks, cuckoo clocks.

In the house: pottery, ceramics, mosaics, tiles, granite counters, metal napkin rings, tea glass holders, faience china, monogrammed sheets, coats of arms, picture frames, blankets.

In the office: desks and leather office armchair, paper holder, elegant paper knife, paperweight, administrative documents, leather briefcase, fine-point pens, pencils and a pencil sharpener, business cards, business paper.

Books: rare and antique leather-bound books, appointment books, history books, architecture books, books on crystals.

Clothing: shoes, belts, corsets, woolens, cashmere shawls and sweaters, fur and leather clothes, designer clothes, mourning clothes.

Work uniforms: overalls, blouses, custom-made business suits, armor.

Used on the feet: orthopedic devices, pumice stones.

Vehicles: wheelbarrows, freight trucks, garbage trucks, trains, hearses, rafts.

Legal documents required to go through customs: passports, visas, green cards, driver's licenses, credit cards.

Also stocks, bonds, funerals.

Locations

Outdoors: infertile or fallow fields. Wastelands. Hilly, mountainous, rocky, uncultivated, or open land. Places that are difficult to reach. Deserts, holes, grottos, obscure valleys, mountains, forests, nature trails, steep mountain slopes, cleavers, cliffs, arêtes, wild land covered with thornbushes and brambles, climbing walls, fences.

Dark and cold locations: caves, churchyards, ruins, quarries where stone is carved, mines, junkyards, abandoned houses or villages, graveyards, dungeons.

Indoors: uncomfortable or poorly furnished rooms, coal cellars, woodsheds, barns, haylofts, foundations, dark corners close to the floor where things can get lost, low ceilings, doors, gates, walls, thresholds.

Also tanneries, manufacturing plants, police stations, shoe factories, detention camps, retreat centers, borders.

Weather

Gray, cloudy, and cold weather. Eastern winds. Extreme conditions (scorching heat or freezing cold).

Colors
Black, dark blue, dark brown, dark gray, eggplant, forest green, snow white, indigo.

Fragrances
Cypress, musk, hyacinth, pine.

Gemstones
Mostly black: aragonite, black diamond, blue coral, garnet, yellow jasper, jet, lepidolite, lodestone, snowflake obsidian, black onyx, black opal, smoky quartz, star sapphire, sardonyx, schalenblende.
Also bricks, granite, plaster, coal, fossils, ivory, porous stones.

Animals
Cloven-footed animals: donkey, goat, pig, camel.
Insects: nonpoisonous spiders, cricket, grasshopper, midge.
Aquatic: eel, toad, pelican, sea turtle.
Nocturnal or underground: Asian palm civet, raccoon, sleeper, owl, bat, bear, koala bear.
Birds: crane, pee wee, thrush, raven, blackbird.
Mythical: unicorn.
Animals actually born in January under Capricorn: gray whale, northern elephant seal, American black bear, eastern gray squirrel.

Parts of the Body
Bones, teeth, skin, joints, knees (synovial fluid), phlegm, spleen, nails.

Archetypes
Elders, fathers, tutors, authority figures, disciplinarians, high fliers, self-made businesspeople, loners, puritans, wise beings (masters).

Professions
Building trades: building contractors, master masons, construction workers, civil engineers, architects, plumbers, locksmiths, people involved in sand, cement, gravel, coal mining, land brokers.

Related to the land: cultivators, shepherds, land owners, crystal dealers, potters.

Related to the government: politicians, workers employed by the state, customs officers, civil servants, policemen, jail keepers, night guards.

People involved with teeth, skin, and bone: dentists, dermatologists, osteopaths, shoemakers, tanners.

People connected to the end of life: undertakers, sextons, priests.

Ascetics: monks, hermits.

Enlightened beings: spiritual masters, sages.

Also business administrators, antiquarians, mathematicians, school directors, grinders, street sweepers, tailors, timekeepers, tinsmiths, chimney sweepers, garbage collectors, grocers, innkeepers.

Hobbies

Practical, quiet, and solitary: music (long hours practicing an instrument), reading serious subject matter, studying.

Enlightenment Tools of Capricorn

States

Alaska, Connecticut, Georgia, Iowa, New Mexico, Texas, Utah.

Cities in the States

Huntsville (AL), Mobile (AL), Prescott (AZ), Fort Smith (AR), Pine Bluff (AR), New London (CT), Tallahassee (FL), Key West (FL), Atlanta (GA), Albany (GA), Savannah (GA), Idaho Falls (ID), Lewiston (ID), Rockford (IL), Cedar Rapids (IA), Dubuque (IA), Sioux City (IA), Paducah (KY), Cumberland (MD), Detroit (MI), North Platte (NE), Jersey City (NJ), Madison (NJ), New York City (NY), Asheville (NC), Hendersonville (NC), Bismarck (ND), Fargo (ND), Cincinnati (OH), Cleveland (OH), Toledo (OH), Enid (OK), Tulsa (OK), Pierre (SD), Austin (TX), Abilene (TX), San Angelo (TX), Salt Lake City (UT), Arlington (VA), Chesapeake (VA), Lynchburg (VA), Newport News (VA), Virginia Beach (VA), Seattle (WA), Charleston (WV), Wheeling (WV).

Countries

Albania, Australia, Burma, Cameroon, Cuba, El Salvador, Haiti, Indonesia, Libya, Poland, Romania, Samoa, Sudan, United Kingdom. Also the United Nations.

World Cities

Brussels (Luxembourg), Bucharest (Romania), Canberra (capital of the Commonwealth of Australia), Delhi (India), Geneva (Switzerland, headquarters of many international organizations including the United Nations), Ghent (Belgium), Mexico City (Mexico), Montreal (Canada), Oxford (U.K.), Port Said (Egypt).

Famous Personalities

Muhammad Ali, Rowan Atkinson, Joan Baez, Maurice Béjart, Humphrey Bogart, David Bowie, Jim Carrey, Pablo Casals, Carlos Castaneda, Paul Cézanne, Jesus Christ, Simone de Beauvoir, Kevin Costner, Patrick Dempsey, Marlene Dietrich, Umberto Eco, Federico Fellini, Ralph Fiennes, Benjamin Franklin, Ava Gardner, Mel Gibson, Cary Grant, G. I. Gurdjieff, Oliver Hardy, Stephen Hawking, Sir Anthony Hopkins, Diane Keaton, Martin Luther King Jr., Rudyard Kipling, Jude Law, Linda Lovelace, Ricky Martin, Henri Matisse, Henry Miller, Kate Moss, Mother Meera, Louis Pasteur, Amanda Peet, Edgar Allan Poe, the cartoon *Popeye, the Sailor*, Elvis Presley, Helena Rubinstein, Albert Schweitzer, Ryan Seacrest, Donna Summer, the comic book *Tintin*, Mao Tse-tung, Maurice Utrillo, Emily Watson, Alan Watts, Daniel Webster, Woodrow Wilson, Tiger Woods, Yogananda.

People

Hindus, Jews.

Apostle

Matthew, the tax collector.

Cartoon/Film Characters

Dumbledore (of the Harry Potter series), Marlin (from *Finding Nemo*), Merlin the Wizard and Sir Bedivere (of the Arthurian legends), Getafix the Druid (of *Asterix & Obelix*), Old Grandet (from Balzac's *Eugénie Grandet*), Schroeder (of *Peanuts*), Scrooge (from Dickens's *A Christmas Carol*), the Tortoise (from Aesop's fable "The Tortoise and the Hare"), the Scarecrow (of *The Wizard of Oz*).

The Capricorn Woman

A Capricorn woman will never daydream about Prince Charming while allowing life to pass her by. When he shows up, she will quietly and happily make space for him, but in his absence, she won't waste her intelligence on things that may or may not come to pass. Don't lie to her or conceal parts of the truth. She doesn't court illusions and she's not an idealist. She believes in hard work, self-sufficiency, and reality.

Don't be fooled into believing she is not a romantic. She is, in her own practical way. When romance is real and she feels emotionally safe that the man she loves will love her back in the same way, she will be the most passionate, caring, and devoted woman you could ever desire. I once met a man who told me he was a poor date but a great husband. That would apply to the Capricorn woman. She will not be at her best on dates (blind dates being the very worst). Once she's past the stage of just getting to know another and defining mutual feelings, she will feel as warm as a panda bear and she will reveal her inner world, the depth of which will enrich you. She also has an eye for recognizing which vulgar stones conceal a diamond. What most would discard, the Capricorn woman will examine and pick up, to reveal its precious contents.

Humor is the key to her heart. Make her laugh and all her good reasons for resisting you will be dispelled. Joy is irresistible to this woman of many subtle moods, some of which could cloud her in sadness and depression for no apparent reason. She just sometimes sees people and situations so clearly that those who are still asleep may resent her for the power of her wisdom.

It is rare that a Capricorn woman would conceal the date of her birth. She doesn't need to because she grows more beautiful with age. Her sense of style is usually conventional and classy, with an insistence on wearing the right labels. Even sick, a Capricorn woman will not relinquish her elegance.

She is good to her children, insists on the right diet and the best education, perhaps even home-schooling them. She can be surprisingly modest for those she loves and she will think of them before she thinks of herself. She will lend an attentive ear to her husband's complaints and to her children's stories, invariably sharing a pearl of wisdom that will comfort their hearts when they've been wounded by the world.

While she is still single, a Capricorn woman's career will be everything to her, but once married and with a family, though she won't necessarily give up her profession, it is likely to take a back seat while she devotes the best part of herself to her loved ones.

She enjoys structure and is a great organizer. She may not be perfect, but she's smart enough to learn from her mistakes. She is the woman the Bible refers to when it says that she will never whisper a bad word behind her husband's back, she will get up earlier than the rest of the family, and she will stay up late to clear the decks for a new day. She is hardworking yet sensual and feminine. When it was said that behind every great man is a great woman, the reference was surely to a Capricorn.

The Capricorn Man

While the Capricorn man is busy becoming CEO of his company, running for Congress, or creating a new bank, he might work around the clock, bring home tons of reports to read on weekends, and share his bed with his computer. You will be tempted to sigh that there is no room in his life for romance. Don't be so sure. The fact that he won't lose his precious time looking for love doesn't mean that his heart doesn't hunger for it. When it knocks on his door, it will never catch him unawares, and even if he looks nothing like Casanova, he will know exactly how to handle it in a way that could make the most reputed seducer turn pale.

The Capricorn man does nothing halfway. A little shy at first, he might make you think that he isn't the most passionate soul around. Think again. His flame, slow at first, will grow steadily with time. Once he determines that you are the one, his intensity and commitment will nurture every romantic fantasy you've ever dreamed of. After reaching his professional goals, he will have all the more time to enjoy the happier side of life that he didn't spend time exploring as a child. Like good wine, this man improves with age.

At home, he will sit at the head of the table with a presence that naturally commands respect. His authority is unlikely to be challenged and his children might both admire and slightly fear him. They will definitely avoid infringing on his rules and they will listen to his wisdom. By the time he welcomes grandchildren, he will have relaxed and he will enjoy a second chance at fatherhood—a much more leisurely one. They will find him a lot more fun than his own children did.

This man is a diamond in the rough. He needs a wife who encourages expressions of affection, reveres family, and also supports his intense ambitions by being an impeccable hostess and accompanying him to the many social functions he attends. His deepest desire is someone whose elegance matches his own, in dress and in spirit. Don't be shocked if seemingly out of nowhere he falls prey to bouts of depression. Like mysterious dark clouds, they hover over his Sun sign like a spell. He is just momentarily saddened and disappointed by life in general and people in particular. Once recharged in silence and aloneness, his inner mastery will shine again, strengthened by the knowledge that beyond the fleeting illusions of reality there is only one, eternal truth.

The Capricorn Child

When I came of age to attend school, my mother was stunned to see me quietly sit down every day after class, and do my homework, without her ever having to utter one word. I was just being true to my Sun sign. It was only when my assignments were complete that I allowed myself to play, usually taking the part of the teacher. When it came time to select a class president, I was always elected.

Being harder on himself than you will ever know, your Capricorn child needs a lot of encouragement. He may pretend he didn't hear the compliment you just paid him or act as if it really didn't matter, but it does. He desperately needs to be told how bright and lovable he is.

He may be demanding and critical of you, making you secretly wonder if the roles haven't suddenly been reversed, making him the parent. A Capricorn child can be counted on to be responsible. Send him to the grocery store and he will promptly return with everything on your list, plus exact change in his hand. Fulfilling tasks supports the sense of purpose he needs to feel he's going somewhere. In his late teens, he will be the designated driver every time and will willingly tutor (for money) the other kids with trouble integrating their lessons.

At a surprisingly young age, Capricorns usually already know what they want to do for a living. Their hobbies are serious and quiet. Most Capricorns are loners. They enjoy silence and solitude. Because they are not particularly outgoing, their awakening to romance could be more difficult than it is for those born under other signs. There is an inherent uncertainty in Capricorns that makes them feel less deserving of love and attention. Once they find someone to their liking who likes them back, they take their involvement seriously, feeling responsible for the other's happiness.

Capricorn children are very ambitious and work hard to attend the best universities and to get as many diplomas as possible. They revere tradition and those who have succeeded before them. They are likely to spend more time with interesting adults than with kids their age, who could be perceived as being a little lightweight.

They need to be encouraged to exercise, as they are quite content to stay home with a book. They don't necessarily feel the inner need to move away from their desk, which will, no doubt, be very neatly organized. The one thing I enjoyed once my homework was done was to sit by the phone and counsel all the kids at school. They knew that after hours I was available to listen. With a pad and pen, I would very seriously take notes while they were telling me all their problems. It made me feel important and needed, but, of course, because I knew way too much about everybody, I was usually "forgotten" when the party invitations were being distributed.

Capricorn children are miniature wizards who, with a wisdom that surpasses their years, are able to perceive clearly what would amaze most adults, if they would only take the time to listen.

Aquarius

Symbol: The Water Bearer

This is the third and last sign to be symbolized by a human being. The Water Bearer is an adult man who pours the waters of knowledge to mankind. Generously shared with humanity, the wisdom of Aquarius helps us shift to the next level in our evolution.

Element: Fixed Air

Fixed air is stagnant air, the atmosphere heavy with new possibilities before the thunderstorm breaks the skies open.

Ruler: Uranus

Uranus was discovered in 1781 as the French and American revolutions were raging from 1789 to 1799 and from 1775 to 1783, respectively. Surrounded by eleven rings, it probably has more than fourteen small moons, as astronomers keep discovering more. Its rotation is most unusual. Because of an almost ninety-degree inclination, Uranus rotates on its side. Its north pole is thus exposed to the Sun for forty-two consecutive years, leaving the south pole in complete darkness during that time, until they exchange positions for another forty-two years. The gas in its atmosphere absorbs all the sunlight colors except for the blue-green hue it presents to us.

Ages of Man

The stage when, after having succeeded in our careers, we either focus on our dreams or share the rewards of our work with humanity.

Character

In nature, this is an unstable time. Winter is not yet over and spring has not yet arrived. Cold and warm days alternate. Thunderstorms erupt out of nowhere while some trees already start bearing leaves.

Aquarians are unusual people, each with his or her own brand of genius, insanity, and idealism. Highly independent, they are ingenious and inventive. They are lovers of humanity and curious by nature. There is no mystery of existence they won't explore, and the stranger, the better. Whether it is UFOs, science, or occurrences defying traditional logic, their bright minds are fascinated by everything coming from the future or the unknown. There is a certain detachment in Aquarians, a faraway, dreamy quality, as well as a natural intuition that strikes like lightning at the most unexpected times.

Highly eccentric, they are also independent, individualistic, and free-thinkers who analyze every behavior much like a scientist. However soft-spoken and calm they appear, there is more than a streak of unconventionality in Aquarians. They dislike routine and control. Disinterested in conventional behavior, they are natural rebels. They cherish their own freedom and are likely to be involved in some humanitarian movement to help the oppressed masses liberate themselves from the chains binding them. Their choices and actions are always deliberate and conscious. Their sense of power and authority invariably departs from established customs.

Attracted to newness and creating their own code of behavior as they move along, they are self-reliant and remain very unaffected by conventional morality. They can even develop sexual preferences based on political or social ideals, with a penchant toward androgyny. Seeking quantity in their experiences, they are natural friends who take a genuine interest in every person who comes their way, though they do so in a rather impersonal manner.

Unique and open-minded, these are refined and positive individuals, attracted to light and positive life concepts. They are the awakeners of the zodiac.

Enlightenment Tools of Uranus

Note: Because Saturn (ruler of Capricorn) was the traditional ruler of Aquarius, his associations are also somewhat relevant for Aquarius. Also, kindly keep in mind that because Uranus is the higher octave of Mercury, some of the associations of these two planets may feel similar.

Day
None.

Number
4.

Metal
Uranium, aluminum.

Shapes/Textures
Mixed, vibrant, pulsating, flashing. Straight or lightninglike lines.

Flavors
Cold, briny, astringent, strange, unusual.

Foods
Deep-frozen, in airtight containers.
Concentrated, scientifically designed meals: nutrition bars.
Most tropical fruit: mangosteen, dragon fruit, durian, star fruit, lychee fruit, jackfruit, ackee, breadfruit, guanabana, kiwi, kumquat, toddy palm seeds, tamatillo, longan, guava, cherimoya, jujube, passionfruit, pepino melon, prickly pear, rambutan, white sapote.
Negatively: irradiated, full of chemicals, highly processed.
Also linseed oil, popcorn.

Herbs/Spices
Those with sharp or unusual flavor, antifatigue, stimulating: bryony root, chicory, ginseng, kola nuts, pokeweed.

Trees/Shrubs
Birthwort, cycad, golden rain tree, screw pine, talipot palm, Barbados pride, red powderpuff tree, tree of heaven, *Medinilla magnifica*, chlorophytum, *Clerodendrum quadriloculare*.

Plants
Hermaphrodite: sea holly.
Also *Curcuma inodora*, chenille plant, "Thai Beauty" caladium, bleeding heart vine, jade vine.

Flowers

Hybrids: "Blue Ice" tall hybrid phlox.

Interesting-looking with very unique features: spider lily, *Pavonia multiflora*, *Costus cuspidatus*, red bromeliad, pineapple ginger, thunbergia, beehive ginger, pineapple lily, "Lobster Claw" heliconia, *Heliconia rostrata*, amaryllis, bird-of-paradise, pelican flower, burbidgea, *Hedychium longicornutum*, Aussie plume, orange coxcomb, *Costa costa*, double fuchsia.

Musical Note

None.

Planetary Dominion

Strikes, sparks, explosions, broken contracts such as divorce, sudden deaths, aerobics, Pilates, experimental science, electricity, laser science, inventions, UFOs, abstractions, paradoxes, excitement, unusualness, the unforeseen and the unexpected, individualism, willpower, originality, eccentricity, independence, free-spiritedness, freethinking, socialism, anarchy, mass media, human rights, revolutions, reforms, New Age technologies, friendship, homosexuality, androgyny.

Angel

Uriel.

Enlightenment Tools of Uranus and Aquarius

Objects

Technologically advanced: cinematographs, electronic gadgets, Skype, iPods, lasers, radars, steam engines, radiology, telephones (particularly wireless and iPhones), satellite television, digital cameras, the Internet, e-mails, videos, computers, antennae, remote controls, walkie-talkies, CDs, DVDs, VHS, gyroscopes, neon signs, fluorescent pens, rainbow-titanium-bullet space pen or horseshoe circular barbell, a multicolored pencil, radioactive substances, magnetic fields, lightning rods, the atomic bomb, scientific equipment, disco balls, flashing lights, blue lights on police cars.

Books and card decks: space travel, aviation, inventions, scientific geniuses, eccentric people, modern art, astrology, astronomy, the Voyager Tarot.

In the house and garden: air-conditioning, hammock, glass tables, inflatable or plastic furniture, modern art, Calder mobiles, Christmas lights, glowing ceiling stars, full-spectrum lightbulbs, tanning beds, lava lamps, plastic shower curtains, sandwich bags, aluminum foil, Tupperware dishes, telescopes, patchwork quilts, rainbow sheets, origami, ikebana flower arrangements, Kirlian photographs of the aura, marbles, pyramid structures, home planetariums, weather vanes, wishing-well planters, solar panels.

Anything inducing spontaneous disintegration: firecrackers, fireworks.

Original clothes: asymmetric, tie-dyed clothing; garments made out of fluorescent, synthetic, or metallic (silver lamé) fabrics; artificial wigs (bright blue, green, purple), green, blue, bright yellow or pink hair dyes; hair gel; dramatic, glittery, or unaesthetic makeup intended to shock; mood rings; peace and love pendants; strange-looking hats; caftans; kimonos; Chinese traditional cheongsam dresses; brocade jackets; rainbow scarves and T-shirts; Swatches; glass and tachyon jewelry.

Vehicles: planes; helicopters; private jets; air balloons; amphibious, electric, or race cars; spaceships; skyrockets; satellites; roller coasters; go-carts; scooters; Vespas; the new Volkswagen Beetle.

Musical instruments: electric guitars, synthesizers, digital pianos.

Also ventriloquist's dummies, remote-control toys, model airplanes.

Locations

Outdoors: rugged ground, freshly plowed earth, big open holes, soil brushed by winds, archaeological digs, quarries.

Places the purpose of which has changed (from residential to commercial or from commercial to industrial, etc.).

Related to transportation: places located near public transportation, railway stations, space and aviation museums, new car fairs.

Related to discoveries: scientific laboratories dedicated to advanced research, chemistry laboratories dedicated to experiments, invention fairs.

Related to lunacy: asylums.

Places that bring people together around a common cause: public baths, clubs, cooperative societies, public institutions, corporations, labor unions.

Related to extraterrestrials: crop circles, other inhabited planets.

All the places where engines are made.

Futuristic architecture: centers where ancient techniques are being modernized, solar houses, modern architecture, modern buildings, sky-rises made with reflective glass.

In and around the house: upstairs rooms, roofs (especially in slate or tile), sunroofs in cars, bedrooms in towers, piazzas, balconies on higher floors, roof gardens or pools.

Weather

Sudden and unexpected weather changes. Wind circulation. Violent storms (tornadoes, cyclones, hurricanes, electrical storms, aurora borealis, rainbows), natural cataclysms (earthquakes).

Colors

Any electric and fluorescent colors, particularly blue, green, and violet.

Fragrances

Frankincense, elemi.

Gemstones

Amazonite, blue lace agate, angelite, aqua aura, azurite, cavansite, chalcedony, danburite, blue goldstone, moldavite, slate, sugilite, tanzanite, violan.

Animals

Unusual birds: birds of paradise, toucan, mynah, penguin.

Also panda bear and mankind.

A few animals actually born in February under Aquarius: gray whale, Dall's porpoise, northern elephant seal, kit fox, eastern and western gray squirrels.

Parts of the Body

Related to the head: the right ear, the pineal gland (third eye), chin.

Lower leg: Achilles tendon, ankles, calves, tibia, fibula.

The ethereal functions of the body: the nervous system (impulses), the body's electromagnetic forces, the aura, the etheric body (the subtle body giving vitality to the physical body).
Also breath, bone growth.

Archetypes
Extraterrestrials, anarchists, rebels, revolutionaries, people ahead of their time, eccentrics, geniuses, humanitarians, inventors, researchers, public figures no longer in office, insane people, utopians, gays, drag queens, people exposed to X-rays, high-frequency tones, earthquakes, or who have been abducted by UFOs, absconders, liberators, robots, pen pals.

Professions
Related to air and space travel: aviators, railroad workers, astronauts, pilots.
All occupations connected with radio, television, the Internet, and communication in general: radio operators, television anchors, computer technicians, broadcasters, electricians.
Modern designers: pyrotechnicists, glassblowers.
Researchers: quantum scientists, chemists, physicists, psychologists, psychiatrists, sociologists.
Committed to engineering perfect bodies: acupuncturists, aerobic teachers, Pilates instructors, personal trainers.
Uncommon employment in general: astrologers, metaphysicians, mesmerizers, phrenologists, occultists, time travelers, UFO researchers, ventriloquists.

Hobbies
The exploration of time travel, UFOs, astronomy, astrology, the future, meeting new friends, aerobics, puzzles, scientific research, coming up with new inventions, abstract painting, tie-dying T-shirts, computer games.

Enlightenment Tools of Aquarius

States
Arizona, Kansas, Massachusetts, Michigan, Oregon.

Cities in the States
Tucson (AZ), Anaheim (CA), Bakersfield (CA), Glendale (CA), San Bernardino (CA), Fort Collins (CO), Jacksonville (FL), Augusta (GA), East St. Louis (IL), Moline (IL), Quincy (IL), Indianapolis (IN), Muncie (IN), Terre Haute (IN), Council Bluffs (IA), Davenport (IA), Topeka (KS), Manhattan (KS), Bowling Green (KY), Louisville (KY), New Orleans (LA), Hagerstown (MD), Lansing (MI), Flint (MI), Jackson (MS), Biloxi (MS), Meridian (MS), Omaha (NE), Carson City (NV), Camden (NJ), Orange (NJ), Manhattan (NY), Raleigh (NC), Columbus (OH), Canton (OH), Dayton (OH), Salem (OR), Corpus Christi (TX), Dallas (TX), Fort Worth (TX), Galveston (TX), Brigham City (UT), Provo (UT), Roanoke (VA), Olympia (WA), Yakima (WA), Fairmont (WV), Parkersburg (WV), Milwaukee (WI).

Countries
Ethiopia, Costa Rica, Gambia, Greece, Grenada, Iran, Liechtenstein, Nauru, Nepal, Sri Lanka, Vatican City, Yugoslavia.

World Cities
Bremen (Germany), Brighton (U.K.), Buenos Aires (Argentina), Hamburg (Germany), Ingolstadt (Germany), St. Petersburg (Russia), Trent (U.K.), Salzburg (Austria), Salisbury (U.K.).

Famous Personalities
Jennifer Aniston, Francis Bacon, René Barjavel, Ed Burns, Princess Caroline of Monaco, Lewis Carroll, Charles Darwin, James Dean, Ellen DeGeneres, Charles Dickens, Christian Dior, Thomas Edison, Mia Farrow, Galileo, Paris Hilton, Michael Jordan, James Joyce, Kitaro, Abraham Lincoln, John McEnroe, Loreena McKennitt, Somerset Maugham, Wolfgang Amadeus Mozart, Paul Newman, Yoko Ono, Ronald Reagan, Franz

Schubert, Shakira, John Travolta, Jules Verne, Oprah Winfrey, Virginia Woolf.

People
Chumash Indians.

Apostle
Thaddaeus-Jude, who took an interest in the people.
Also the angelic realm.

Cartoon/Film Characters
Alyosha (of Fyodor Dostoyevsky's *The Brothers Karamazov*), Agent Codie Banks, Snoopy (of *Peanuts*), Too-Ticky and the Hattifatteners (of *The Moomins*), Sir Bors (of the Arthurian legends; he wouldn't kill a fellow man), Professor Calculus (of *The Adventures of Tintin*), the Loch Ness Monster, Sherlock Holmes, Eugene the Jeep (of *Popeye*), the Tin Man (from *The Wizard of Oz*), R2-D2 (of *Stars Wars*), Mr. Magorium and Eric Applebaum the Hat Collector (of *Mr. Magorium's Wonder Emporium*), the Wonder Emporium itself.

The Aquarius Woman
One of my aunts is a typical Aquarius. Although she resides in Finland, that doesn't prevent her from regularly bumping into people who knew her half a century ago when she lived in Japan. Regardless of what time it is, at night, in winter, my Aquarian aunt can be seen out planting little trees and gathering the dead leaves that cover the frozen ground. Really close to no one, she nonetheless has a mile-long list of friends. Whenever someone's name is mentioned, we can be sure she has that person's picture in one of her albums lining a whole wall in her apartment.

If you are not afraid of an independent and highly unique woman, then the Aquarius woman is for you. She will definitely keep you on your toes and do things that may seem strange, such as storing pencils in the fridge, or walking backward down the stairs. Her interests keep changing and she constantly brings new people into her life—friends she just made, mostly eccentrics like herself, who walk to the beat of their own drummer.

Even though there could be something a little impersonal and idealistic in the way she expresses her emotions, there is no doubt that she is faithful and loyal to her one true love. She is an Air sign, remember? This means that her freedom is sacred. Never in a million years dictate her moves or impose traditional role models on her. Air cannot be trapped, and neither should she. If caged, she will simply rebel and flee without ever looking back, feeling neither remorse nor sadness.

Motherhood can be a little bewildering to her. Her tendency is to treat her children more like interesting human beings and friends than in a nurturing or protective way. Having a family won't deter her from her own life and interests, which at times may bring her far from the home fire. Defending global causes for people she doesn't know personally is more natural to her than intimacy.

With her extraterrestrial beauty, she is a unique and fascinating individual coming straight from the future, her normal abode.

The Aquarius Man

The Aquarius man is something of a holy innocent. Because friendship is paramount to him, he can seem asexual. He isn't, but a fascinating conversation with someone whose personality is unusual is much more likely to arrest his heart than sexual vibes or romance, which could scare him away.

One very good Aquarian friend of mine is a superior chef. His restaurant is always full of friends and his receptions at home gather no less than a few hundred people at a time. He is kindhearted and very generous. Despite the crowds in his life and a very hectic schedule, he is a devoted husband and father of three Aquarius children whom he treats as the individuals they are. Always interested in others, he often surprises me with keen perceptions that he seems to have pulled from thin air. Although he is grounded, practical, and responsible, his transparent blue eyes often have a faraway look. His dream is to tour South America for six months on his motorcycle with a couple of friends, and just enjoy the taste of total freedom.

An Aquarius man can be something of a mystery. Detached, emotionally cold, or impersonal at times, he can treat his lover as his best friend and can momentarily forget all about her as he becomes fascinated by the mind of a new person. Although loving only one person doesn't come too naturally to the Aquarian male, his interest is momentarily captivated by someone else purely on a platonic and intellectual level. Breathlessly kissing on a couch in a dimly lit room is less comfortable to him than being in a room full of friends.

There is a touch of genius in this free-spirited man who laughs in the face of tradition and does things his way without ever caring about what others think. If you are open-minded enough to welcome his otherworldliness, you may discover horizons you never even knew could exist.

The Aquarius Child

As a child, an Aquarius professional gymnast friend of mine got expelled from every school he attended because of his unusual habit of flinging from tree to tree.

Another little Aquarius boy I know, every night, without ever waking up, sits up, wraps himself in his blanket, and meditates with his fingers interlocked in silence, completely immobile, for about half an hour. Still asleep, he resumes his horizontal position until morning. At school, he takes a genuine interest in all his classmates. He helps those who are having trouble and confronts others on their lies.

An Aquarius child is a little genius who loves scientific encyclopedias, anything related to space, biographies, and the description of varied cultures. Intrigued by mechanics, he is likely to tear your alarm clock apart to figure out its inner workings and come up with the elaborate model for a time machine. Science fiction appeals to his vast imagination. For Halloween, an extraterrestrial costume is a must.

His strong will won't bend to yours. Whatever you had in mind, it might be best to forget it. He defies convention and does as he pleases. Without ever taking the same road twice, he never does anything the way it is expected of him. More rigid people might find this nerve-racking, but if you are open-minded and flexible, you will be pushed out of any box you may have unconsciously fallen into.

More than a little absentminded, he might be diagnosed with attention deficit disorder (ADD). His attention span is short. Led by flashes of inspiration, he lives in the future. What grabs his attention is elusive.

He may spend more time daydreaming about some complicated invention than concentrating on his homework. And because he is focused on why his teacher tilts her head when she asks a question, what she is actually teaching could be lost on him. His logic resonates to strange universal patterns that science will confirm in a few decades.

Instinctively sensing that what is to be already was, he is aware that there is no past, present, or future—just one eternal moment.

PISCES

(FEBRUARY 18–MARCH 20)

Symbol: The Fish

Swimming in opposite directions and yet bound together by a silver cord, the fish of Pisces are elusive. In nature, fish come in all sorts of shapes, sizes, and colors. There are more than twenty-five thousand species. They live in ever-changing environments full of rocks, algae, colors, and magic. Their senses are highly developed and they are believed to discern colors as well as we do. Most swim with the current, yet some, such as salmon, go against it. Most are cold-blooded, but some, such as sharks, are hot-blooded. Most live only in water, but some, such as warm-blooded aquatic mammals for brief periods of time, can leave it. There is always this duality in Pisces: taking the path of least resistance or expressing their genius.

Element: Mutable Water

This is ever-moving water, the water of oceans that ebbs and flows, evasive, mysterious water that can never be fully closed in on.

Ruler: Neptune

Neptune was discovered in 1846 as the spiritist movements were emerging. (Allan Kardec's *The Spirits' Book* was first published in 1857. He made the masses aware that spirits existed and could be contacted through specially trained mediums.) Neptune remains a mystery. It is surrounded by blue-green gas, and all we know is that its core is ocean-like and rocky. It rotates around the Sun in 165 years and has two Moons.

Ages of Man
When we reach enlightenment, fusion with the divine, oneness.

Character
In nature, this is the time of the year when snow melts, revealing budding new plants. The earth is soggy and wet, and the still, cold air starts warming up. The boundaries between being still asleep and waking up are unclear. Although it's not spring yet, winter is definitely dissolving. There is a softness in the air—the promise of all that is to come.

The last sign of the zodiac, Pisces combines Aries' idealism, Taurus' indolent calm, Gemini's intelligence, Cancer's sense of humor, Leo's nobility, Virgo's attention to detail, Libra's fair and objective judgment, Scorpio's mystical insight, Sagittarius' generosity, Capricorn's wisdom, and Aquarius' humanism.

Pisceans are sensitive beings with many artistic talents. Pisceans draw their inspiration from other dimensions. More genius composers and dancers are born under that sign than under any other. Their visions invariably transmit subtle information received from invisible realms.

Because of their extreme sensibility, there is always a danger of undoing in Pisces. Their tendency, at times, might be to escape the harshness of reality and dream their lives rather than experiencing them. Submerging themselves in movies, songs, or, in extreme cases, alcohol, helps them drown the misery they so acutely sense around them. But when in supportive emotional environments, they are able to channel their finely tuned senses for the betterment of humanity.

They instinctively understand everyone around them as well as every situation. Their souls are gentle, imaginative, and inspired with an affinity for the abstract and the mystical. Dreamers and natural shamans, they are compassionate, psychic, and selfless. Their connection with the spiritual realms gifts them with medium and psychic abilities. Their innate connection to the divine connects them to the oneness of all that is.

Enlightenment Tools of Neptune

Note: Jupiter was the traditional ruler of Pisces. Some of the associations listed in Sagittarius can apply to Pisces. Kindly note also that Neptune is the higher octave of Venus. Some of Venus' associations (in Taurus and Libra) are also relevant for Pisces.

Day
None.

Number
7.

Metals
Neptunium, platinum (stainless, dense, precious metal), lithium (very light), white gold.

Shapes/Textures
Nebulous, chaotic, transcendental, with rhythmical curves. Gaseous, liquid, mysterious, elusive, indefinable, difficult to analyze.

Flavors
Sweet, subtle, seductive, intoxicating.

Foods
Fish: salmon, trout, halibut, cod, sardines, snapper, tuna, sea bass, mahi-mahi, sole, tilapia, flounder.
Seaweed: dulse, kelp, nori, wakame, kombu.
Sweet: sugarcane, rhubarb, cotton candy.
Seeds: hemp.
Fasting for spiritual purposes.

Herbs/Spices
Mystical herbs inducing dreams: *Calea zacatechi, Alepidea amatymbica, Silene capensis,* synaptolepsis, peyote, *Lophophora williamsii,* jimson weed.

Also goldenseal, kava.
Poisons: hemlock, arsenic.

Trees/Shrubs
Cananga tree, linden tree, staghorn sumac tree, silk tree, star magnolia tree, Judas tree, Japanese maple tree, bird-of-paradise tree, fringe tree, pussy willow, Hong Kong orchid tree, rubber tree.

Plants
Symbiotic or parasites: lichen, golden polypody.
Used for their perfumed flowers: sweet gum (liquidambar).
Plants used as drugs: opium poppy, marijuana, hallucinogenic mushrooms, tobacco.
Aquatic: algae, reed.
Also ming aralia, ponytail palm, variegated raphis palm.

Flowers
Ephemeral or fragile: cosmos, poppy, bat flower, *Maxillaria pulchra*, blue pendant ginger, *Cattleya bowringiana*, *Brassavola nodosa*, *Bletia purpurea*, *Caularthron bilamelatum*, pink verbascum, *Sobralia decora*, Amazon lily, shell ginger, ginger lily, chalice vine, snowdrop, centradenia, Alberta splash.
Aquatic: lotus.
Those the essence of which is extracted: lavender.
Also silk flowers.

Musical Note
None.

Planetary Dominion
Covert alliances, secrets, artistic skills, music, photography, sleep, dreams, idealism, fantasy, hallucinations, everything that is vague and nebulous, the unconscious, spirituality, meditation, mysticism, psychic abilities (mediumship, clairvoyance).

Angel
Azrael or Asariel.

Enlightenment Tools of Neptune and Pisces

Objects
Physical
Artistic: films, photos, cameras, music (particularly New Age and trance), dance, poetry.

Anything creating illusion: synthetic fabrics, fake money, fake fur, gemstone imitations (rhinestones), implants, veneers, hair extensions, pastiches, wigs, colored contact lenses, plastic (particularly transparent), counterfeit money, yellow cedar.

Transparent and shining fabrics: thin veils, extra-fine lace, mull.

Clothes: princess dresses, wedding gowns, wedding veils, transparent capes, silk trains, mull scarves, lace baby dolls, orchids or feathers as hair ornaments, shiny hairpins, delicate and discreet jewelry, fine transparent high-heeled shoes.

Materials: fine gravel, limestone.

Related sleep: sleeping aids, earplugs.

Supports to psychic abilities: crystal balls, Ouija boards.

Anything related to the ocean and swimming: goggles, swimming suit, surfboard, palms of the hand, snorkeling gear, underwater eye mask, glass-bottom boat to observe the ocean life, boats, sand.

In the house: Oriental rugs, delicate china, spiraled shells in which the tides can be heard, ship models, ship in a bottle, aquarium, Dead Sea salts for the bath.

String and/or slightly off-key instruments: harps, Parsifal bells, sitar, out-of-tune piano or guitar.

Also alcohol, drugs, gas, anesthetics, oil, solvents, rubber.

Nonphysical
Involving deceit: optical illusions, sacrifice, betrayals, nonviolent thefts, substitutions, propaganda, frauds, bankruptcies, disappearances.

Related to spirituality and psychic abilities: ego dissolutions, the divine, the sacred, spiritual realms, spiritualism, what lies beyond the veil, sym-

pathy, compassion, meditation, levitation, unconditional love, dreams, hypnosis, trance, intuition, psychic abilities, telepathy, shamanism, sleep, coma, etheric healing, reflexology, parapsychology.
Also unsolvable mysteries, trust funds.

Locations

Outdoors: dumping grounds, fertile plains welcoming to retreat centers.

Mysterious: haunted houses, dungeons, houses falling apart particularly in bad neighborhoods or in areas prone to floods.

Involving water: oceans, pool water, water holes attractive to birds, land subject to inundations, maritime museums, giant aquariums.

Related to spirituality: places of spiritual retreat, prayer, and meditation, monasteries.

Places of forced retreat: prisons, hospitals, orphanages, dormitories, retirement homes, asylums, rehabilitation centers (drugs, alcohol), ghettos, concentration camps, slave quarters.

Charitable institutions using mostly volunteers: AA, Salvation Army, foster care, YMCA, FreeArts, hostels, benefit associations.

Places where we tend to escape reality: breweries, pubs, cinemas, dance halls, smoking areas.

Indoors: low ceilings, floors, and what covers them: wall-to-wall carpets, linoleum, hardwood floors, well-furnished small rooms, black rooms (for X-rays or photography), rooms with barred windows, meditation rooms, cellars.

Weather

Clouds, fog, dust, smoke, mist, drizzle.

Colors

Transparent, shimmering, iridescent, pearly, polished, blurry, shifting, tender, smooth colors, including aquamarine, light blue, vibrant sea green (of the Caribbean Sea), lavender mauve, soft pearl grays, peach, shell pink, pure glistening white.

Fragrances
Ambergris, ginger, lavender, myrrh, opium, storax, ylang-ylang.

Gemstones
Aquamarine, amethyst, yellow calcite, pink chalcedony, charoite, coral (blue and white), fluorite (clear, green, and purple), white jade, green jasper, kyanite, larimar, nephrite, seraphinite.

Animals
Fish of all kinds: salmon, starfish, seahorses, goldfish.
Most exotic saltwater fish: angelfish, anthias, *Borbonius anthias,* batfish, butterfly fish, chromis, cardinals, clown, yellow tang, declevis butterfly, garibaldi damselfish.
Marine animals: sand dollar.
Water mammals: dolphins, whales.
Water birds: seagulls, flamingos, pelicans.
Animals expressing unconditional love: dogs.
Animals actually born in March under Pisces: Dall's porpoise, American marten, fisher, wolverine, northern river otter, sea otter, northern raccoon, northern elephant seal, western gray squirrel, mountain beaver, pygmy rabbit.

Parts of the Body
Feet and toes, the glandular system, the gastro-abdominal system, the lymphatic system, the pituitary gland, the synovial fluids, the tarsus and metatarsus bones, the thalamus, mucus, genes.
Also the emotional or astral body (the subtle body that, bridging the physical to our mind, is the seat of our emotions).

Archetypes
People whose origins are unclear: orphans, bastards, ghosts.
Deceitful people: con artists, counterfeiters, bootleggers, kidnappers,
Outcasts: beggars, slaves.
People living a fantasy: hypochondriacs, amnesiacs, escapists, dreamers, drug and alcohol addicts.

Inspired people: idealists, visionaries, mystery investigators, music and movie lovers, mystics, geniuses.

Professions
Industries: the fishing industry, the oil industry.

In politics: democratic and popular movements, socialist and Communist parties, election campaigns.

Artists: character actors, film producers, impressionist painters, musicians, composers (particularly of New Age music), dancers, photographers, illusionists.

People working in the drug, alcohol, gas, or refuse businesses: drug dealers, chemists, wine merchants, barmen, garbage collectors.

Professions connected to the ocean: hydraulic engineers, underwater divers.

Related to the feet: foot surgeons, reflexologists (foot massage therapists).

Related to places of isolation: jail keepers, hospital staff.

Requiring secrecy: spies, secret agents.

Related to the unconscious or the spiritual realms: mediums, channelers, hypnotherapists, psychics, monks.

Hobbies
Appealing to the imagination, artistic, rhythmic, by the ocean: dancing, dreaming, meditating, listening to soft music, watching an inspiring film, painting, taking photographs, sleeping, receiving a psychic reading, doing yoga or tai chi, writing or reading poetry, sitting by the ocean, swimming with dolphins, writing in a diary, receiving a foot massage.

Enlightenment Tools of Pisces

States
Florida, Maine, Nebraska, Ohio, Vermont.

Cities in the States
Phoenix (AZ), Yuma (AZ), Sacramento (CA), St. Petersburg (FL), Evansville (IN), Fort Wayne (IN), Frankfort (KY), Lake Charles (LA), Shreve-

port (LA), Augusta (ME), Bangor (ME), Lewiston (ME), Fall River (MA), Lowell (MA), New Bedford (MA), Battle Creek (MI), Dearborn (MI), Minneapolis (MN), St. Cloud (MN), Hattiesburg (MS), Independence (MO), Springfield (MO), Helena (MT), Billings (MT), Butte (MT), Missoula (MT), Lincoln (NE), Reno (NV), Sparks (NV), Atlantic City (NJ), Bridgeton (NJ), Hempstead (NY), Yonkers (NY), Grand Forks (ND), Akron (OH), Klamath Falls (OR), Medford (OR), Allentown (PA), Pawtucket (RI), Myrtle Beach (SC), Sioux Falls (SD), Amarillo (TX), San Antonio (TX), Ogden (UT), Price (UT), Portsmouth (VA), Huntington (WV), Madison (WI), Eau Claire (WI), Green Bay (WI), La Crosse (WI), Laramie (WY).

Countries

Ghana, Mauritius, Monaco, Morocco, the Netherlands, St. Lucia, Taiwan (China).
Also the Gobi and Sahara deserts.

World Cities

Alexandria (Egypt), Birmingham (U.K.), Bournemouth (U.K.), Cardiff (U.K.), Casablanca (Morocco), Dublin (Ireland), Jerusalem (Israel), Lisbon (Portugal), Regensburg (Germany), Santagio de Compostela (Spain), Seville (Spain), Warsaw (Poland).

Famous Personalities

The Academy Awards, Ansel Adams, Prince Albert of Monaco, Michelangelo, Drew Barrymore, Sandro Botticelli, Edgar Cayce, Frédéric Chopin, Glenn Close, Copernicus, Albert Einstein, Hubert de Givenchy, Handel, George Harrison, Patricia Hearst, Jennifer Love Hewitt, Victor Hugo, William Hurt, Jon Bon Jovi, Ted Kennedy, Queen Latifah, Téa Leoni, Jerry Lewis, Liza Minnelli, the Mother, David Niven, Rudolf Nureyev, Pythia (Oracle at Delphi), Maurice Ravel, Auguste Renoir, Rimsky-Korsakov, Seal, Dr. Seuss, Svetlana Stalin, John Steinbeck, Rudolph Steiner, Antonio Vivaldi, Elizabeth Taylor, George Washington, Rachel Weisz, Bruce Willis.

People
Gypsies, Basques.

Apostle
Judas Iscariot, who betrayed Christ.

Cartoon/Film Characters
Cinderella, Nemo (of *Finding Nemo*), Ariel (of *The Little Mermaid*), The Fisher King (of the Arthurian legends), Dorothy (of *The Wizard of Oz*), Giselle (of *Enchanted*), Jonathan Livingston (of Richard Bach's *Jonathan Livingston Seagull*), the Little Mermaid (of Hans Christian Andersen's "The Little Mermaid").

The Pisces Woman
There is something elusive and mysterious about the Pisces woman. She is dreamy and not above wishing upon a star. A lover of music and poetry, she is a true romantic who knows how to create a special atmosphere. Selfless at heart, she will help a friend in need and rescue stray animals. She is soft, gentle, and sensitive, yet also strong and independent when necessary. The epitome of femininity, she is the princess described in fairy tales, complete with the charm and unique powers. Her magic is tangible. She knows how to talk to animals, babies, and plants alike and would be no foreigner to fairies and elementals, were they to sit on her lap. Her eyes reflect the dreamy, ethereal quality of the distant spheres of consciousness she knows so intimately. Her wisdom is ancient and her soul remembers visiting many realms, visible and invisible.

She is an artist and a creator. Children adore her. She usually chooses flowing, exotic dresses that expand her imagination and enhance her natural beauty. Content to read a novel or watch a movie, she also loves to meditate, play the piano, cook, and be with her lover. She will never try to compete with the man in her life and she knows instinctively how to bring out the best in him, making him feel strong and cherished. Her seduction is subtle, with an enduring, exotic perfume. She can be everything her mate wants her to be and more. The Pisces woman is the women of all the other signs wrapped up in one. Mystical and elusive, she also needs aloneness to travel through time and space, gathering all the elements that enrich her inner visions. She is a very special lady of many talents.

The Pisces Man

A very close Piscean friend of mine is a district attorney. Unbeknownst to his staff, he also writes screenplays and novels. In his free time, he travels the world, paints, decorates his house, is a superb photographer, dreams of getting a dog, enjoys a large circle of good friends, rides his bicycle on the beach, and organizes rallies. Unusual? Not really. A Piscean man, no matter how successful he is in his career, remains a dreamer at heart. A born romantic, he will create dinners that will make his loved ones feel cherished. There will be flower arrangements on each table and wine will flow while good music warms the atmosphere, enhanced by candles. The Piscean man is particularly sensitive to suggestion. Trust him and he will prove you right. Don't, and his behavior will justify your worst fears. When he sinks into a blue mood, wear your most sexy dress, a charming smile, and suggest a change of scenery. He will soon see again the world in brighter colors.

Beauty entices him. So do warmth and elegance. He is an attentive lover and a kind man in whom others easily confide, knowing he will never judge another without having walked a few miles in that person's moccasins. Because he is able to join them in their realities, children enjoy him too. He knows how to draw a whale and make it alive, or how to build a boat in the sand and make it float on the ocean to a thousand mysterious and exotic destinations.

His occasional need for aloneness should be respected. Too much togetherness can erode the subtle magic of his love. He may even occasionally not tell the whole truth, not out of deceit, but because he needs to protect the private garden of his dreams. These are very innocent lies that are best left without comment.

The Pisces man has many moods and many talents lurking under the ever-changing surfaces of his inner oceans. His life mirrors the many inner shifts that gradually bring him ever closer to the fusion with the divine that haunts his soul.

The Pisces Child

The Pisces child is a delightful child to raise. Trigger his imagination, surround him with love and music, and he will grow into a sensitive, balanced human being. Support him in his wish to learn a musical instrument. His understanding of notes and harmonies seems to stem from another lifetime. He also has a deep affinity for light and crystals. A mobile with all sorts of bright, cheerful colors hanging above his bed or a lava lamp is a must. He will spend hours enraptured by the subtle shadows drawn on the walls of his bedroom.

He is a natural lover of animals. A little cat or a dog he can take care of and cherish will become his own special confidant. He makes friends easily, without stopping at differences in races or language barriers.

The little girls are attracted to angel clothes, and the little boys, to magical heroes. These children are charming and usually quiet. They enjoy their aloneness and know how to create their own imaginary world to keep them company.

Pisces children love water. Visits to the ocean, searching for shells on the beach, or splashing in the family pool bring delight to their young hearts.

Discipline does not come naturally to them. Although they don't always understand rules, these free-spirited children need boundaries. They may also require some gentle guidance to learn how to respect others' possessions. Their instinct is that everything should belong to anyone as needed.

These are very special children with obvious psychic abilities. They feel and know what remains unsaid around them. They were born with the natural talent of seeing beyond appearances into the soul of truth.

4

Enlightenment Using the Astrological Tools

for Enlightenment of the Other Signs

Now you're armed with suggestions on how you can use the enlightenment tools of your own sign to reinforce who you already are. For example, a Pisces using lavender essential oil (lavender is one of the flowers of Pisces) enhances his/her basic spiritual qualities. Or, by wearing a forest-green sweater, a Capricorn reinforces the discipline and structure of his/her Sun sign.

But we are more than just our Sun signs. We each are all the signs and all the planets, in different measures. You can further enhance your life using the other eleven signs of the zodiac. For example, to develop more balance and harmony, use the associations of your opposite sign. These pairs of opposites are:

1. Aries-Libra

2. Taurus-Scorpio

3. Gemini-Sagittarius

4. Cancer-Capricorn

5. Leo-Aquarius

6. Virgo-Pisces

Dynamic, straightforward, enthusiastic Aries is brought back to balance through Libra's and Venus' enlightenment tools. Whenever angered or impulsively propelled to action, if an Aries holds or wears a rose quartz stone or necklace, a feeling of peace will bring him/her into his/her heart. Or when Leo feels insecure, tapping into the enlightenment tools of Aquarius—for example, reading a book on the Chumash Indians (the people associated with Aquarius)—may help bring things into perspective.

Regardless of your sign, you can integrate the qualities of any other sign into your life by working with any other sign's enlightenment tools. For example, if you want to add more glamour to your life, consider using some of the Leo's enlightenment tools, or the enlightenment tools of the Sun, Leo's ruling planet (as found in Chapter 3), in your daily routine. Wear the color gold or gold jewelry. Burn a cinnamon-scented candle. Visit a wild animal reservation. Spend quality time with your cat. These enlightenment tools will make you more aware of your ability to shine, your generosity of spirit, your love of life, your warmth, and your playfulness.

To further refine the use of the eleven other signs' enlightenment tools, you should be aware that each sign highlights a particular area of life for each of the other eleven signs. Depending on what you wish to enhance in your life, for easy reference, here's a list of what each planet and the sign it rules help enhance:

- The enlightenment tools of ARIES, ruled by Mars, enhance dynamism, spontaneity, and courage.

- The enlightenment tools of TAURUS, ruled by Venus, enhance love, sensuality, and patience.

ENLIGHTENMENT
USING THE
ASTROLOGICAL
TOOLS FOR
ENLIGHTENMENT OF
THE OTHER SIGNS

167

• The enlightenment tools of GEMINI, ruled by Mercury, enhance consciousness, multitasking, and communication skills.

• The enlightenment tools of CANCER, ruled by the Moon, enhance sensitivity, a sense of security, and imagination.

• The enlightenment tools of LEO, ruled by the Sun, enhance glamour, playfulness, and creativity.

• The enlightenment tools of VIRGO, ruled by Mercury, enhance efficiency, practical intelligence, and attention to details.

• The enlightenment tools of LIBRA, ruled by Venus, enhance relationships, peace, and love.

• The enlightenment tools of SCORPIO, ruled by Pluto, enhance power, depth, and passion.

• The enlightenment tools of SAGITTARIUS, ruled by Jupiter, enhance abundance, luck, and adventurousness.

• The enlightenment tools of CAPRICORN, ruled by Saturn, enhance discipline, persistence, and wisdom.

• The enlightenment tools of AQUARIUS, ruled by Uranus, enhance uniqueness, friendship, and freedom.

• The enlightenment tools of PISCES, ruled by Neptune, enhance compassion, artistic abilities, and mysticism.

THE HOUSES

We can now introduce the concept of houses. Houses mirror the twelve signs of the zodiac. The twelve signs are obtained by dividing the Earth's yearly rotation around the Sun by twelve. In contrast, each house symbolizes a particular area of life. Numbered from I to XII, counterclockwise, they are based on the division by twelve of the Earth's daily rotation upon itself. Each house represents a different area of life experience. I previously made an analogy with the theater. The planets are the actors. The signs they're in are the clothes they wear. The houses are the particular locations where the scene unfolds.

The traditional meanings assigned to each of the twelve houses are as follows:

I: Personal appearance.

II: Money (personal values and resources).

III: Communication.

IV: Home.

V: Creativity, romance, and children.

VI: Health, pets, and work.

VII: Marriage.

VIII: Sexuality, joint finances, and transformation.

IX: Long-distance travel, philosophy, and religion.

X: Career.

XI: Friendships.

XII: Subconscious.

These associations can seem arbitrary. But we need to remember that everything in astrology is totally logical. The twelve houses parallel, or mirror, the twelve signs:

ENLIGHTENMENT
USING THE
ASTROLOGICAL
TOOLS FOR
ENLIGHTENMENT OF
THE OTHER SIGNS

169

I mirrors dynamic Aries, with his leadership abilities and slight self-absorption.

II mirrors patient Taurus, whose values are very grounded and material.

III mirrors curious Gemini, who is always eager to learn and share information.

IV mirrors sensitive Cancer, who needs the security and nurturing of a family.

V mirrors creative Leo, who breathes romance and needs to be center stage.

VI mirrors practical Virgo, who insists on health and good nutrition.

VII mirrors loving Libra, whose life revolves around relationships and creating peace.

VIII mirrors powerful Scorpio, who is fascinated by sexuality, death, and wealth.

IX mirrors philosophical Sagittarius, who is so keen on traveling and understanding the meaning behind experiences.

X mirrors ambitious Capricorn, whose life is mostly dominated by his career.

XI mirrors humanitarian Aquarius, who makes friends anywhere he goes.

XII mirrors psychic Pisces, who enjoys the more mystical aspect of life.

We could further link the twelve houses up to the twelve evolutionary stages of the growth of a plant from seed back to seed. Let us, for example, take the life cycle of a green bean:

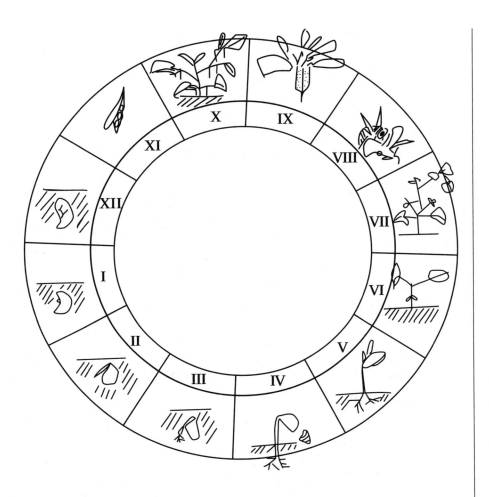

I. The seed starts its development.

II. The emergence of a little sprout.

III. The growth of little roots.

IV. The emergence of the rooted plant aboveground.

V. The development of leaves.

VI. The fully developed leaves.

ENLIGHTENMENT
USING THE
ASTROLOGICAL
TOOLS FOR
ENLIGHTENMENT OF
THE OTHER SIGNS

171

VII. The blooming into flowers.

VIII. The pollination of the flower by a bee.

IX. The flower slowly transforms into a green bean pod.

X. The plant is covered with green bean pods.

XI. Each bean pod ripens, letting its seeds fall on the ground.

XII. The seeds are buried into the soil, where they will each start a new cycle.

Each of the twelve growth stages of the bean relate directly to stages or specific aspects of our life. Here's a close look at what each house symbolizes.

I. PERSONAL APPEARANCE (THE SEED STARTS ITS DEVELOPMENT).

• Our physical appearance.

• Our perception of life.

• Our sense of personal power.

• The impact we have on our environment.

II. MONEY (THE EMERGENCE OF A LITTLE SPROUT).

• Our values.

• Our sense of security (finances).

III. COMMUNICATION (THE GROWTH OF LITTLE ROOTS).

• Our intellectual skills and mental faculties (elocution, letter or document writing).

• Short trips.

• Our relationships to siblings, cousins, and neighbors.

IV. HOME (THE EMERGENCE OF THE ROOTED PLANT ABOVEGROUND).

• The foundation of our lives.

• What makes us feel protected (our home).

• Our connection to our father and ancestors in general.

V. CREATIVITY, ROMANCE, AND CHILDREN (THE DEVELOPMENT OF LEAVES).

• Self-confidence.

• Creativity.

• Our capacity to play and be joyful (hobbies).

• Financial speculations and investments.

• Romance and freely shared emotions.

• Our relationships with children.

• Our boyfriends and girlfriends.

VI. HEALTH, PETS, AND WORK (THE FULLY DEVELOPED LEAVES).

• Personal growth.

• Health/nutrition/how well we take care of our bodies.

• Our relationship with colleagues at work.

• Our relationship with small pets.

VII. MARRIAGE (THE BLOOMING INTO FLOWERS).

• Close associations based on a common vision.

• Marriage (or if single, our chances of attracting the right partner).

• The positive conclusion of open conflicts.

• Our spouse.

VIII. SEXUALITY, JOINT FINANCES, AND TRANSFORMATION (THE POLLINATION OF THE FLOWER BY A BEE).

• Sexuality.

• Self-transformation.

• Finances shared with others (spouse, inheritances, business associates, taxes, insurances).

• Skills brought over from past lives.

• Our live-in lover.

IX. LONG-DISTANCE TRAVEL, PHILOSOPHY, AND RELIGION (THE FLOWER SLOWLY TRANSFORMS INTO GREEN BEAN PODS).

• Our faith and philosophy of life.

• Our athletic skills.

• Our philanthropic aspirations.

• Higher education (university level).

• Long-distance traveling and our connection to other cultures.

• Public speaking, writing, publishing.

• Our involvement with the law.

• Our connection to foreigners.

• Our relationship to God.

X. CAREER (THE PLANT IS COVERED WITH GREEN BEAN PODS).

• Our aspirations in life (career).

• How we handle discipline and responsibilities.

• Our boss.

• Our relationship to our mother.

XI. FRIENDSHIPS (EACH BEAN POD RIPENS, LETTING ITS SEEDS FALL ON THE GROUND).

• Long-term dreams.

• What makes us happy.

ENLIGHTENMENT
USING THE
ASTROLOGICAL
TOOLS FOR
ENLIGHTENMENT OF
THE OTHER SIGNS

175

- Involvement in group activities.

- Our friends.

XII. SUBCONSCIOUS (THE SEEDS ARE BURIED INTO THE SOIL, WHERE THEY WILL START A NEW CYCLE).

- Our subconscious.

- Our spiritual self (meditation).

- Our need for retreat.

- The transmutation of karma.

- Our relationship to large animals (horses).

LISTS OF THE SIGNS AND WHICH HOUSES ARE RULED BY WHICH SIGN

By now you should feel very comfortable with your Sun sign and how it relates to your life. Your Sun sign is determined by the time of the year you were born. For example, someone born on January 17 has his Sun in Capricorn. Someone born on November 15 has her Sun in Scorpio. The Sun sign gives the basic coloration of your character.

You also have a rising sign, or ascendant, which adds nuances to your basic temperament. This is the sign that was rising on the eastern horizon at the moment of your birth. This is calculated either by a professional astrologer or through any astrology computer program. It requires your full birth data:

1. Date of birth (month, day, year).

2. Time of birth (as exact as possible).

3. Place of birth (the latitude and longitude of the city in which you were born).

Knowing your rising sign will help you explore your personality more deeply.

As we come to the lists of how the twelve houses of your personal Sun sign and rising sign relate to the twelve signs of the zodiac, know that you'll be able to make practical use of these lists for enlightenment. There are several steps you can take:

1. Refer to the list of the houses.

2. Use the lists in the pages that follow and find your sign and your rising sign.

3. Determine which part of your life you would like to enhance and see which sign will help you do that optimally.

4. Go to the enlightenment tools for that sign in Chapter 3.

5. Blend the enlightenment tools of that sign with the ideas offered in the fourth part of Chapter 2, called "Ideas for the Practical Use of the Astrological Tools for Enlightenment."

Specific practical examples follow this list.

IF YOU ARE ARIES OR ARIES RISING (ARIES ASCENDANT), THE ENLIGHTENMENT TOOLS OF:

• Aries enhance the affairs and the people ruled by the 1st house.

• Taurus enhance the affairs and the people ruled by the 2nd house.

• Gemini enhance the affairs and the people ruled by the 3rd house.

• Cancer enhance the affairs and the people ruled by the 4th house.

ENLIGHTENMENT
USING THE
ASTROLOGICAL
TOOLS FOR
ENLIGHTENMENT OF
THE OTHER SIGNS

- Leo enhance the affairs and the people ruled by the 5th house.

- Virgo enhance the affairs and the people ruled by the 6th house.

- Libra enhance the affairs and the people ruled by the 7th house.

- Scorpio enhance the affairs and the people ruled by the 8th house.

- Sagittarius enhance the affairs and the people ruled by the 9th house.

- Capricorn enhance the affairs and the people ruled by the 10th house.

- Aquarius enhance the affairs and the people ruled by the 11th house.

- Pisces enhance the affairs and the people ruled by the 12th house.

IF YOU ARE TAURUS OR TAURUS RISING (TAURUS ASCENDANT), THE ENLIGHTENMENT TOOLS OF:

- Aries enhance the affairs and the people ruled by the 12th house.

- Taurus enhance the affairs and the people ruled by the 1st house.

- Gemini enhance the affairs and the people ruled by the 2nd house.

- Cancer enhance the affairs and the people ruled by the 3rd house.

- Leo enhance the affairs and the people ruled by the 4th house.

- Virgo enhance the affairs and the people ruled by the 5th house.

- Libra enhance the affairs and the people ruled by the 6th house.

- Scorpio enhance the affairs and the people ruled by the 7th house.

- Sagittarius enhance the affairs and the people ruled by the 8th house.

- Capricorn enhance the affairs and the people ruled by the 9th house.

- Aquarius enhance the affairs and the people ruled by the 10th house.

- Pisces enhance the affairs and the people ruled by the 11th house.

IF YOU ARE GEMINI OR GEMINI RISING (GEMINI ASCENDANT), THE ENLIGHTENMENT TOOLS OF:

- Aries enhance the affairs and the people ruled by the 11th house.

- Taurus enhance the affairs and the people ruled by the 12th house.

- Gemini enhance the affairs and the people ruled by the 1st house.

- Cancer enhance the affairs and the people ruled by the 2nd house.

- Leo enhance the affairs and the people ruled by the 3rd house.

- Virgo enhance the affairs and the people ruled by the 4th house.

- Libra enhance the affairs and the people ruled by the 5th house.

- Scorpio enhance the affairs and the people ruled by the 6th house.

- Sagittarius enhance the affairs and the people ruled by the 7th house.

- Capricorn enhance the affairs and the people ruled by the 8th house.

- Aquarius enhance the affairs and the people ruled by the 9th house.

- Pisces enhance the affairs and the people ruled by the 10th house.

ENLIGHTENMENT
USING THE
ASTROLOGICAL
TOOLS FOR
ENLIGHTENMENT OF
THE OTHER SIGNS

IF YOU ARE CANCER OR CANCER RISING (CANCER ASCENDANT), THE ENLIGHTENMENT TOOLS OF:

• Aries enhance the affairs and the people ruled by the 10th house.

• Taurus enhance the affairs and the people ruled by the 11th house.

• Gemini enhance the affairs and the people ruled by the 12th house.

• Cancer enhance the affairs and the people ruled by the 1st house.

• Leo enhance the affairs and the people ruled by the 2nd house.

• Virgo enhance the affairs and the people ruled by the 3rd house.

• Libra enhance the affairs and the people ruled by the 4th house.

• Scorpio enhance the affairs and the people ruled by the 5th house.

• Sagittarius enhance the affairs and the people ruled by the 6th house.

• Capricorn enhance the affairs and the people ruled by the 7th house.

• Aquarius enhance the affairs and the people ruled by the 8th house.

• Pisces enhance the affairs and the people ruled by the 9th house.

IF YOU ARE LEO OR LEO RISING (LEO ASCENDANT), THE ENLIGHTENMENT TOOLS OF:

• Aries enhance the affairs and the people ruled by the 9th house.

• Taurus enhance the affairs and the people ruled by the 10th house.

• Gemini enhance the affairs and the people ruled by the 11th house.

- Cancer enhance the affairs and the people ruled by the 12th house.

- Leo enhance the affairs and the people ruled by the 1st house.

- Virgo enhance the affairs and the people ruled by the 2nd house.

- Libra enhance the affairs and the people ruled by the 3rd house.

- Scorpio enhance the affairs and the people ruled by the 4th house.

- Sagittarius enhance the affairs and the people ruled by the 5th house.

- Capricorn enhance the affairs and the people ruled by the 6th house.

- Aquarius enhance the affairs and the people ruled by the 7th house.

- Pisces enhance the affairs and the people ruled by the 8th house.

**IF YOU ARE VIRGO OR VIRGO RISING (VIRGO ASCENDANT),
THE ENLIGHTENMENT TOOLS OF:**

- Aries enhance the affairs and the people ruled by the 8th house.

- Taurus enhance the affairs and the people ruled by the 9th house.

- Gemini enhance the affairs and the people ruled by the 10th house.

- Cancer enhance the affairs and the people ruled by the 11th house.

- Leo enhance the affairs and the people ruled by the 12th house.

- Virgo enhance the affairs and the people ruled by the 1st house.

- Libra enhance the affairs and the people ruled by the 2nd house.

ENLIGHTENMENT
USING THE
ASTROLOGICAL
TOOLS FOR
ENLIGHTENMENT OF
THE OTHER SIGNS

- Scorpio enhance the affairs and the people ruled by the 3rd house.

- Sagittarius enhance the affairs and the people ruled by the 4th house.

- Capricorn enhance the affairs and the people ruled by the 5th house.

- Aquarius enhance the affairs and the people ruled by the 6th house.

- Pisces enhance the affairs and the people ruled by the 7th house.

IF YOU ARE LIBRA OR LIBRA RISING (LIBRA ASCENDANT), THE ENLIGHTENMENT TOOLS OF:

- Aries enhance the affairs and the people ruled by the 7th house.

- Taurus enhance the affairs and the people ruled by the 8th house.

- Gemini enhance the affairs and the people ruled by the 9th house.

- Cancer enhance the affairs and the people ruled by the 10th house.

- Leo enhance the affairs and the people ruled by the 11th house.

- Virgo enhance the affairs and the people ruled by the 12th house.

- Libra enhance the affairs and the people ruled by the 1st house.

- Scorpio enhance the affairs and the people ruled by the 2nd house.

- Sagittarius enhance the affairs and the people ruled by the 3rd house.

- Capricorn enhance the affairs and the people ruled by the 4th house.

- Aquarius enhance the affairs and the people ruled by the 5th house.

- Pisces enhance the affairs and the people ruled by the 6th house.

IF YOU ARE SCORPIO OR SCORPIO RISING (SCORPIO ASCENDANT), THE ENLIGHTENMENT TOOLS OF:

- Aries enhance the affairs and the people ruled by the 6th house.

- Taurus enhance the affairs and the people ruled by the 7th house.

- Gemini enhance the affairs and the people ruled by the 8th house.

- Cancer enhance the affairs and the people ruled by the 9th house.

- Leo enhance the affairs and the people ruled by the 10th house.

- Virgo enhance the affairs and the people ruled by the 11th house.

- Libra enhance the affairs and the people ruled by the 12th house.

- Scorpio enhance the affairs and the people ruled by the 1st house.

- Sagittarius enhance the affairs and the people ruled by the 2nd house.

- Capricorn enhance the affairs and the people ruled by the 3rd house.

- Aquarius enhance the affairs and the people ruled by the 4th house.

- Pisces enhance the affairs and the people ruled by the 5th house.

IF YOU ARE SAGITTARIUS OR SAGITTARIUS RISING (SAGITTARIUS ASCENDANT), THE ENLIGHTENMENT TOOLS OF:

- Aries enhance the affairs and the people ruled by the 5th house.

- Taurus enhance the affairs and the people ruled by the 6th house.

- Gemini enhance the affairs and the people ruled by the 7th house.

ENLIGHTENMENT
USING THE
ASTROLOGICAL
TOOLS FOR
ENLIGHTENMENT OF
THE OTHER SIGNS

- Cancer enhance the affairs and the people ruled by the 8th house.

- Leo enhance the affairs and the people ruled by the 9th house.

- Virgo enhance the affairs and the people ruled by the10th house.

- Libra enhance the affairs and the people ruled by the 11th house.

- Scorpio enhance the affairs and the people ruled by the12th house.

- Sagittarius enhance the affairs and the people ruled by the 1st house.

- Capricorn enhance the affairs and the people ruled by the 2nd house.

- Aquarius enhance the affairs and the people ruled by the 3rd house.

- Pisces enhance the affairs and the people ruled by the 4th house.

IF YOU ARE CAPRICORN OR CAPRICORN RISING (CAPRICORN ASCENDANT), THE ENLIGHTENMENT TOOLS OF:

- Aries enhance the affairs and the people ruled by the 4th house.

- Taurus enhance the affairs and the people ruled by the 5th house.

- Gemini enhance the affairs and the people ruled by the 6th house.

- Cancer enhance the affairs and the people ruled by the 7th house.

- Leo enhance the affairs and the people ruled by the 8th house.

- Virgo enhance the affairs and the people ruled by the 9th house.

- Libra enhance the affairs and the people ruled by the 10th house.

- Scorpio enhance the affairs and the people ruled by the 11th house.

- Sagittarius enhance the affairs and the people ruled by the 12th house.

- Capricorn enhance the affairs and the people ruled by the 1st house.

- Aquarius enhance the affairs and the people ruled by the 2nd house.

- Pisces enhance the affairs and the people ruled by the 3rd house.

IF YOU ARE AQUARIUS OR AQUARIUS RISING (AQUARIUS ASCENDANT), THE ENLIGHTENMENT TOOLS OF:

- Aries enhance the affairs and the people ruled by the 3rd house.

- Taurus enhance the affairs and the people ruled by the 4th house.

- Gemini enhance the affairs and the people ruled by the 5th house.

- Cancer enhance the affairs and the people ruled by the 6th house.

- Leo enhance the affairs and the people ruled by the 7th house.

- Virgo enhance the affairs and the people ruled by the 8th house.

- Libra enhance the affairs and the people ruled by the 9th house.

- Scorpio enhance the affairs and the people ruled by the 10th house.

- Sagittarius enhance the affairs and the people ruled by the 11th house.

- Capricorn enhance the affairs and the people ruled by the 12th house.

- Aquarius enhance the affairs and the people ruled by the 1st house.

- Pisces enhance the affairs and the people ruled by the 2nd house.

ENLIGHTENMENT
USING THE
ASTROLOGICAL
TOOLS FOR
ENLIGHTENMENT OF
THE OTHER SIGNS

185

IF YOU ARE PISCES OR PISCES RISING (PISCES ASCENDANT), THE ENLIGHTENMENT TOOLS OF:

• Aries enhance the affairs and the people ruled by the 2nd house.

• Taurus enhance the affairs and the people ruled by the 3rd house.

• Gemini enhance the affairs and the people ruled by the 4th house.

• Cancer enhance the affairs and the people ruled by the 5th house.

• Leo enhance the affairs and the people ruled by the 6th house.

• Virgo enhance the affairs and the people ruled by the 7th house.

• Libra enhance the affairs and the people ruled by the 8th house.

• Scorpio enhance the affairs and the people ruled by the 9th house.

• Sagittarius enhance the affairs and the people ruled by the 10th house.

• Capricorn enhance the affairs and the people ruled by the 11th house.

• Aquarius enhance the affairs and the people ruled by the 12th house.

• Pisces enhance the affairs and the people ruled by the 1st house.

Yes, it's a wealth of information, but you don't need to commit all these lists to memory. Use this book as a reference point to make the changes you want in your life using the enlightenment tools. Here's how:

EXAMPLE 1

You are Taurus or Taurus Rising and want to enjoy a more enlightened marriage-type relationship:

1. From the house list earlier in this chapter, you can see that marriage is depicted by the 7th house.

2. From the lists just given, you realize that Scorpio enhances the affairs of that house for you.

3. Go back to the section on Scorpio in Chapter 3 and read carefully all the enlightenment tools of Scorpio.

4. Go through the list of the practical uses of the enlightenment tools in the fourth part of Chapter 2.

5. Blend the ideas in both chapters and come up with your own creative ideas.

For example:

- Spend time in Denver, Colorado.

- Plant rhododendrons in your garden.

- Wear labradorite jewelry.

Example 2

You are Capricorn or Capricorn Rising and want to enjoy enlightened creativity as well as positive relationships with children:

1. From the house list earlier in this chapter, you realize that both these affairs are ruled by the 5th house.

2. From the lists just given, you'll see that Taurus is the sign that rules your 5th house.

3. Going back to the Taurus section in Chapter 3, read through the enlightenment tools for Taurus.

ENLIGHTENMENT
USING THE
ASTROLOGICAL
TOOLS FOR
ENLIGHTENMENT OF
THE OTHER SIGNS

187

4. Going to Chapter 2, also read through the practical suggestions to use these enlightenment tools.

5. Blend what you read in both chapters and come up with your own creative ideas.

For example:

- Surround yourself with heavy sculptures.

- Wear fine linen clothes.

- Choose pale blue or pink drapes for your art studio.

- Dab some spikenard behind your knees.

EXAMPLE 3

You are Pisces or Pisces Rising and you want to reach enlightenment in your finances:

1. From the house list earlier in this chapter, you'll see that finances are ruled by the 2nd house.

2. From the lists just given, you'll realize that your 2nd house is ruled by Aries.

3. In the Aries section in Chapter 3, read again all the enlightenment tools of Aries.

4. In Chapter 2, go through the practical ideas on how to use the various enlightenment tools.

5. Blend the two chapters and come up with your own creations.

For example:

- Wear red clothes (Aries' color) when going to the bank.

- Create a money altar dedicated to Samael (Aries' angel).

- Choose Tuesdays to balance your checkbook or pay your bills.

- Have the photo of a ram as a screen saver.

ONENESS MEDITATION

In the same ways that a prism reflects light through its various facets, each degree of the zodiac is an aspect of the divine.

Every day of the year, as seen from the Earth, the Sun progresses by one degree. Every month, it changes sign. In one year, the Sun appears to have gone through the 360 degrees of the zodiac and its twelve signs.

If we meditate every day at the exact same time, we get an inner experience of each aspect of creation. The best moments would be the exact time of sunrise, when we can greet the dawn of a new day, or at sunset, when we can release with gratitude the gifts that were given to us in the last twenty-four hours.

In one year, we shall have had an opportunity to experience directly every aspect of our divinity.

ENLIGHTENMENT
USING THE
ASTROLOGICAL
TOOLS FOR
ENLIGHTENMENT OF
THE OTHER SIGNS

189

STAIRWAY TO

ENLIGHTENMENT

IN THE YEARS

2009-2012

5

Why 2012? The Mayan Calendar Made Easy
and the Concrete Meaning of Ascension

The most widely used calendar today is the Gregorian calendar. Based on the yearly revolution of the Earth around the Sun, it was devised in 1582 by Pope Gregory XIII. It assigns a specific date to each year, month, and day, providing us with the grid that structures our perception of reality.

The Mayan calendar is unique in that it is not related to any planetary motion. Purely spiritual, it provides us with a special map to the evolution of human consciousness.

It is important to understand that the ancient Mayans had two major calendars:

1. A personal calendar.

Also called the Short Count or the Tun calendar, it is 360 days long. Each day has a meaning and is sacred. Our life purpose is revealed by the day on which we were born. Every 52 Tuns (52 x 360 days), all debts were banished and the Mayans started over.

2. A sacred calendar.

Also known as the Long Count or the Tzolkin calendar, it is 260 days long. The number 260 is obtained by multiplying the 13 deities the Mayans had by the 20 aspects of creation (signs). To the Mayans, 13 and 20 were sacred numbers.

This calendar is based on the cycles of days multiplied at each level by 20, with the exception of the Tun level, which is obtained by multiplying the Uinal period by 18. It leads to the following five divisions:

- Kin: 1 day.

- Uinal (1 Kin x 20) = 20 days.

- Tun (1 Uinal x 18) = 360 days.

- Katun (1 Tun x 20) = 7,200 days.

- Baktun (1 Katun x 20) = 144,000 days.

This is the divine calendar, the source of all the prophecies. What makes this calendar particularly relevant is that it ends on December 21, 2012. Indications of what lies beyond that date are almost nonexistent. A suggestion is made to October 21, 4772, stating that we would celebrate the anniversary of King Pacal of Palenque's accession to power. Also known as Pacal the Great, this long-reigning Mayan king was deified after his death. The monuments of Palenque are his legacy. This date, being almost three thousand years in our future, would confirm that 2012 is only the end of one cycle of evolution, after which another one will begin.

In what follows, this is the only calendar with which we shall be concerned.

The Sacred Mayan Calendar

The Mayan calendar began at 0.0.0.0.0. (0 Baktun, 0 Katun, 0 Tun, 0 Uinal, 0 Kin). In our Gregorian calendar, this corresponds to August 11, 3114 BC, which for the Mayans marked the beginning of divine cosmic creation. The year 3114 BC was the end of the Stone Age and the beginning of the Bronze Age:

- Sumer and Egypt emerged as civilizations.

- Cuneiform and hieroglyphic writing appeared.

- The first pyramids and temples were built.

- Bronze was invented.

While the Gregorian calendar that we use every day has no specific end date, the Mayan calendar is made of a series of complete cycles that each have an end. It describes nine basic Cycles of Creation leading us from the Big Bang about sixteen billion years ago until the present time, through the appearance of the first animals, to the first primates, to the first humans, through spoken language, followed by written language and industrialism.

A full cycle consists of 13 Baktun (13 Baktun, 0 Katun, 0 Tun, 0 Uinal, 0 Kin), which equals 1,872,000 days, or 5,125.36 years.

Then it just takes a little math to find the end date of the calendar, or the end date of this particular cycle. Add 5,125.36 years—the calendar's full cycle—to the calendar's start date of August 11, 3114 BC. That brings us to an end date of December 21, 2012.

So far, the Mayan calendar has described in great detail everything humanity has experienced for the past billions of years. The entire calendar looks like a pyramid, with 9 levels, each 20 times shorter than the previous one. Since January 5, 1999, we have been in the Galactic Cycle of Creation, which lasts through October 28, 2011. It is 12.8 years long. The acceleration of the evolution of consciousness is already tangible.

On October 29, 2011, we shall enter the very last cycle, the Universal

Cycle of Creation, which lasts 260 days and ends on December 21, 2012. Some students of the Mayan calendar have wondered which of these two dates, October 28, 2011, or December 21st, 2012, is the correct end. Both are correct. This could be likened to the moment of the spring equinox on March 21, which is the official beginning of spring. In February, with warmer days and trees starting to burst with flowers, we may already feel that spring has arrived; in April, we may wonder if we aren't still in winter, despite our calendar stating otherwise!

This very last year, starting on October 29, 2011, and ending on December 21, 2012, will be the year of "the last chance" for many. I'm among those who contend that the final date of ascension is 12.21.2012. Here are my reasons:

- The numerology of that date is spectacular. Only made of 0, 1s, and 2s, it also adds up to 11, which is the number of mastery, and for that reason cannot be reduced to simple digits.

- It occurs at the exact time when the Sun enters Capricorn (the winter solstice) at 3:12 PST or 6:12 EST, which is also numerologically perfect, made of 1, 2, 3, or 6 (2 x 3).

- After studying the correlation between the Mayan calendar and Western astrology, I find that the planetary configurations in the December 21, 2012, chart are so unique that there is no doubt in my mind that this is the precise end date.

But really, the exact mathematical end date shouldn't matter that much. We need to remember that we each have free will and are on an individual journey. Some of us will reach enlightenment even sooner than the end of the Mayan calendar. December 21, 2012, is simply the landmark date when a critical mass of people will realize their divinity and become conscious cocreators.

The meaning of the end of the Mayan calendar has also been the source of much discussion. It doesn't mean the end of the world or the ruination of everything you see today. Instead, on that date, the solar plane will come in perfect alignment with the galactic center. The Earth will be completely surrounded by the Milky Way. A cosmic portal will open, leading us back to our divine truth. One world age will officially end, allowing another one to begin.

In the past, our choices were simple. All we had to check in the morning was our mailbox. Then came P.O. boxes and voice mails, followed by faxes, e-mails (with sometimes two or three addresses), and text-messaging on cell phones. The rapid evolution of technology allows us today to receive communications in ways that didn't even exist only a few decades ago.

As we progress toward 2012, the manner in which our thoughts create our reality will become more and more obvious. There will be "instant karma," meaning that the consequences of our actions become visible more and more immediately. All that is possible will occur simultaneously. The tapestry of our lives will be woven with miracles.

And because we shall be free at all times to manifest anything we want that is in harmony with the laws of the universe, there will be no need for a calendar, hence its end.

But, of course, these wonderful things won't happen without us. If we remain skeptical, if our doubts are stronger than our faith, if our fears are stronger than our love, then we shall create a very different reality for ourselves. Enlightenment is a conscious choice we each need to make. When we do, there will be no limit to the happiness and peace we shall experience.

THE DAYS AND NIGHTS OF THE MAYAN CALENDAR

The very last part of the Mayan calendar is the Galactic Cycle of Creation. It is composed of seven days and six nights. Interestingly enough, this echoes Creation as described in the Bible, which also took seven days and six nights. (These dates are based on Carl Johan Calleman's *The Mayan Calendar and the Transformation of Consciousness*.)

First Day: January 5, 1999–December 30, 1999
ruled by the God of Procreation

First Night: December 31, 1999–December 24, 2000
ruled by the God of Wind

Second Day: December 25, 2000–December 19, 2001
ruled by the God of Sunrise

Second Night: December 20, 2001–December 14, 2002
ruled by the God of Dance

Third Day: December 15, 2002–December 9, 2003
ruled by the God of Water

Third Night: December 10, 2003–December 3, 2004
ruled by the Goddess of the Moon

Fourth Day: December 4, 2004–November 28, 2005
ruled by the Goddess of Rain

Fourth Night: November 29, 2005–November 23, 2006
ruled by the God of Intoxication

Fifth Day: November 24, 2006–November 18, 2007
ruled by the God of Fire

Fifth Night: November 19, 2007–November 12, 2008
ruled by the God of Death

Sixth Day: November 13, 2008–November 7, 2009
ruled by the God of Flowers

Sixth Night: November 8, 2009–November 2, 2010
ruled by the God of Healing

Seventh Day: November 3, 2010–October 28, 2011
ruled by the God of Manifestation

Astrology is always based on beginnings. The very first moment of any reality could be likened to the seed that contains within it the whole tree. Whether it is the moment when a newborn draws its first independent breath, the laying of the first brick of a building, the signing of an important contract, or the first time a question is asked, a map of the heavens—an astrological chart—is calculated. Using the precise date, place, and time for the start of anything, it reveals its potential.

I wanted to see if Western astrology would confirm the Mayan calendar. Erecting a chart, or a map of the heavens, for the beginning date at 12 A.M. of each of the days and nights in the Galactic Cycle (except for the Ascension chart, which occurs on December, 21, 2012, at the exact moment of the Winter Solstice), I was blown away by what I found.

Each of the charts contains a very special configuration detailed in the chapters to come. The only chart in which nothing stands out is the one of the seventh day, but there's a reason for that too, which I shall explain in Chapter 9. The charts each point to very specific changes we need to manifest in our lives.

The fulfillment of the birth of the whole new, positive, and magical reality promised by the end of the Mayan calendar—Ascension—requires that we become aware of what is really at stake.

Ascension comes from *ascending*. It means becoming "lighter" or "of the light." For example, consuming organic, natural, raw vegetarian foods, or thinking happy, positive thoughts, contribute to raising our frequencies. More examples of practical steps we can take in our daily lives are given in Chapter 12.

THE CONCRETE MEANING OF ASCENSION

We reach Ascension when we realize that we are one with the divine. This is an individual process. The year 2012 is when a critical mass of people will reach that level of consciousness. It is not the end of the world, but the end of *one* world or experienced reality, a world based on fear, control, drama, scarcity, and pain.

In 2012, all our cycles of incarnations come to their natural conclusion. The year 2012 could be likened to a final exam in school. Some of us will be expelled, others will have to take the class again, and some of us will graduate with honors. We get to choose which category we fall into by making the lifestyle changes proposed in Chapter 12. Every moment of the next few years counts.

Those who will be expelled:

In past lives, all the parts we denied in ourselves dissolved into what could be likened to black holes. We reincarnated fragmented. Some people may be so fragmented that no matter how much love and consciousness we pour into them, they may be too far gone to absorb any of it sufficiently to continue in the emerging reality. The Earth is a living entity. In her need to heal, she will now accept only those who heal with her. Those who insist on perpetuating lies, violence, fear, negativity, destruction, and hatred will not be allowed in the new world we are creating. This is why we could witness catastrophes that, in a few hours, wipe thousands of people off the planet.

Those who will have to take the class over:

Some who woke up too late but still want to change will be given that opportunity, in a parallel reality, at a slower rate, until the end of the next big evolutionary cycle.

Those who will graduate with honors:

Those who are awake and actively doing their best to heal themselves, others, and our planet will reach enlightenment. We do not individually have to wait for 2012 for this to happen. It could happen anytime between now and 2012. The year 2012 is when humanity will have reached a critical mass that will lift humanity to the next level. It will be an exciting time, a time when all the old, limiting/limited consciousness won't have a hold anymore and miracles will be part of ordinary existence.

Ascension occurs in the Age of Aquarius. This sign, symbolized by two parallel waves, describes two realities that coexist separately from one another.

Those who prefer a world of fear, war, and lies will reside in that dimension of destruction, while those of us who refuse that creation will not have to live in that hell. These two worlds will exist simultaneously, without ever meeting. (You'll read more about these worlds in Chapter 6 when you discover the prophecies of John of Jerusalem.)

We can understand this by comparing it to Mystery Schools (schools where people are initiated to metaphysical knowledge). They are invisible to those who aren't ready to be initiated. A higher frequency is only visible to those who vibrate, or resonate, at that level. For example, angels who vibrate at the highest level cannot be seen by people who are in anger, distrust, and fear (as they have lower frequencies). But people whose hearts are open, who radiate love, peace, and joy (therefore having higher frequencies), are blessed to feel and physically see angels. Another example would be a television set. You can own one and never in your life see a violent or negative program simply because you choose not to watch. This doesn't mean that horror films aren't projected simultaneously on other channels, but these are not the ones you tune in.

The sacred society we are creating vibrates so high that it is naturally protected from those who are of a lower frequency. We are already now experiencing natural separations. People who remain stuck in their dramas and attached to their fears don't feel comfortable around higher-vibrating individuals. They usually leave on their own or cannot even relate to higher-vibrating people at all and their paths don't cross anymore.

The exciting journey that we are on is that we shall create everything as good and happy as we could ever imagine. "But what about my work, my wife, my husband, my house?" you may ask. If in those relationships there is mutual support, growth, enrichment, freedom, and happiness, we shall continue evolving together. But if they are a constant cause of friction and pain, we can only resolve them by taking full responsibility with the very simple meditation offered by Dr. Ihaleakala Hew Len (www.hooponopono.org): "I'm sorry, please forgive me, I love you, thank you." With the energy of asking for forgiveness, even for what may seem to be coming to us from the outside, and sending love and gratitude, there is no difficult situation that cannot be turned around. It will either be healed so that we can pursue that particular relationship on a whole new level, or it will naturally dissolve, leaving space for a partnership that is more conducive to higher growth and happiness.

As we approach 2012, the pace of life will continue to accelerate. We download an ever-increasing amount of information at a faster rate. Our thinking goes into overload, eventually shutting down and forcing us to rely solely on our intuition. Focusing our priorities on what brings us peace, happiness, and abundance creates more peace, more happiness, and more abundance.

Our relationships are changing. Many people have been single for sometimes several years. This is part of the whole process. We cannot rely on another to complete us. We have to find that completeness from within. It is only when each of us will be a pillar standing in its own right that we shall meet our spirit partner—the being with whom we were created as one at the beginning of time before the separation of male and female. He/she is the other pillar of the temple between which life can flow.

Spending months or sometimes years alone is an essential part to being able to attract our right mate. It is only when we realize that we don't need another to make us happy that we become complete in our own right. And that's the requirement to attracting the right partner and enjoying life with them. It is about becoming all that we are on our own, first, before we enjoy life with a partner.

The number 2 is ruled by the Moon. Starting in 2000, women are the keepers of the wisdom. Previously, starting in 1000—1 being ruled by the Sun—it was the men who were in charge. If we were created complementary in our bodies, in our psyches, living at the same time, on the same planet, it does not make sense that we should be at odds with each other. We are meant to ascend together, as couples. The sexuality we shall then experience won't be a one-chakra, one-body affair, but a multibody, multichakra sacred celebration. (*Chakra* is the Sanskrit term meaning "wheel" or "disk." There are seven major chakras or energy centers, located at major points of the human nervous system, and corresponding to specific acupuncture points. They can be likened to portals between our inner and outer worlds through which we radiate and receive energy.) When church leaders condemned sex as sinful, they knew exactly what they were doing: if the people were allowed a positive expression of their sexuality, with love, without hiding or feeling guilty, they would realize how powerful they truly were and thus they would be very difficult to control.

There is a fun and powerful exercise we can do to attract the right person in our lives. First buy a blank notebook.

1. On a Monday, start making a list in that notebook of all the qualities you'd like to find in the person you want to share your life with. Think of every area of life (family, hobbies, money, work, travel, children, sex, education, sense of humor, and so on). Everything should be written positively. For example, if you don't want someone who drinks alcohol, write down, "Someone who is sober, is respectful of his/her body, who treats his/her body like a temple." (And don't assume anything. The universe sometimes has an interesting sense of humor. A friend of mine created a list to attract the right apartment. She wanted a spiraling staircase, which she got—except she forgot to write that she also wanted a second floor. There was her spiraling staircase in a corner of her one-floor apartment, leading nowhere, as a decoration!) When you are done with your list, tape together the pages so when you open your notebook the next day, you will see two new blank pages and you won't be able to read what you wrote the previous day. Tuesday, start all over. You may write the same things, different things, or some things may be omitted. Each day is a new day. When you're done, again tape your pages so that on Wednesday you won't be able to read what you wrote previously. Continue for five days in a row. If one day you don't have much time, still write in a few ideas. On the weekend, leave your notebook alone.

2. For week two, continue the same process, leaving your notebook alone on the weekend.

3. For week three, do the same thing again. The idea is to go deeper and deeper into your subconscious, thinking of all your past relationships, what worked and what didn't, thinking of relationships you admire or relationships seen in films or read in novels. It is an extremely empowering journey.

4. On Monday of the fourth week, you will cut all your tape and read your whole notebook from beginning to end, as if it were someone

else's. Tuesday, do nothing. Wednesday, make an exhaustive list of everything that came up in the three previous weeks. Even if something was mentioned only once, but feels important to you, it should be part of your final list. Once that list is established (with everything expressed in a positive manner), you may throw your notebook away. It has served its purpose. Make two copies of your list—one that you will place in a beautiful box—it's your order to the Universe. The second copy you will read every night before going to sleep, thanking the Universe for this person already being in your life. As you do that, create the emotion of already being in love, already living with this person, and a miracle is guaranteed to occur. Remember, our feelings create our reality. If we believe in something strongly enough, as if it has already happened, it will concretize in physical reality.

Money can be another area of major manipulation. Ruling the world, money has caused wars, thefts, betrayals, and murders. We must stop focusing on scarcity and start creating the emotion of already being wealthy beyond measure. At this time we shall manifest all the abundance we deserve.

There is a wonderful practice that we can all benefit from doing. It was taught to me by a divine mother from Singapore. It only works with banknotes. Don't try this with checks and credit cards, as it could backfire. When you are about to spend paper money ($1, $5, $10, and so on) hold it by its lower left-hand side corner between the thumb and index of your left hand. Stare at it, silently saying to it:

You and I are inseparable.
Go and feed the starving.
Go and clothe the naked
And come back to me a millionfold.

Then spend it immediately—that part is essential. You may also in the morning bless as a group all the dollar bills in your wallet and then bless them individually as you are spending them. That blessing will touch all the people through whose hands the bill circulates. It is guaranteed to come back to you with millions more because you changed your whole relationship to money.

Another fun abundance exercise is to play with the fake million-dollar bills from www.getyourmillionshere.com to help you create the emotion of wealth.

We will see more barters as we reach 2012 and beyond. With no exchange of money, we completely bypass taxes. Everybody works and we each receive what we need.

Where we live will also be of the utmost importance. We need to feel happy on the land we occupy and in harmony with the people around us. We may choose higher, more mountainous locations and prefer like-spirited communities where we can help each other.

We are ascending with, and in, our bodies, not without them. We need to nurture them with good nutrition, sufficient sleep, and exercise in harmony with our physical and spiritual nature. The simpler and more natural, organic, and raw our foods are, the better. That's how Mother Earth intended us to eat. Fruits and vegetables should be ripened naturally and not processed and canned in dark factories. Growing old and sick is also part of the consciousness we are leaving behind. We now have the ability to regenerate our bodies at a cellular level, causing the life span now considered to be normal to be extended by several hundred years.

All living creatures as well as the Earth also are ascending. Bees are not going extinct. They have already ascended, waiting for us in the parallel reality that all of us who will reach enlightenment will move into naturally as we become more and more of the light. Pets at this time are very powerful teachers and masters. Animals are not remaining submissive and silent in the face of mistreatment. Plants are refusing pesticides. The Earth wants its waters to be clear and pure again. If we own land, we should start growing our own herbs, fruits, and vegetables, and if we live in an apartment, we should begin sprouting seeds for nutrition.

The quality of our water is vital. We should install a water purifier and/or activator and at the very least charge our water with crystals, positive affirmations, and on purple plates (kindly refer to Chapter 12 for more information on the purple plates). Water carries our memory and using microwaved water or foods is like cutting out all the letters in a page, throwing them into the air, and hoping to be able to read what has randomly fallen on the ground.

These are exciting times and we should not give in to fear. The doomsday scenarios will only exist for those who focus on them. If we stay tuned in a frequency of positive, healing energy, love, and oneness, there are no limits to the miracles we can create and attract to ourselves. And yes, much may be stripped away in our lives, but if it can be taken away, it never was ours. We need to remember that we are not our bank account, we are not our relationship, we are not our profession, we may even not be whom we have been conditioned to believe that we are. So, who are we? That's the fascinating journey that we are traveling on until 2012. It is a journey into the unknown because nothing in humanity's past has prepared us for the magic that is coming. We are individually and collectively creating one moment at a time, one choice at a time.

Before I explain in more detail what you can expect in each of the years leading us to 2012, there is a special prophecy of which you need to learn. A thousand years ago, John of Jerusalem had a vision that, if we care to listen, will change our lives forever and lead us to our true destiny.

With great clarity, John of Jerusalem reveals the pitfalls of which we need to become aware in order for the enlightenment promised by the Mayan calendar in 2012 to occur.

6

The Prophecies of John of Jerusalem

(1042–1120)

Our current place in the Mayan calendar—the cycle between 1999 and 2011—is the one in which our ethics have to be in perfect order to reach enlightenment. This is where the prophecies of John of Jerusalem come in. He offers a missing link between the Mayan calendar and our concrete day-to-day living. He makes us aware of the pitfalls we are facing and the dangers that could prevent us from reaching the promised enlightenment.

Very little is known of John of Jerusalem, who most probably is the same person as Jean de Mareuil or Jean de Vézelay. He may have been a Knight Hospitalier. (After the First Crusade, the Muslims authorized the creation of a Latin-rites church as well as a hospital in Jerusalem. The Knight Hospitalier order's primary purpose was to protect the ever-increasing number of pilgrims going to the holy city, the church, and the hospital.) John of Jerusalem is thought to have contributed in 1099 to the liberation of Jerusalem, which had been invaded twenty years earlier by the Turks. It is in that city that he is believed to have received his vision.

The prophecies came to light again in 1994, when a strange little book was published in Paris by Jean-Claude Lattès. The book, *Le Livre des Prophéties: Le Troisième Millénaire Révélé*, was attributed to John of Jerusalem. The prophecies within the book had been discovered four years earlier by Professor Galvieski in the archives of the Zargosk Monastery near Moscow.

Despite the controversy that shrouds their authenticity, the prophecies rang completely true to me, striking me as the most important prophetic message I had ever come across.

The book begins with a fifty-line prologue that, among other predictions, describes the discovery of the American continent, the United Nations of Europe, and the United Nations of America. It is followed by two parts.

Part I consists of thirty paragraphs, each made up of between five and eleven lines. It's entitled, "At the beginning of the year thousand following the year thousand." That translates into 2000, the third millennium.

Part II consists of only ten paragraphs. It's entitled, "When the year thousand following the year thousand will come into full bloom." This part to me describes what will happen beyond 2012 after the Ascension process.

Years went by and I almost forgot about this book and the prophecies within it until I started giving seminars on the astrology of Ascension. As more and more material was flooding my consciousness, John of Jerusalem's prophecy came back to me so vividly that I had to dig that text out and read it again. Contrary to Nostradamus's prophetic quatrains, which, allowing much room for interpretation, remain cryptic at best, the unequivocal simplicity of John's words written nearly five centuries before leaves no space whatsoever for imagination.

Like the first time, rereading his words simply blew my mind. Thirteen years had gone by. No longer the story of some hypothetical future, it was describing perfectly what all the news channels and newspapers across the world report every single day.

The world we are now experiencing several years into the new millennium is exactly as John of Jerusalem, about nine centuries ago, had foreseen it.

Part I

Part I goes back and forth between seven major topics:

1. The Abuse of the Earth's Resources

"Nature's path will be abandoned" (I-17)*

We live in homes with artificial light. We eat processed foods. For the smallest nearby errand, we use our car. The stress of our lives is such that we no longer take time to smell the flowers or take a stroll on the beach. We need exercise equipment to stay in shape. The soil is so depleted that in order to have all the vitamins we need, it is essential that we absorb all sorts of supplements. The air we breathe is polluted. We drink bottled water that has absorbed chemicals from plastic containers. We apply poison to our skin under the guise of lotions, perfume, and makeup. Some over-the-counter medications cite death as one of their side effects! Do I need to continue?

"The sun will burn the earth." (I-23)
  "The air will become burning hot." (I-12)

With the destruction of the "good" ozone in our atmosphere and as global warming progresses, causing the melting of the ice caps, we are experiencing dramatic climate changes all over the planet.

"The water will be fetid." (I-12)
  "The illnesses of the water, the sky, and the earth will hit." (I-21)

The quality of our water is questionable at best. In some cities and in many countries, tap water carries dangerous diseases. Chemicals are being sprayed in our already polluted air, causing lung disease. The more antibiotics we use, the more indestructible viruses become.

"The fields will be empty." (I-3)
  "No fields to cultivate." (I-20)

* *Note:* The Prophecies of John of Jerusalem, as they appear in this book, were translated by the author from French. They are in some cases paraphrases instead of a strictly literal translation of the text.

THE PROPHECIES
OF JOHN OF
JERUSALEM

209

"The earth will be naked and sterile." (I-12)

"There won't be enough bread for all." (I-3)

"Many men will have hunger tighten their stomachs." (I-4)

"Man will have changed the face of the earth, he will have excavated the soil and the sky." (I-12)

John of Jerusalem clearly says that this state of affairs didn't just happen. Man, by messing up nature's laws, created this state. We still have food in our fields, but for how long? Climate changes freeze many fruit trees, destroying valuable crops. Our pets recently died en masse to call our attention to the fast food they were being fed—which included meat from their own species. The industrialized sugar given to bees to lower the costs of mass production has killed them. Bees have already disappeared in more than twenty-four states, completely upsetting the ecological balance. The consequences are extremely serious. Lack of pollination means that our food supply will soon be scarce.

"Man will have turned the animals into beasts shaped by his will, destroying numerous species. He will have changed the laws of life." (I-25)

The animal kingdom is no longer respected or honored. Chickens are raised and forced to lay eggs in torturous conditions. Cattle are fed hormones before being slaughtered in barbaric circumstances. Wolves are shot from helicopters. Dolphins dramatically die, caught in huge fishing nets. The new invention of our mad scientists is meat cloning. Many species, such as the disappearing bees, in an effort to confront us with the living hell we are creating for ourselves, have chosen to leave our dimension and shift to the next, thus ascending before we do.

2. Destruction of Cities by War and the Elements

"The desert will corrode the land and water will be deeper and deeper like a deluge one day, the very next, the soil will dry up." (I-21)

"The sea will raise like boiling water, engulfing towns and shores. Entire continents will disappear. Men will take refuge in the heights." (I-23)

Terrible droughts and fires have already devastated many localities (the Witch Fire in California in 2007), while dramatic tornadoes and storms have hit others (the tsunami in Thailand, Hurricanes Katrina and Rita in New Orleans and the southeast United States, all in 2005).

"The earth will shake in various locations." (I-22)

"Each city will be Sodom and Gomorrah." (I-1)

"The houses will be destroyed or stolen." (I-9)

"Towns will cave in, mud will submerge the villages, fire will destroy the new Romes." (I-22)

Sodom and Gomorrah, cited in the Bible, refer to two cities that once upon a time existed southeast of the Dead Sea and were suddenly destroyed by fire. Less than a decade into the twenty-first century, there have already been thirty major earthquakes around the world, killing more than half a million people. Compare these numbers to about forty-five major earthquakes in the whole of the twentieth century, claiming the lives of about one million people, and about eighteen major earthquakes in all the centuries before, there clearly is an alarming increase. The Earth is a living entity. Earthquakes are her way of dealing with her diseases, which are caused by our lack of respect. And, of course, when reading this vision, we cannot help but be reminded of the tragic events on September 11, 2001, in New York City. When the Twin Towers collapsed in flames, thousands of people died in one instant.

"Mass movements will push people from one country to another." (I-16)

Entire peoples have been forced by political and economic conditions to leave their countries of origin. Let us mention among many others the Mexican immigrants, the number of whom in the United States has doubled between 1990 and 2000, now reaching almost five million.

3. Man's God Complex

"Man will believe himself to be God." (I-27)

"Man will want the power of God. He will know no limit." (I-2)

"The only law will be one's own." (I-3)

"There will be neither order nor rule." (I-8)

"He will set himself up as the Master and monarch of forests and herds." (I-12)

"Men will no longer surrender to God's law." (I-18)

When man acts as if nature were his to tame, use, and abuse, man is setting himself up to be the devil's apprentice. Deforestation is destroying the precious natural balance provided to the whole planet by the rain forests. Overgrazing is creating intense desertification in China and many other countries. Once more, the pressure to make more money is overriding ecological considerations, further threatening life.

"Hatred will flood the lands." (I-9)
  "Like poison, fear will lie in every heart." (I-18)
  "Distrusting everything, he will feel fear." (I-30)
  "Blinded, conquered by anger and jealousy, man will hit with the capacity to destroy everything around him." (I-27)
  "Jews and Allah's children will oppose each other." (I-28)
  Fear is the opposite of love. It comes from judgment and is a form of attack. We feel the need to defend ourselves. We erect walls against others. We separate ourselves. Wars begun in the twenty-first century are still raging in various parts of the globe:
  In Asia and the Middle East:

• Since 1983, the Sri Lanka civil war.

• Since 2001, fighting in Afghanistan.

• Since 2003, the war in Iraq.

In Africa:

• Since 2005, the war in Chad.

• Since 2006, fighting in Somalia.

Infamous bombings are hitting Europe:

• Train bombings in Madrid in March 2004.

• Bombings in London's Underground and bus system in July 2005.

And Asia:

- The Mumbai train bombings in India in July 2006.

4. *Optical Illusions and Delusions of Grandeur*

"False prophets will gather the blinded men." (I-7)

"The merchants of illusions will come, offering the poison. It will destroy the bodies and rot the souls. And those who will have mixed that poison to their blood will be like trapped wild animals. They will rape, extort money, and steal. Life will become an everyday apocalypse." (I-4)

Poison is in the water in our own houses, in the irradiated foods we eat, in the smog and smoke rising above the Earth, in the toxic particles found in the air we breathe. It is also in the intensely disturbing magnetic fields created by our cellular phones, television sets, computers, dishwashers, microwave ovens, laser beams, and electronic gadgets. And if that wasn't enough, we are being bombarded by advertisements convincing us that we are neither as young, as slim, nor as beautiful as we should be. In order to erase our age or lose unsightly fat, we're told we need to inject our bodies with more poison (breast implants, organ enlargements, Botox). Science does not really know the long-term effects of these products because no one has used those chemicals long enough. Millions of people throughout the world are enslaved to illegal drugs. This leads to a downward spiral of robberies, prostitution, and murders to obtain the ever-increasing amounts of money required to satisfy addiction.

"Men will know how to give life to mirages. Senses will be fooled and they will believe they are touching what doesn't exist. Man won't be able to separate what is from what isn't. He will get lost in false labyrinths." (I-24)

IMAX theaters recreate life as a 3-D experience, yet it is not real. Our sound systems allow us to listen to music as if we were in a concert hall, but we're not; instead, we are alone in our room. Digital images are so clear that we could swear we're outdoors, hearing the buzzing of the bee on the flower, but we're not. We are just staring at a flat picture reproduced on paper or recreated on a computer screen.

John of Jerusalem goes on to describe how innocent and *"blinded"* (I-7) we are, *"misled"* (I-24), *"held prisoners"* (I-14), and *"believing to be free . . . are true slaves"* (I-15) led into *"the abyss."* (I-14)

Computers, for example, were meant to serve us and help us gain time. Sure, on one level, they enable faster communication and an expansion of the mind. But they also enslave us. They require more and more complex knowledge, are constantly outdated by new technology, and are formidable tools of mass control. There is no privacy anymore. Any personal e-mail can potentially become a weapon against our freedom.

Microwaves are another example of what takes us farther away from nature. Supposed to make our lives easier, they really create chaos in our bodies. Microwaves shock particles. All the memory contained in the water content of microwaved foods is forever disturbed. What we then absorb is genetically transmuted, chaotic, and, ultimately, dead. And if we are what we eat, couldn't this account for the depression, fears, loss of meaning, and apathy so many people suffer from today?

5. The Abuses of Sexuality and of Children; Also, the Homeless

"Each will shut their eyes to not see the women being raped." (I-9)

According to Women's Rape Crisis Center statistics, in 2006–2007 in the United States alone, there was a forty percent increase of rape. Rape is a weapon of war. Gang rape against women has been resorted to in every conflict, on every continent:

- In Europe: Nazi Germany, Cyprus, Bosnia-Herzegovina, Croatia.

- In Asia: Bangladesh, Cambodia, China, Tibet.

- In Africa: Liberia, Somalia, Uganda, Algeria, Rwanda.

- In the Caribbean: Haiti, Peru.

"Everyone will try to climax all one can." (I-5)
"The father will take pleasure with the daughter, the man with the man,

the woman with the woman, the old with the pubescent child, and this will happen in the eyes of all. But the blood will turn impure. The evil will spread from bed to bed." (I-6)

Sexual promiscuity has spread like wildfire. Loveless sex with people we don't know or we hardly know is commonplace and can have devastating consequences on an emotional, spiritual, and physical level. In fact, John of Jerusalem clearly foresaw the AIDS epidemic.

"The child will be sold . . . Pleasure will be taken in the newness of his skin. The child's sacred weakness will be forgotten." (I-13)

"He will be hunted down for pleasure and sometimes his body will be sold." (I-26)

Child prostitution is a huge epidemic. It doesn't solely exist in Burma, Thailand, or South Korea. It also plagues the United States, where thousands of lost and despaired children every year are caught in the nets of pimps who, ruling with fear, turn them into sex slaves.

"There will be reason to fear for man's child. Poison and despair will be on the lookout for him. He will have been selfishly desired only for oneself . . . he will be threatened by brain death. He will live in games and mirages . . . No one will have taught him hope nor action." (I-26)

"No master will guide the child." (I-5)

According to the Los Angeles Homeless Services Coalition, in 2007 alone, 3.5 million people (1.35 million of whom are children) experienced homelessness. Children under the age of eighteen account for thirty-nine percent of the homeless population. Forty-two percent of these are under the age of five. Many children grow up without any real value system or role model. They may be born in broken families or raised by single parents who don't have time because they have to work three jobs to make ends meet. Or perhaps their parents are simply neglectful. Without a solid emotional foundation, these children indiscriminately absorb the violent images and sounds transmitted by Game Boys, computers, iPods, or television. Cellular phones are known to cause cancer and brain tumors, especially in young children. (Award-winning Mayo Clinic–trained neurosurgeon Dr. Vini Khurana says he believes a link between mobile phones and certain brain tumors will be proven in the next decade—a belief supported by warnings to citizens by the French and German governments and the European Environment Agency.) Without true, loving guidance, many children hang out in malls or on the street, where they become the targets of pimps and drug dealers.

"Families will be like separated grains that nothing can unite. Without any ties, people will roam all over the place without any guide." (I-17)

"Many men . . . wandering, penniless, humiliated and despaired . . . [will be] without a home." (I-20)

"Men in multitudes excluded from human life, neither rights, nor roof, nor bread, naked, will sell their bodies." (I-29)

Single people as well as whole families lack a roof to protect them. Whether it is because of illness, postwar trauma, the abuse of drugs, or drastic economic troubles, jobless and without any money, they survive at the edge of society.

6. Financial Greed

"Whoever will enter the temple, will encounter merchants." (I-1)

"He will want to possess always more . . . because his head is lost in mirages." (I-30)

We are living in a consumer-based society. For a closer look at what we have become, take a look at a twenty-minute animated film created by Free Range Studios with Annie Leonard (www.storyofstuff.com). It will forever change your understanding of what advertisements and stores really are about.

"Gold will be in blood." (I-1)

"Man will create merchandise out of everything. Each thing will have its price: trees, water, and animals. Nothing will be given, everything will be sold. All man will be worth is the weight of his flesh. His body will be exchanged like a piece of meat." (I-11).

Our lack of vision and greed encourage quick fixes such as the destructive practice of illegally selling one's organs for money.

"Although he sleeps on bags full of grain [man] will only give a handful as

alms and what he gives with one hand, he will take back with the other."
(I-10)

A fear-based society creates the need for self-preservation, which in turn leads to selfishness. A lack of understanding that we are all one justifies the belief that what we give to another will deprive us. Nothing could be farther from the truth. The law of abundance states that what we generously give with an open heart comes back to us a millionfold.

7. The Secret World Government

"A black and secret order will emerge. Its law will be hatred and its weapon, poison. Always wanting more gold, it will extend its reign to the whole earth."
(I-19)

"It is monarchs devoid of faith who will reign. They will command innocent and passive human crowds. Their faces will be hidden and their names kept secret. Their fortified castles will be lost in the forests. They will decide the fate of everything and everyone. No one will participate in their orders' gatherings." (I-15)

"The just and the weak will suffer its [the black order's] rule. The powerful will serve it." (I-19)

"The sight and spirit of men will be held prisoners." (I-14)

"The sword will defend the snake." (I-1)

"The predators will gather them in flocks to better lead them into the abyss."
(I-14)

"At the end of the path, will be the abyss." (I-2)

"Man's masters will betray him and there will only be bad shepherds."
(I-30)

In ancient Egypt, pharaohs were both spiritual and political leaders. This was the last time that church and state were one. John of Jerusalem foresaw the Secret Government, also referred to as the shadow government. Created by a powerful elite, this largely faceless, self-financing, self-perpetuating organization operates outside of constitutional laws. With the CIA at its core, it has, in recent history, relied on the help of the Mafia and former Nazis to plot the assassinations of world leaders and, through torture and murder, it has overthrown governments (Iran, Cuba, Vietnam, Chile, Cambodia). Above the law, its powers exercised beyond public scrutiny, conducting covert operations without external control, the Secret Government remains untouchable. The fate of all resides in the hands of a few who, in a spirit of warfare and beyond accountability to public institutions, act with total immunity. What is occurring behind the scenes is exposed in an amazing film, *Zeitgeist* (www.zeitgeistmovie.com). The film confirms John of Jerusalem's predictions flawlessly. What we are not aware of could literally enslave our souls and kill us.

Although Part I describes a very barbaric reality, the prophecy doesn't leave us on a bleak note. As we recognize the dangers we face, we shall have the power to transmute most of them and manifest Part II of this vision.

PART II

Although there is no specific date, to me, this part of the prophecy describes the state both humanity and the Earth will reach after Ascension. I therefore take it that John of Jerusalem is speaking of 2012 and beyond. The full extent of his vision may not occur until the middle of the third millennium, but we shall be well on our way after 2012.

Part II of John of Jerusalem's prophecy is short but sweet. It begins, "When the year thousand coming after the year thousand will come into full bloom," and goes on to describe in ten paragraphs an age when humanity, awakened to its spiritual dimension, will enjoy pure happiness.

"Faith will show a new vigor. After the dark days of the beginning of the second millennium, happy days will open." (II-36)

The Earth will be healed. Efforts are being made in many locations to plant trees again:

"The forests will once again be dense and the deserts will have been irrigated. The waters will have become pure again. Earth will be like a garden." (II-37)

The power of prayer can reverse the pollution of entire lakes, as described in research by Dr. Masaru Emoto in his book *The Hidden Messages in Water.*

"Man will watch over all that lives. What he soiled, he will purify. He will feel that all of Earth is his home. Thinking of tomorrows, he will be wise." (II-37)

"And the earth will be in order." (II-36)

The first millennium, which started with 1, the Sun's number, was ruled by men. The year "two" thousand is ruled by the Moon, the divine mother. We shall see more and more women reach positions of high authority. Some countries already have a woman president. For example, Finland, with Tarja Halonen.

"Woman will come and grab the scepter. She will be the great master of the times to come and what she will think, she will impose upon men. She will be the Mother of the year two thousand. After the Devil's days, she will pour the lukewarm softness of the Mother . . . She will be beauty." (II-35)

One thousand years before the invention of television, radio, and the Internet, John of Jerusalem predicted that:

"Each person will step in regulated synch with others. One will know everything that is happening in the world." (II-38)

An era of abundance will come:

"Man will open his heart and his wallet to the more resourceless." (II-38)

"Man will have learned how to give and share." (II-39)

"Roads will go from one side of the Earth to the other and to the sky on the other side." (II-37)

John of Jerusalem clearly describes submarines, scuba diving, planes, and space shuttles. Yet it also seems that our bodies will develop in such a way as to render those means of transportation unnecessary:

"The body of man will be magnified and skillful." (II-34)

"Men will be able to dive deep into waters. Their bodies will be new and they will be fish. And some will fly higher than the birds." (II-33)

Past and future will hold no secrets to our clairvoyance and expanded consciousness. We shall return to a state of oneness:

"He will remember what was and he will know how to read what is to come." (II-40)

"He will have unraveled the secrets possessed by the Ancient Gods." (II-34)

"Finally, only one language will be spoken by all." (II-31)

The society we are recreating is one of beauty and magic:

"He will have conquered the sky. He will create stars in the large, deep blue sea." (II-32)

"With the power and the gush of a spring, he will create. He will teach his knowledge to the masses and the children will know the earth and the sky more than anyone before them." (II-34)

"He will have built new cities in the sky, on the earth, and on the sea." (II-40).

Humanity, says John of Jerusalem, will live in peace and harmony, with love and joy in its heart:

"People will love and share, dream and give birth to dreams." (II-35)

"Man will know the spirit of each thing. Stone or water, the body of the animal or someone's look." (II-34)

"Man will experience a second birth. Spirit will seize upon the crowd of men who will commune in fraternity." (II-36)

"He will know that what hits one, wounds the other." (II-31)

We shall be fully healed:

"Illnesses will be treated before they manifest. Each person will be his own and others' healer." (II-38)

Our bodies, regenerated at a cellular level, will live hundreds of years:

"Men will live as long as the oldest of men whom the Sacred Books speak about." (II-33)

"Because man will have in his life lived many lives, he will no longer fear his own death and he will know that Light will never go out again." (II-40)

Immersed in fear, believing what their senses show them, unaware of their personal power, caught in self-inflicted limitations, some people will think they have no other option but to descend farther and farther into the hell described in Part I of John of Jerusalem's prophecy.

Let us never forget that we have free will.

No matter what our circumstances look like, we need to become conscious that we are a hundred percent responsible for our reality. Even that which seems beyond our conscious control, isn't. We create what we see. At any given moment, we can also make the choice to see things differently and thus manifest a whole truth.

We can take the warnings offered in John of Jerusalem's prophecy, combined with the precise time line given by the Mayan calendar, and use them as a guide for our actions in the years to come. They are a reminder that while we encounter challenging circumstances and face difficult choices, the only path to everlasting peace and happiness is enlightenment. As we consciously choose to replace fear with love, the transformation of our inner reality necessarily shifts the world around us. Indian philosopher Mahatma Gandhi expressed this beautifully: "Be the change you want to see in the world."

For those who will choose enlightenment, I will in the next chapters detail every year from 2009 to 2012 in general and for each sign. I will offer the guidelines to expanding our awareness. Through precise portals at specific dates, this is the stairway leading from the dark, apocalyptic scenery painted in Part I of John of Jerusalem's prophecy to Part II, the glorious reality after Ascension.

KINDLY NOTE:

I'll be introducing some new concepts and terms in the following chapters.

CHIRON

Chiron is an asteroid located between Saturn and Uranus. While it is not associated to a specific sign, it offers some similarities to Virgo. Chiron represents our wounds and our capacity to heal both ourselves and others. It is the bridge between the known (Saturn) and the unknown (Uranus)—between the old and the new.

Eclipses

Eclipses occur when the Sun, the Moon, and the Earth come in complete alignment. One celestial body casts a shadow on another, thus making it seem as if it has disappeared. A lunar eclipse can only occur at the full Moon, when the Earth is between the Sun and the Moon. The Earth casts its shadow across the Moon, making it look like it has disappeared, or eclipsed, from our sky. A solar eclipse can only occur at the new Moon, when the Moon is between the Sun and the Earth. The Moon is in front of the Sun, blocking it in such a way that, from Earth, we cannot see the Sun anymore. It is only an optical illusion, of course, but one that has tremendous significance. An eclipse is always a time of major realizations and change, the results of which are usually apparent within one month of the date of the eclipse. Whatever happens on those days is final and irreversible.

My interpretations of eclipses are based on the images offered in a book called *The Sabian Symbols in Astrology*, written in 1953 by Marc Edmund Jones, who is known as the "dean of American astrology." In 1925, Jones worked with Elsie Wheeler, a crippled young girl who was very gifted and psychic. She channeled 360 pictures—one for each of the 360 degrees of the zodiac. What makes these images particularly significant is that due to her young age and infirmity, her world experience was extremely limited. Most of the images she received were completely outside her conscious understanding.

Aspects

Aspects are the specific angular distances (relationships) between the planets. The aspects are obtained by:

- Dividing the zodiacal wheel by 1 (conjunction 0 degrees)—a fusional relationship.

- Dividing the zodiacal wheel by 2 (opposition 180 degrees) or by 4 (square 90 degrees)—a more challenging relationship.

• Dividing the zodiacal wheel by 3 (trine 120 degrees) and 6 (sextile 60 degrees)—a harmonious relationship.

• There is also one extra division of 150 degrees, the quincunx, which is an aspect of change. One hundred–fifty degrees corresponds to 5 signs. Every 5 signs, we find two signs which have no connection with each other (for example, neither Aries and Virgo or Gemini and Scorpio are of the same element, nor the same mode of transmission of that element, and are about as different from one another as they can be). Symbolized by a see-saw, this is an aspect of change and requires that we find an equilibrium between vastly different elements within our environment and our own nature. When two planets are joined by an aspect, their principles blend according to the quality of the aspect. If planets are words, when they are joined to another, a sentence is formed.

CONFIGURATIONS

Aspects linking more than two planets are called "configurations." As you will notice in the following pages, except for one day—the 7th day developed in Chapter 9, the beginning of each new "day" and "night" in the Mayan calendar is marked by the presence of a few special configurations, which are as follows:

T SQUARE

Two planets in opposition (180-degree angle) are each squaring (90-degree angle) a third planet. This creates the feeling of a "three-legged" table. A challenge is revealed that is resolved through the missing "fourth leg," the point opposite the planet that is squared by the two planets in opposition with each other. The discomfort forces us to find creative solutions and thus grow.

GRAND TRINE

Three planets are trining each other (120-degree angle). This is a very harmonious and flowing configuration, one that feels comfortable, the reward of past positive deeds. The only danger is that its level of ease could entice us to rest on our laurels and stop seeking more in our lives.

SEMI-GRAND SEXTILE

Two planets are in opposition (180-degree angle) to each other, and two more are between those two. The four planets are each linked to the next one by a 60-degree angle (sextile aspect).

For example, if the Sun is at 15 degrees Aries and the Moon is at 16 degrees Libra, they are in opposition to each other. Now, if we also have Mars at 15 degrees Gemini and Saturn at 15 degrees Leo, the Sun is not only in opposition with the Moon, but in Sextile with Mars, which is in Sextile with Saturn, which is in Sextile with the Moon. Together, those four planets form at Semi-Grand Sextile. This is a very creative aspect. It is as harmonious as the Grand Trine but it isn't as static. There is a sense of movement and a positive wish to progress in a flowing manner. These planets stimulate each other.

YOD

Also called "Finger of God," this is a very unique configuration involving three planets, two of which are in Sextile to each other (60-degree angle), both pointing to the third one by quincunx (150-degree angle).

For example, if Mars is at 0 degrees Aries and Mercury is at 0 degrees Gemini, Mars and Mercury are in Sextile to each other. If Pluto is at 0 degrees Scorpio, it is in quincunx (150-degrees) to both Mars and Mercury, which point at it. This is a configuration of destiny. It reveals a very special life path as well as the best way to fulfill one's highest purpose.

RETROGRADE

From our viewpoint on Earth, all the planets, except the Sun and the Moon, which are never retrograde, sometimes seem—for a period going from a few weeks to a few months—to go backward. It is caused by their speed of rotation relative to the Earth's. This optical illusion has great meaning in astrology. That planet's principles are expressed more inwardly. We may remember aspects of ourselves we had forgotten or never had an opportunity to develop. The rhythm of life seems to slow down, enabling us to ask ourselves questions we had never thought about.

THE DATES

When an aspect occurs more than once, this doesn't mean that nothing happens between those dates. They describe a whole cycle. The first period could be likened to a knock on the door; the second, to sitting down and having a conversation; and the third one, to the digestion of the information exchanged.

Each date is explained in astrological terms (which planets are linked by which aspect, or in which sign a specific eclipse falls). If this makes it easier for you, skip the technicalities and simply read the dates and their interpretation.

When two or three specific dates are given, it doesn't mean that a particular transit (planetary aspect or relationship between two planets or particular cosmic event) occurs only on those dates. They mark the whole period during which an influence is going to be felt. For example: Saturn Quincunx Chiron (February 3 through August 31) means that we shall experience that energy from the beginning of February all the way to the end of August. Sensitive people can even feel it starting one to two months before that period until about one to two months after its completion (as early as the beginning of December 2008 through the end of October 2009).

Additionally, the dates given hereafter are in Eastern Standard Time (EST). Depending on your time zone, there may be up to a twenty-four-hour variation.

THE ASTROLOGICAL SYMBOLS

THE PLANETS:

☉ Sun

☽ Moon

☿ Mercury

♀ Venus

♂ Mars

♃ Jupiter

♄ Saturn

⚷ Chiron

♅ Uranus

♆ Neptune

♇ Pluto

THE SIGNS:

♈ Aries   ruled by Mars ♂

♉ Taurus   ruled by Venus ♀

♊ Gemini   ruled by Mercury ☿

♋ Cancer   ruled by the Moon ☽

♌ Leo   ruled by the Sun ☉

♍ Virgo	ruled by Mercury ☿
♎ Libra	ruled by Venus ♀
♏ Scorpio	ruled by Pluto ♇
♐ Sagittarius	ruled by Jupiter ♃
♑ Capricorn	ruled by Saturn ♄
♒ Aquarius	ruled by Uranus ♅
♓ Pisces	ruled by Neptune ♆

A beautiful way to learn more about the signs and the planets, their meanings and how you can personally integrate them in your daily lives, is to draw each one of these symbols on an index card and carry it in your pocket for any length of time. You will see that, for example, while you are working with the Pluto card, you will start having intense experiences. Working with the Venus card will attract more peaceful and loving circumstances. Or you may enlarge any of these symbols and hang them in your bedroom to "dream" those energies into your life.

In Chapters 7 to 10, you will find the charts of the various stages or portals that humanity will be going through between 2009 and 2012. You are welcome to activate this process both for yourself and collectively, by placing little crystals on each, wherever you intuitively feel drawn. There is no right or wrong here. These crystal placements will keep changing as your inner vision leads you into a deeper understanding of your own divine truth.

7

2009

DELINEATION OF THE CHART OF THE SIXTH DAY

OF THE MAYAN CALENDAR

(NOVEMBER 13, 2008–NOVEMBER 7, 2009)

AND THE PLANETARY CONFIGURATIONS IN 2009

2009

In numerology, 2009 (2 + 0 + 0 + 9) equals 11. Being a master number, 11 cannot be reduced to 2.

This 11 year is a year of mastery when we shall realize that we are not bound by the limitations we may have identified with. We are infinite, beautiful, and powerful. Our capacity to manifest anything that is in alignment with the highest good of the universe is unlimited.

THE SIXTH DAY OF THE MAYAN CALENDAR

Special Configurations
Grand Trine between Saturn, Jupiter, and the Moon

2009 is a year of peace. We reap the rewards of much effort. There is stability in our domestic affairs. Our sense of family expands to inte-

6th Day in Mayan Calendar

Natal Chart
Thursday, November 13, 2008
12:00:00 AM EST
New York, New York
Tropical   Koch True Node

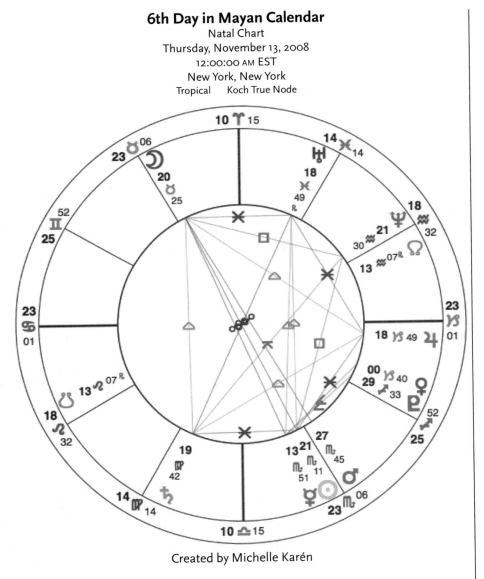

Created by Michelle Karén

grate friends we feel deeply related to at the soul level. We are likely to live in a place that is private when we need to retreat from the world, but that does not isolate us from the like-spirited people we cherish. It feels secure while affording us the space to keep expanding and traveling. It could even be in another state or a country that feels like a nest. The lo-

2009
DELINEATION OF
THE CHART OF THE
SIXTH DAY OF THE
MAYAN CALENDAR

229

cations we are likely to favor are a bit remote, higher up on hills or in the mountains, with a view.

T Square between the Sun, Neptune, and the Moon

This year brings the need to integrate spiritual principles into our daily lives. As we spiritualize ordinary activities, our consciousness expands. For example, we can silently send love and blessings while standing in line at the post office or we can treat an aggressive person with compassion. We become masters—enlightened or liberated spiritual teachers who are one with the divine, such as Jesus Christ or Buddha—by listening to our hearts and acting with generosity and joy. Our capacity to manifest extraordinary realities stems from this inner understanding.

Semi-Grand Sextile between Saturn, the Sun, Jupiter, Uranus, and the Moon

What needs to be transformed becomes obvious. This is a particularly creative configuration that balances discipline, expansion, and change, freeing us from old conditionings. Shifts occur by raising the frequency of our present circumstances.

Envelope between Saturn, the Sun, Uranus, and the Moon

Seen in a superficial way, our relationship to authority, change, ourselves, and our home and family seems flowing and harmonious. However, inner conflicts are lurking under the surface. They create the tension necessary to seek another level of evolution. Our need to express our uniqueness is likely to be blocked by more conventional structures from which we need to free ourselves. It is also necessary that we resolve that which is not completely in balance within ourselves and that we observe the areas of our lives where we may have overcompensated in an attempt to hide a subtle sense of inadequacy.

In Western Astrology
Uranus and Neptune in Mutual Reception (in Each Other's Sign; Since December 31, 2003–March 12, 2011)

In these eight years, we are transmuting into human dolphins. These aquatic mammals have the natural ability to X-ray each other. Any lack of balance or disease is immediately visible to them, which leaves no room for lies or manipulation. As we become more sensitive to the energy fields of others, our perceptions go beyond what another person may be trying to hide or may not even be conscious of. This is an exciting time when our psychic abilities are gradually developing, allowing us to perceive dimensions that were previously hidden.

Jupiter in Aquarius (January 5, 2009–January 17, 2010)

Ecology remains at the forefront of our concerns this year. There could be some breakthroughs in science and music that revolutionize the way we understand our connection to the rest of humanity. Philanthropic movements bring like-spirited people together from all over the world. Humanity's objective is of a high order, with an insistence on independence. Our social life expands. New, dynamic friendships and group associations are greatly enhanced. We feel the need to bring justice to mankind and create situations where all win.

Solar Eclipse 6°29' Aquarius (January 26)

Eclipses always bring us to points of no return. In the Sabian Symbols, this degree is described as "A child is seen being born out of an egg." This particular eclipse is the birthing of our truth. We are emerging into a whole new dimension, where all that we thought could not be challenged will be undone, forcing us to learn everything new. As we find our marks, we also discover aspects of ourselves and our lives that we never knew existed.

Saturn Quincunx Chiron (February 4, August 31)

As we truly commit to life, our wisdom and our natural sense of authority bloom. By daring to imagine that things can be different, we transform what was limiting. We need to create a clear inner vision of what we want and feel in our emotions that it has already happened for it to manifest.

Saturn Opposition Uranus (February 5, September 15)

The old order comes crashing down as the new rushes in. In the face of a mounting need for freedom, independence, and the manifestation of our individuality, limiting structures can no longer maintain their facades. Revolutions, revolts, and rebellions will occur, destroying conditioned boundaries. Out of that chaos, a new organization—more in alignment with our divine truth—will emerge.

Lunar Eclipse 20°52' Leo (February 9)

We could mistakenly think that we have the whole truth when we only have a partial understanding of it. This degree is described in the Sabian Symbols as "Intoxicated chickens dizzily flap their wings trying to fly." Sometimes a little knowledge can be more damaging than none. It is important that we exercise caution and remain alert. If we lose ourselves too rapidly in a dream, no matter how beautiful it is, we won't reach the heights that are only accessible through patience, endurance, and diligent inner work.

Jupiter Quincunx Saturn (March 22, August 19, February 5, 2010)

During these few months, life could be a bit of a roller coaster. Our wishes to expand are likely to feel delayed by limitations. If we do not allow those ups and downs to derail us from our long-term goals and if we adopt a practical, realistic approach to those challenges, we are guaranteed professional and personal advancements, as well as prosperity.

Pluto Retrograde (April 4–September 11)

If we don't allow difficult circumstances to discourage us, empowerment is ours. Even if everything around us seems to be crumbling down, we need to remember who we really are. We are not our job, nor our relationships, nor our money, but we are expressions of the divine.

Jupiter Conjunct Chiron (May 23, July 22, December 7)

We give meaning to our lives as we take risks. This is a time when faith, optimism, and the belief in abundance lead us beyond our wildest expectations and literally enable us to manifest miracles. We are able to bring about social and personal reforms that lead us into the extraordinary.

Jupiter Conjunct Neptune (May 27, July 10, December 21)

Even normally nonreligious and nonbelievers change their minds and start recognizing the oneness of which they are a part. This transit brings compassion, generosity of spirit, and much joy. The law, religion, long-distance traveling, music, art, and philosophy directly benefit from our intuitive and spiritual insights. We could be drawn to a form of mysticism. This is a time when we are likely to be attracted to another country to which we feel a very strong spiritual connection. As we visit this location, memories of a past life could return.

Neptune Retrograde (May 28–November 4)

For our spiritual life to bloom, it is important that we spend more time outdoors and enjoy Mother Earth. As we connect to the simplicity of nature and find magic in a blade of grass, the sound of the waves crashing against a rock, and the feeling of the breeze caressing our check, we can deal more easily with the demands of our material reality. We can find joy in our responsibilities and access the wisdom with which we can inspire others.

Chiron Retrograde (May 30–October 31)

Healing is brought by the deep understanding that we are not alone and that we are protected. As we conquer our lesser instincts and rise to a higher state of consciousness, we can help those who are still struggling. From our own wounds comes our magic.

Jupiter Retrograde (June 15–October 12)

More of what has been lurking behind the scenes, particularly in the area of politics, the law, and religion, is revealed. Some people are likely to be unmasked for their ulterior motives and for misleading others. We could also witness natural disasters such as fires. Many could feel their lives are empty, yet despite seeing no sense in life, they will keep moving forward. As they do, the future starts looking much brighter and a feeling of peace and protection will overcome them.

Uranus Retrograde (July 1–December 1)

Perversion and the abuse of power in certain organizations become so apparent that people are inspired to join forces with like-spirited people. We will see the emergence of communities where people help each other and grow as a unit while respecting each other's uniqueness. We become more acutely aware of the importance of pursuing our own interests and fulfilling our dreams.

Lunar Eclipse 15°32' Capricorn (July 7)

The Sabian Symbols describe this degree as being "School grounds filled with boys and girls in gymnasium suits." We are still very much in a learning process and are reminded not just to train our minds and our spirits, but also our bodies. Ascension necessitates that we take very great care of our physical bodies. Sufficient sleep, harmonious exercise, cleansing, good nutrition, and organic foods (raw and unprocessed when possible, to be as nature offers them) are essential for us to become of the light.

Solar Eclipse 29°26' Cancer (July 21)

In the Sabian Symbols, this degree is "A daughter of the American Revolution." Our freedom of expression is the gift of all our ancestors who rebelled against abusive power and social oppressions. We are the products of all who came before us, and of our own selves in past lives and other dimensions. It is important to never take our privileges for granted. They are presents to be nurtured.

Lunar Eclipse 13°35' Aquarius (August 5)

The Sabian Symbols describe this degree as "A train entering a tunnel." Once again, darkness is testing us. But at the end of this passage is light. We need to have faith that what is disappearing, being destroyed or removed, was not for our highest good. What is ours can never be taken away. No matter what the circumstances around us are at any given moment, our inner trust should be our strength.

Saturn Quincunx Neptune (September 12)

Realism and mysticism meet, giving birth to powerful visions and idealistic endeavors. Activities that were hidden and people who were seeking secrecy are likely to be exposed. Knowledge derived from initiations undergone in past lives is likely to emerge, giving us deeper insights into universal truths.

Saturn in Libra (October 29–April 6, 2010, and July 21, 2010–October 4, 2012)

Those who still haven't found their spirit partner will find him or her under this transit. This is a time when our romantic relationships are solid and grounded in reality. We are attracted to people with substance, and we approach partnerships with a desire to give and receive cooperation, support, and enrichment. Working in harmony with others is a priority, as is being creative in a productive manner. Our judgment is sound and we are able to resolve residual emotional inhibition. Loneliness and isolation are feelings that won't exist anymore as we understand that we are never separated from one another. Relationships that were karmic in essence and have outlived their purpose will dissolve. Many true marriages between soul-related beings are formed under this beautiful transit, while existing good and growth-promoting relationships are strengthened.

Saturn Square Pluto (November 15, January 31, 2010, August 21, 2010)

Difficult circumstances involving social, economic, and political conditions could retard progress. In the face of power plays, criminal activities, and natural disasters, we are tested in our ability to uproot ancient obsessions and transmute any past selfishness.

Lunar Eclipse 10°21' Cancer (December 31)

In the Sabian Symbols, this degree is "A clown caricaturing well-known personalities." We are ending this year on a note of tremendous fulfillment. Scarcity does not exist. Success or fame are not limited to a chosen few, but can be accessed by all. The abundance of life is such that we can become anything we choose. As we tap into our inner wealth, the bounty of life is ours to manifest.

8

2010

DELINEATION OF THE CHART OF THE SIXTH NIGHT

OF THE MAYAN CALENDAR

(NOVEMBER 8, 2009–NOVEMBER 2, 2010)

AND THE PLANETARY CONFIGURATIONS IN 2010

2010

In numerological terms, this is a 3 year (2 + 0 + 1 + 0 = 3), bringing expansion, travel, and adventure. Our faith, enthusiasm, and optimism open many exciting doors. The people we meet help us discover new horizons. We search more actively for meaning and purpose.

THE SIXTH NIGHT OF THE MAYAN CALENDAR

Special Configuration

There are two reinforced squares between Saturn, the Sun, Mercury, Pluto, and Jupiter. This is a very subtle configuration made of two squares (90-degree angles) and three semi-squares (45-degree angles).

6th Night in Mayan Calendar

Natal Chart
Sunday, November 8, 2009
12:00:00 AM EST
New York, New York
Tropical   Koch True Node

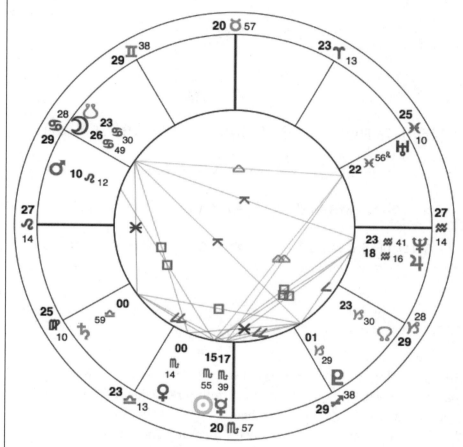

Created by Michelle Karén

Squares, which are a division by 4 of the zodiac, are traditionally considered to be challenging. Similar to the steps of a stairway, they require effort on our part, giving us a chance to move out of our comfort zone.

The power for change in this configuration is profound. An inner revolution is occurring that forces us to touch the core of our being. It will feel difficult only if we resist the transformations that need to take place. As we reexamine our thoughts, get rid of old beliefs, and trash distorted perceptions (refer to Chapter 12, "Practical Steps to Enlightenment," at the end of this book), we have the opportunity to develop a healthier sense of ourselves.

In Western Astrology
Saturn Retrograde (January 13–May 30)

This retrogradation helps unmask those in positions of authority who only serve their own agenda and not for the good of the people. It reveals false power. More and more like-spirited people are likely to be drawn to meditation through which they reveal their inner beauty and wisdom. The growing awareness that true power comes from within and not without creates the building blocks of the new society that is emerging.

Solar Eclipse 25°01' Capricorn (January 15)

In the Sabian Symbols, this degree is described as "A nature spirit dancing in the iridescent mist of a waterfall." The veil between the visible and the invisible is thinning. We become more directly aware of the existence of other dimensions and the spiritual beings (angels, archangels, ascended masters) who assist our evolution from other realms. We thus accomplish more with less effort.

Jupiter in Pisces (January 17–June 5, and September 10–January 22, 2011)

In the next few years, we increase our generosity, kindness, and compassion toward those less aware or less fortunate than ourselves. As we tap more deeply into our spiritual resources, our emotions and our imagination fuel our creations in ways that magically transform our lives.

Saturn Square Pluto (January 31, August 21)

Kindly refer to 2009.

2010
DELINEATION OF
THE CHART OF
THE SIXTH NIGHT
OF THE MAYAN
CALENDAR

Jupiter Quincunx Saturn (February 5)

Kindly refer to 2009.

Jupiter Sextile Pluto (February 6)

As we get rid of old conditionings and shift what was stagnant in our lives, powerful opportunities for new beginnings appear. We are likely to feel more benevolent and tolerant than usual. Trust and positive co-operation create beautiful expansions in anything related to the law, higher education, and religion. A long-distance trip could completely change our consciousness. We could even decide to emigrate for social or political reasons.

Neptune Conjunct Chiron (February 17)

As we understand how our thoughts have created our reality, we heal. The wisdom found in forgiveness transmutes our emotional wounds.

Pluto Retrograde (April 6–September 13)

These few months mark a transition. We are ready to leave the old and enter the unknown. Much is being reformed in both our inner and outer lives. We are moving forward with both eagerness and vigilance.

Saturn Reenters Virgo (April 7–July 20)

Saturn has been in Virgo since September 2007. We are becoming more aware of the need to heal our mother, the Earth, and to honor her resources. The next few months are our final chance to reverse the abuse that has been taking place for too long. Supporting organic farming and recycling as much as we can and stopping pollution wherever possible become primary concerns.

Saturn Quincunx Chiron (April 12, July 21)

Kindly refer to 2009.

Chiron Enters Pisces (April 20–July 19)

We are becoming more and more aware of our spiritual kinship with all living entities. The notion that we are all one doesn't feel like an abstract concept anymore. Forms of mystical healing are spreading like wildfire.

Saturn Opposition Uranus (April 26, July 26)

Kindly refer to 2009.

Saturn Quincunx Neptune (May 2, June 27)

Kindly refer to 2009.

Jupiter Opposition Saturn (May 23, August 16, March 28, 2011)

Existing structures are going through a period of readjustment. The obstacles limiting our wish for expansion are transmuted by wisdom and patience.

Uranus in Aries (May 27–August 13)

We set ourselves free from restrictive circumstances by acting in an impetuous and impulsive manner. Our need for independence is impulsive and lacks subtlety.

Neptune Retrograde (May 31–November 6)

The more we are in touch with our inner vision and our personal wisdom, the more protected we are. As we recognize that our true strength lies in our inner wisdom, the magic of life becomes available to us.

2010
DELINEATION OF
THE CHART OF
THE SIXTH NIGHT
OF THE MAYAN
CALENDAR

241

Chiron Retrograde (June 4–November 5)

Beyond the variety of choices available to us, during this period a unifying principle emerges from our deeply embedded past.

Jupiter Conjunct Uranus (June 8, September 18, January 4, 2011)

This is a time of progressive ideas, independence, and restlessness. We don't accept things so readily and we need to rock the status quo in both our lives and our environment. Exciting opportunities to travel and further our education open new dimensions. Legal breakthroughs are likely to occur.

Lunar Eclipse 4°50' Capricorn (June 26)

In the Sabian Symbols, this degree is described as "Indians on the war-path. While some men row a well-filled canoe, others in it perform a war dance." While we honor and claim our personal spiritual power, our fighting spirit remains on alert, making us ready for every eventuality.

Uranus Retrograde (July 5–December 5)

This is a powerful time to manifest our uniqueness. The clearer and the more focused our choices are, the faster we can become everything that we are.

Solar Eclipse 19°23' Cancer (July 11)

This is a time of happiness. The image associated with this degree in the Sabian Symbols is "Venetian gondoliers giving a serenade." We enjoy life by appreciating its gifts.

Chiron Reenters Aquarius (June 4–February 8, 2011)

Chiron entered Aquarius in January 2006. This is the last time before 2012 that Chiron is in that sign. Our dreams and visions are shaping the new society into existence.

Saturn Reenters Libra (July 21–October 5, 2012)

Kindly refer to 2009.

Jupiter Square Pluto (July 24, August 3, February 25, 2011)

This is a time of new beginnings requiring much reorganization. A tremendous reform of society is at hand.

Uranus Reenters Pisces (August 13–March 11, 2011)

Uranus has been in Pisces since March 2003. This is its last period in that sign.

Channeling and visionary philosophies are flourishing everywhere. As they introduce us to a different understanding of what we thought was our reality, we are forced to look at traditional religion in a whole new light. A deeper alignment with our higher selves dramatically increases our intuition and, in some cases, psychic abilities.

Lunar Eclipse 29°22' Gemini (December 21)

In the Sabian Symbols, this degree is described as "A parade of bathing beauties before large beach crowds." Through personal excellence we are raising the bar for the whole of humanity.

2010
Delineation of
the Chart of
the Sixth Night
of the Mayan
Calendar

243

9

2011

Delineation of the Chart of the Seventh Day

of the Mayan Calendar

(November 3, 2010–October 28, 2011)

and the Planetary Configurations in 2011

2011

In numerological terms, this is a 4 year $(2 + 0 + 1 + 1 = 4)$, a stepping-stone year into the new reality that we are creating. Sudden and unexpected changes are likely to occur.

The Seventh Day in the Mayan Calendar

No Special Configuration

We should not be fooled into believing that nothing will happen this year, but instead should consider that we have complete free will. What we shall manifest is our choice. We are learning firsthand what it means to be cocreators. The highest possible reality can only come into being through wisdom, a pure heart, and loving intentions.

7th Day in Mayan Calendar

Natal Chart
Wednesday, November 30, 2010
12:00:00 AM EST
New York, New York
Tropical   Koch True Node

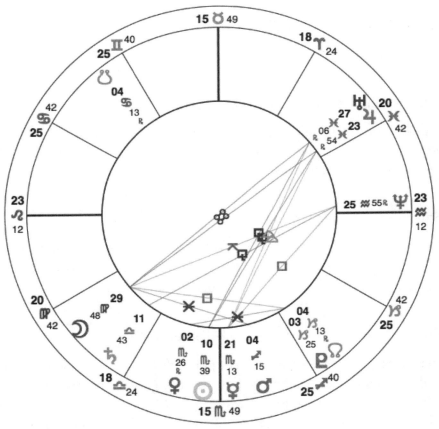

Created by Michelle Karén

In Western Astrology
Solar Eclipse 13°38' Capricorn (January 4)

The Sabian Symbols assign the following image to this degree: "An ancient bas-relief carved in granite remains a witness to a long-forgotten culture." Time is not linear. Past, present, and future occur simultaneously. Thus, in a parallel reality, any civilization that ever was, still exists.

2011
Delineation of
the Chart of
the Seventh Day
of the Mayan
Calendar

245

Eclipses are always landmarks beyond which the circumstances of our lives will never be the same. This particular eclipse requires that we stop identifying with old sufferings, distortions, and dramas so that we may remember our magnificence.

Jupiter Conjunct Uranus (January 4)

Kindly refer to 2010.

Jupiter Reenters Aries (January 22–June 4)

Unlikely to respect the status quo, our personal expression is blunt. With the excitement of a pioneer starting a new adventure, we use every opportunity to dynamically forge ahead.

Saturn Retrograde (January 26–June 12)

During these three weeks we are being asked to reexamine and transform the limitations we have accepted as being inevitable. As we realize that our boundaries are self-created, our true liberation begins.

Chiron Reenters Pisces (February 8–February 2019)

In the years to come, we are entering a blissful state of conscious union with the divine. Our healing abilities are emerging from our depths. We now have the chance to tear down once and for all the walls that have kept us in the illusion of separation. Recognizing that beyond skin color, culture, or creed we are different expressions of the same God leads to experiencing the oneness that is the essence of enlightenment.

Jupiter Square Pluto (February 25)

Kindly refer to 2010.

Uranus Reenters Aries (March 11–March 6, 2019)

In the years to come, any remaining oppression becomes intolerable. Aggressive and direct actions impulsively destroy outdated institutions. Whole crowds violently rebel against old, binding conditionings. As the past is burned down, a new sense of freedom is enjoyed.

Jupiter Opposition Saturn (March 28)

Kindly refer to 2010.

Neptune Reenters Pisces (April 4–August 4)

These few months are particularly magical. We can feel that we are floating in a state of bliss. Beauty permeates our vision, enabling us to see the best both in others and in our circumstances. We are able to recognize that even what seems imperfect really is in divine order. We seek peace, music, the solace of the ocean and meditation. We are drawn to like-spirited beings who share our sense of the sacred. As we move into a space where the veil between the visible and the invisible is thinner, we see in transparency into other people's minds and hearts. Telepathy becomes an overwhelming reality, making it much more difficult to lie or play games.

Pluto Retrograde (April 9–September 16)

Many established structures visibly start to crumble down, governments change, nations fall. The wealthy and untouchable are not immune to destruction anymore. World power is shifting hands. This is the end of the control of a few over the masses. The need to participate in a total reform of society becomes a deep motivation for many. As the old makes way for the unknown, a feeling of exhilaration awakens.

Solar Eclipse 11°02' Gemini (June 1)

"A negro girl fights for her independence in the city," says the Sabian Symbols about this degree. As we empower ourselves, no discrimina-

2011
Delineation of
the Chart of
the Seventh Day
of the Mayan
Calendar

247

tion or limitation can stand in our way. The more we express our truth without fear, the less likely we are to be engulfed by those forces who would squish our identity to keep us under their control.

Neptune Retrograde (June 3–November 9)

During these months, we become particularly sensitive to vibrations. Our compassion and ability to see the sacred in our environment enable us to directly channel information from higher spheres of consciousness. As the veil separating various realms of existence thins, we develop telepathy and hear the music of the spheres. (The *music of the spheres* refers to the harmonies created by the various proportions of the celestial bodies in their relationship to each other. This philosophical concept, developed by Greek mathematician Pythagoras, was furthered by astrologer-astronomer Johannes Kepler. British composer Greg Fox, in an experiment conducted in 2006, proved that planets each have a certain pitch. He made the harmonies of the spheres audible in a CD called *Carmen of the Spheres*.) Composers and painters are inspired to create very unusual works. Nurturing ourselves—breathing, sleeping, dreaming, meditating, and being present to the present—contributes further to bringing magic to this plane. Love is expressed unconditionally.

Jupiter Enters Taurus (June 4–June 11, 2012)

During these twelve months, we are becoming very concerned with the state of the Earth. We are collectively engaged in healing the climate and curbing pollution. Those who can are growing their own vegetable gardens. We need to eat the foods offered to us by nature—organic, raw fruits, uncooked vegetables, herbs, honey, and sprouts—that we can grow in our own kitchen. Our values are practical. We are no longer spending money we don't have. Our financial resources are not made of plastic but of real coins. We more and more shall trade services. This will provide us all with what we need and allow us to value everyone's work without any money exchange. We are interested in the practical uses of what we learn. Developing new methods of healing, understanding how to take care of the Earth and value her resources, studying the laws of abundance and attraction, are all seen as important applications of our intelligence.

Chiron Retrograde (June 8–November 10)

During these months, self-transformation becomes a mass obsession. Healing ourselves individually, healing society, and healing the Earth become a collective priority. An ever-increasing mass of people is already awakened. Still more are getting caught in this immense vortex of energy that is spinning faster and faster, making realities collide. The fact that past, present, and future were never separate becomes an obvious reality. As the world keeps accelerating with a multitude of options happening simultaneously, we cannot but reach a point of utter stillness where ultimate healing occurs.

Jupiter Sextile Neptune (June 8)

We become actively involved in humanitarian movements for peace. Our spirituality is almost mystical, bringing exhilaration to our hearts. We may feel inspired to create altars or meditation rooms in our homes. Our positive expectations create prosperity and happiness. As we share our abundance with those less privileged, all expand. Our power and mastery grow in direct proportion to our ability to rise above illusions. We once again envision humanity's future with faith and joy.

Lunar Eclipse 24°23' Sagittarius (June 15)

The Sabian Symbols describe this degree as "A chubby boy on a hobbyhorse." We create the reality we want by seeing and feeling as if it's already happened. This eclipse is the portal beyond which no positive dream will remain unfulfilled.

Solar Eclipse 9°11' Cancer (July 1)

"A large diamond in the first stages of the cutting process" is the Sabian Symbols' description of this degree. We have now recognized our co-

2011
DELINEATION OF
THE CHART OF
THE SEVENTH DAY
OF THE MAYAN
CALENDAR

249

creating abilities and we have seen the divinity residing within. Nothing can hold us back from manifesting what is the highest good of all.

Jupiter Sextile Chiron (July 2, December 6, February 14, 2012)

The new social order is built with faith, optimism, a feeling of expansion, and much enthusiasm. As one outgrown structure after another disappears, we can start aiming at objectives lying beyond the material plane. We are reaching into our own immortality and transcendence.

Jupiter Trine Pluto (July 7, October 28, March 12, 2012)

The social reforms occurring with this transit transform what is no longer necessary in our changing reality. Insurances and taxes could be greatly impacted and even disappear completely. As the mysteries of life, death, and God are revealed, the masses become more and more enthusiastic about spirituality and its practical applications in daily life. Psychic faculties develop as a side effect of this grand awakening. Domestic circumstances are also changing. Our family is no longer limited to those of our blood, but comes to integrate as well all those to whom we feel our souls are connected.

Uranus Retrograde (July 9–December 10)

Independence and spontaneity increase during these few months. Our uniqueness becomes our strength. As we free ourselves from all boundaries, we become the pioneers of the new beginnings.

Neptune Reenters Aquarius (August 4–February 3, 2012)

Psychic awareness, intuitive insights, and the yearning for enlightenment accompany this position. We are putting the "meta" back into physics. Science is rediscovering what was commonplace in Lemuria and Atlantis, such as laser therapy, the power of words, and that the planets emit sounds. Premonition dreams are powerful and should be heeded.

Jupiter Retrograde (August 30–December 25)

Concerns surrounding the state of the Earth are occurring at this time. Global warming, pollution, and the handling of waste, food, and water supplies could all come to the forefront simultaneously, forcing us to find creative solutions, and fast. We also need to unburden ourselves from excess material possessions. Anything we haven't used in more than six months should be recirculated. Living abundantly is no longer viewed as the acquisition of more "stuff." Our prosperity is in direct proportion to what we value spiritually and to our positive ability to use our inner resources.

Solar Eclipse 2°37' Sagittarius (November 25)

In the Sabian Symbols, this degree is symbolized by "Two men playing chess." Two opposing forces are in competition, using clever strategies to outdo each other. Let us not forget light and darkness. Each defines the other, but they are different aspects of the same reality. Whatever the problem is, love is the only answer.

Lunar Eclipse 18°08' Gemini (December 10)

"A large archaic volume reveals a traditional wisdom," say the Sabian Symbols. Despite the newness of the society we are creating, its roots go back to the beginnings of humanity, before all the distortions and manipulations. We see the purity of this ancestral knowledge and gain wisdom that we are now unearthing again from the depths of our being. And as we reintegrate that meaning into our lives, we discover that those things ancient are also of the future.

2011
Delineation of
the Chart of
the Seventh Day
of the Mayan
Calendar

251

10

2012

Delineation of the End of the Mayan Calendar

(October 29, 2011–December 21, 2012)

Ascension Chart

(December 21, 2012)

and the Planetary Configurations in 2012

2012

This is a 5 year $(2 + 0 + 1 + 2 = 5)$, a year when much information becomes available. It is a year of change and movement. If we are to reach liberation, this is our last chance to transmute what remains of the old consciousness. Because the last hour is often the darkest, the intensity of the challenges that will appear can seem at times—particularly during the summer—difficult to bear. But let us not forget: nothing is pre-

Last Year in the Mayan Calendar

Natal Chart
Saturday, October 29, 2011
12:00:00 AM EDT
New York, New York
Tropical   Koch True Node

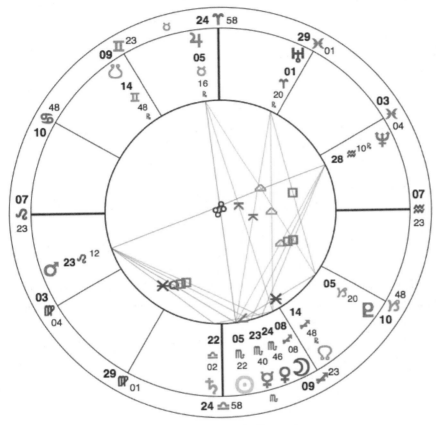

Created by Michelle Karén

sented to us that we cannot handle. We chose to be here at this magnificent time in the evolution of humanity, fully aware of what would await us. The more we embrace what presents itself to us, one obstacle at a time, with integrity and courage, the faster we shall remove the blocks separating us from enlightenment.

2012
DELINEATION OF
THE END OF THE
MAYAN CALENDAR

The Mayan calendar is comprised of seven days and six nights. One ending occurs on October 28, 2011, which is the end of the seventh day.

I am presenting the chart as starting the following day at midnight because I consider the last 14 months—until the Winter Solstice in 2012—as the year of the "last chance," where those who were at the edge will join the flow of evolution and ascend with a massive amount of people all over the planet.

Special Configuration
A double T Square between Mars, Neptune, and Mercury Conjunct Venus:

Our willpower is dissolving, allowing us to touch a much deeper and more magical aspect of ourselves. We are more in harmony with Nature and could communicate with animals and plants in ways that surprise us and open us to a previously unknown wealth of information. We are in tune with the invisible and able to see the beauty around us. We understand others and the situations we find ourselves confronted with intuitively. Our thinking is in essence deep and loving. We express ourselves with compassion. Our actions are motivated by tremendous sensitivity. Powerful insights allow us to reach beyond the surface into the mystery of existence and our own spiritual roots.

In Western Astrology
Neptune Reenters Pisces (February 3–January 27, 2026)

During this time, we acutely experience our spiritual dimension. Our attunement with higher spheres of consciousness is tangible. Our dreams are vivid and our imaginations, inspired. Our mystical state of mind enables us to see beauty everywhere around us. Music is soothing, as are silence and art (particularly dance and photography). We can feel the need to adopt a slower pace, allowing more space for daydreaming and meditation. The magic we feel permeating the atmosphere connects our souls with transcendent states of being. As the veil separating the more materialistic world and the higher realms gently dissolves, we are able to read energy and feel the unknown.

Jupiter Sextile Chiron (February 14)

Kindly refer to 2011.

Jupiter Trine Pluto (March 12)

Kindly refer to 2011.

Pluto Retrograde (April 10–September 18)

Our sense of responsibility is strong. We need to use our power constructively and with great integrity. As we reach a state of unconditional love, the whole of society is also purified.

Pluto Sextile Chiron (May 12, September 6)

Our ability to regenerate is powerful at these times. There is likely to be great healing in our understanding of sexuality, immortality, and the positive use of power. Dangers test our strength and courage. Thanks to our penetrating insights into others and the circumstances around us, we are able to transform what is not of the light.

Jupiter Quincunx Saturn (May 16, December 22)

Our desire for broader, adventurous horizons may meet with obstacles that limit our expansion. This forces us to ground ourselves and become stronger. Outgrown structures are smoothly and gradually dissolving. New organizations are slowly replacing them.

Solar Eclipse 0°20' Gemini (May 20)

This degree is described in the Sabian Symbols as "A glass-bottomed boat reveals undersea wonders." As the veil separating us from other dimensions is removed, the beauty and the magic we discover expand our horizons.

Lunar Eclipse 14°08' Sagittarius (June 4)

The Sabian Symbols refer to this degree as being "The groundhog looking for its shadow on Groundhog Day, February 2." As legend would have it, if a marmot emerging from its lair on February 2 fails to see its shadow, it means clouds are hiding the sun, implying that spring is near. If it sees its own shadow, it needs to return to his hibernation for another forty-two days. The day of this eclipse is like Groundhog Day, marking an important turning point. We need now to assess exactly where we are: Have we completed our homework? Is there still something within ourselves that needs to be shifted? If we feel clear and happy, we can look forward to joyful and lighter days. If there is still something in our lives that creates difficulties, it is important that we transform it as quickly as possible.

Neptune Retrograde (June 4–November 11)

During these months, meditation brings subtle insights. Our attunement to the spiritual realms leads to a deeper understanding of the sacredness of life. The fact that we are all one becomes clearer as our experience of unconditional love deepens. Music, painting, silence, and solitude bring solace to our souls. Our dreams at night could be particularly powerful. We are inspired to create more beauty and peace around us.

Jupiter Enters Gemini (June 11–June 26, 2013)

Our curiosity knows no limits at this time. We want to know everything. The portal to other dimensions is wide open, offering us insight into concepts that were previously hidden. Our broad-mindedness leads us to investigate the most varied topics. As we enthusiastically share this knowledge, other people's intellectual horizons are vastly enriched.

Chiron Retrograde (June 12–November 14)

The roots of the wounds we may still carry lie deep within ourselves. Contemplation, isolation, and silence bring healing. As we examine the consequences of our actions, a chance is given to erase any remaining karma.

Uranus Square Pluto (June 24, September 19)

This time is likely to be intense. We are now dealing with no less than collective karma requiring an ultimate transformation. All the darkness needing to leave our plane could make a last attempt to save itself. Disruptive events directly linked to evil, corruption, and social, economic, and political upheaval test our survival skills and our capacity to be emotionally transparent. Our spiritual strength is likely to be challenged by negative magic, the use of dark occult, sexual powers, and natural cataclysms such as cyclones, tsunamis, and volcano eruptions. We need to stay grounded in our own light to recognize that these changes are a chance for a new beginning. As we remain clear on who we are and what kind of world we are creating, progressive reforms and revolutionary innovations lead to unfamiliar yet positive new circumstances.

Jupiter Square Neptune (June 25)

Under this transit, we should beware of anything that is too good to be true. Spiritual illusion could sweep us off our feet into dangerous directions. False prophets could mislead us. Illusions that we have already reached our destination could blind us to the necessity of continuing our inner work. At this point in time, we need more than ever to use our judgment. All that glitters is not gold. If our inner voice tells us that something is ever so slightly off, we should listen carefully. A lack of vigilance could make us fall prey to false Christ consciousness—false light appearing real. We need to focus on what is in front of us, in full presence each moment, far away from idealistic daydreams encouraging us to escape reality.

Uranus Retrograde (July 13–December 13)

This is a period to assert our independence and pioneering spirit. Unexpected and destructive cataclysmic events could occur. What was still holding us in the old consciousness suddenly passes. Rebellion and the need for freedom from old structures press us forward in impatient and disruptive ways. A new order emerges out of chaos.

Jupiter Quincunx Pluto (July 18, December 20)

At these times, we need to cultivate integrity, patience, and humility. Strange psychic phenomena could occur, testing our spiritual clarity and emotional strength. We could see projections that don't exist but are specifically manufactured to create fear in us and make us feel vulnerable. We need to remember that no matter what the reality around us seems to be, we are immensely powerful. Fear is the opposite of love. When we focus on love, we become invincible to fear. As we draw on our faith and inner connection to the divine, no amount of dark manipulation can have a hold on our spirit.

Jupiter Sextile Uranus (July 21)

Unexpected new spiritual concepts arise at this time. Our consciousness broadens through psychic visions. Major scientific breakthroughs free us from previously limited beliefs. Sudden opportunities change our daily routine and project us into a whole new dimension.

Jupiter Square Chiron (July 24)

Religious fanaticism and the temptation to play God are great dangers to individuals and to entities such as governments at this time. If we channel our sense of injustice into great humanitarian causes, our visions and aspirations for a better world can have a transformative impact on society. Traveling brings healing. No matter how profound the destruction around us may seem, if we maintain our faith, rely on our wisdom, and listen to our inner guidance, invisible doors miraculously open right in front of us. As we keep focused on the highest good, we radiate the spiritual authority needed to inspire those who would fall prey to negative power extremes. Envisioning the positive attracts it into our lives.

Pluto Sextile Chiron (September 6)

Kindly refer to May 12.

Saturn in Scorpio (October 5–December 23, 2014)

In the next two years, our sense of purpose is strong and focused. The intensity of our emotions can lead us to a whole new understanding of sexuality. As we become aware of the energy exchanges occurring during physical intimacy, we experience sex no longer as a one-chakra, one-body experience but as a multichakra, multibody adventure. While making love with love to our right partner, we can find ourselves traveling through our past lives.

Saturn Trine Neptune (October 10)

Governmental institutions, the banking system, and corporate businesses are dissolving in their traditional form, gradually integrating spiritual principles. Meditation, yoga, and contemplative practices spiritualize our daily lives, helping us approach practical issues in a whole new light. Our intuitive insights deepen our perceptions, which are mature and grounded in reality. We can have lucid dreams and develop an awareness of our past lives.

Solar Eclipse 21°56' Scorpio (November 13)

The Sabian Symbols describe this degree as being "Hunters shooting wild ducks." Although this seems to be a law of nature—that some are predators and others are prey—this doesn't need to be. We do not require meat to survive. When we absorb what was killed, we are eating fear, death, and violence. This eclipse is our chance to truly connect with the spirit of animals, plants, and the Earth with respect and gratitude.

Saturn Quincunx Uranus (November 15)

A new society is emerging, integrating fresh new ideals with the best of the old society. The need for freedom is balanced by a sense of discipline. More people are directly in touch with their intuition. Original scientific inventions and creative ideas expand our lives into exciting, uncharted territory.

Saturn Trine Chiron (November 16)

At this time, far from being restrictive, limitations should be seen as our chance to consolidate our mastery. Even if we still have to face darkness in and around us, we should remember that darkness is what defines light. The more secure and grounded we are, the more efficient the last social reforms will be. As we embrace everything that we are and all that surrounds us, we radiate authority, grace, wisdom, and peace.

Lunar Eclipse 6°40'Gemini (November 28)

In the Sabian Symbols, the image associated with this degree is "A well with bucket and rope under the shade of majestic trees." Three weeks from the final Ascension date, we have found the transparent waters of knowledge. We can drink and replenish ourselves on every level. As our body regenerates, so do our heart and our soul.

Jupiter Quincunx Pluto (December 20)

Kindly refer to July 18.

FINAL CONCLUSION OF THE MAYAN CALENDAR

Special Configurations

There are two intertwined yods, or "fingers of God." It is extremely rare to see two such perfectly intertwined yods. This is a creative, karmic configuration that places us in alignment with our true destiny.

Ascension

Natal Chart
Friday, December 21, 2012
6:12:00 AM EST
New York, New York
Tropical   Koch True Node

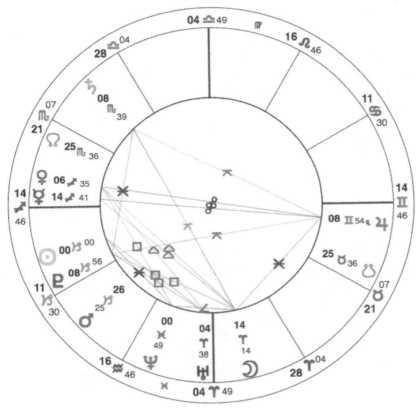

Created by Michelle Karén

Between Saturn and Pluto Pointing toward Jupiter

This yod signifies unearthing our true power and knowing that we are not alone. As we dynamically move toward the future and create positive values, we are being supported in our efforts by invisible, loving forces, such as angels and spiritual guides. All the limitations of the past—power plays, obligations, duties, responsibilities, authority, hard work—dissolve. Relationships are just of the light. They are totally supportive of our growth, in unconditional love, respect, kindness, and enthusiastic adventurousness.

A Very Wide Yod between the Moon and Jupiter Pointing toward Saturn

The second yod points toward focus, concentration, and discipline leading us to mastery. As we let go of old habits, release conditioned emotional responses that no longer serve us, and choose a lifestyle integrating organic foods, a lack of clutter, clean closets, positive thoughts, and enriching relationships, we reach enlightenment.

Ascension (December 21)

A critical mass reaches enlightenment. There will be celebrations around the planet on very special vortices (the chakras of the Earth—power points such as Sedona, Arizona, the Machu Picchu in Peru, the Pyramids in Egypt or Mexico, Hawaii, and Glastonbury in England, to name only a few), further helping shift the old energies that have been lagging behind. As in every event joined by millions of people across the world, the joy, peace, and freedom will be multiplied exponentially.

Jupiter Quincunx Saturn (December 22)

Kindly refer to May 16.

Saturn Sextile Pluto (December 26)

Brought about by much effort and focus, our lives are starting over in a completely different dimension. This is a reincarnation without changing bodies. It is a complete regeneration all the way to the cellular level, leading to new beginnings in every area of our lives.

11

THE MAYAN CALENDAR AND THE SIGNS

This chapter gives details on how each sign experiences the next four years leading to ascension. To get a clearer picture, read in Chapter 3 both your Sun sign and your rising sign (ascendant).

My interpretations are organized by category, following the order of the astrological houses, which I discussed in Chapter 4:

I: Personal appearance

II: Money

III: Communication

IV: Home

V: Creativity, romance, and children

VI: Health, pets, and work

VII: Marriage

VIII: Sexuality, joint finances, and transformation

IX: Long-distance travel, philosophy, and religion

X: Career

XI: Friendships

XII: Subconscious

Between 2009 and 2012, each sign will go through changes in each one of the twelve categories in this list, but at different times and in various measures. Overall, for example, for some signs, such as Cancer or Cancer Rising, as well as Leo or Leo Rising, the emphasis will be more on relationships. Others, such as Capricorn or Capricorn Rising as well as Aquarius or Aquarius Rising, will go through the greatest changes in their personal appearance and financial situation. And for others still, such as Aries or Aries Rising and Taurus and Taurus Rising, the greatest shifts will be apparent in career and friendships.

In the great tapestry of life, by each playing our part, we contribute to the whole symphony of evolution.

2009–2012 FOR ARIES AND/OR ARIES RISING

I. PERSONAL APPEARANCE

June 6, 2010–September 7, 2010 (Jupiter in Aries)
January 22, 2011–June 4, 2011 (Jupiter in Aries)

Your self-confidence is at its height. In your wish to expand, you contemplate far-reaching goals that could lead you to climb the highest mountain—either literally or symbolically. You are drawn to generously share your knowledge. And because you impress others as being full of life, enthusiasm, and exuberance, you draw much attention and luck to yourself. During these periods, your positive code of ethics supports a

ENLIGHTENMENT

264

strong desire to lead a spiritual life. High aspirations and vast visions inspire you to greater accomplishments.

May 27, 2010–August 13, 2010 (Uranus in Aries)
March 11, 2011–March 6, 2019 (Uranus in Aries)

In a wish to discover your own truth, you are likely to revolutionize your personal appearance. Your insistence on independence could lead you to creating your own style. Your need for freedom, happiness, and excitement are so enhanced that you may walk away from that which had become too stale or predictable in your life. During these periods, you definitely emerge as a leader with highly original and inventive new insights. As you undergo a radical self-transformation, you are likely to rise as the champion of some major social change.

> *During those four periods, the enlightenment tools of Jupiter (Sagittarius) and Uranus (Aquarius) help you bring light to your personal appearance.*

II. MONEY

June 4, 2011–June 10, 2012 (Jupiter in Taurus)

If you are wise with the money you earn and if you share your bounty with others, this is a period of great financial abundance. Money comes effortlessly to you. Your success is related to long-distance traveling. A strong sense of honesty and straightforwardness accompanies your business dealings. Your ability to "sell" yourself is greatly enhanced. Your philosophical and spiritual resources contribute to your sense of security.

> *Between June 2011 and June 2012, the enlightenment tools of Jupiter (Sagittarius) help you bring light to your financial affairs.*

III. Communication

December 21, 2010 (Lunar Eclipse in Gemini)
June 1, 2011 (Solar Eclipse in Gemini)
December 10, 2011 (Lunar Eclipse in Gemini)
May 20, 2012 (Solar Eclipse in Gemini)
November 28, 2012 (Lunar Eclipse in Gemini)

These days mark a shift in the way you express your ideas and in how your thoughts are received by others. What has changed will be visible within a month of the eclipse dates.

> *During these many eclipses, the enlightenment tools of Mercury (Gemini) help you bring light to your daily life and your mental abilities.*

June 11, 2012–June 26, 2013 (Jupiter in Gemini)

Your relationships with brothers, sisters, cousins, and neighbors become deeper. These are wonderful periods for writing, exchanging information, short-distance travel, and furthering your education. You could be tempted to go back to school to acquire a skill that will empower your life. Learning widens your horizons. There is a playfulness related to children, a need to practice outdoor sports with them and to expand their minds.

> *From June 2012 to June 2013, the enlightenment tools of Jupiter (Sagittarius) help you bring light to your communication, intellectual skills, and relationships with brothers and sisters.*

IV. Home

July 21, 2009 (Solar Eclipse in Cancer)
December 31, 2009 (Lunar Eclipse in Cancer)
July 11, 2010 (Solar Eclipse in Cancer)
July 1, 2011 (Solar Eclipse in Cancer)

Within a month of these four dates, the possibility of a move or of a drastic change in your living circumstances is indicated. There is an emphasis on your relationships with your parents. You are likely to better understand your roots and what has made you who you are.

During these eclipses, the enlightenment tools of Cancer and the Moon help you bring light to your home.

V. Creativity, Romance, and Children

February 9, 2009 (Lunar Eclipse in Leo)

Within a month of this date, your creative expression will change radically, integrating some powerful and exciting new elements. A new birth could occur, symbolically and literally. If you are single, you could be swept off your feet by an exciting romantic prospect—someone who deeply connects with your heart. More intimacy is likely to occur in an existing relationship, leading to a greater depth of involvement.

In February 2009, the enlightenment tools of Leo help you bring light to your creativity, romance, and in your relationship with your children.

VI. Health, Pets, and Work

Since September 3, 2007 until October 29, 2009 (Saturn in Virgo)
April 7, 2010–July 20, 2010 (Saturn in Virgo)

During these two periods, it is mandatory that you take great care of your health. Alarm signals should not be overlooked. Eat wholesome, organic foods and exercise properly. There could be added responsibilities in your work requiring increased efficiency, focus, and reorganization.

During these two periods, the enlightenment tools of Saturn (Capricorn) help you bring light to the areas of work, health, and relationships with pets.

VII. Marriage

October 29, 2009–April 6, 2010 (Saturn in Libra)
July 21, 2010–October 4, 2012 (Saturn in Libra)

For those of you who are still single, the next three years bring a solid, mature relationship. Grounded in reality, it is reliable and will be there for a long time. Those already in a relationship have a chance to change what needs to be changed and to solidify what is good and enriching. A sense of restriction could accompany marriage, forcing you to a deeper commitment that may require patience and wisdom. Limitations should not be projected onto your partner but should instead be seen as a chance to recognize and transmute fears within yourself.

During these three years, the enlightenment tools of Saturn (Capricorn) help you bring light to the areas of marriage and intimate relationships.

VIII. Sexuality, Joint Finances, and Transformation

October 5, 2012–September 18, 2015 (Saturn in Scorpio)
November 13, 2012 (Solar Eclipse in Scorpio)

In 2012, particularly around November 13, 2012, you are likely to want to seriously investigate death and the afterlife. Esoteric knowledge will also appeal to you as you start remembering ancient wisdoms that were buried within you. Your attitude toward sexuality is likely to be passionate and deeply transformative, with the ability to travel through time and space. There may be more responsibilities involved in joint finances, leading to a chance to solidify any matter related to taxes, insurance, or inheritance.

Between October 2012 and September 2015, the enlightenment tools of Saturn (Capricorn) and Scorpio transform sexuality and joint finances.

IX. Long-Distance Travel, Philosophy, and Religion

June 15, 2011 (Lunar Eclipse in Sagittarius)
November 25, 2011 (Solar Eclipse in Sagittarius)
June 4, 2012 (Lunar Eclipse in Sagittarius)

Within one month of these three dates, a journey out of state or to a foreign country could be life-changing. It will most likely affect your philosophy of life and transform your connection to religion. It could also inspire you to write a book and lead you to conference-speaking or teaching. You may also be drawn to furthering your education and deepening your connection with your higher mind.

On these eclipses, the enlightenment tools of Jupiter and Sagittarius help you bring light to long-distance travel, philosophy, and religion.

X. Career

July 7, 2009 (Lunar Eclipse in Capricorn)
January 15, 2010 (Solar Eclipse in Capricorn)
June 26, 2010 (Lunar Eclipse in Capricorn)
January 4, 2011 (Solar Eclipse in Capricorn)

A very special opportunity is likely to be offered to you on these eclipse dates, the repercussions of which will unravel for an entire month. This may lead to more responsibilities and a definite advancement in your career, or, if you have been unhappy, it could bring a complete change.

On these dates, the enlightenment tools of Capricorn help you bring light to your career.

Since January 19, 2007 until January 4, 2009 (Jupiter in Capricorn)

The first week of January ends a period of two years that brought much luck to your career. The more ethical you are in your business dealings, the greater the rewards will be. Exciting opportunities lead to tremendous expansion related to other states, foreign countries, or foreigners.

During that period, the enlightenment tools of Jupiter (Sagittarius) help you bring light to your career.

Since November 28, 2008 until November 21, 2024 (Pluto in Capricorn)

During this time, there are drastic changes in your career. Outmoded ambitions are torn and rebuilt differently. Tremendous power behind the scenes leads to great responsibilities, which dramatically improve your social status. You are likely to be the agent of a major reform in society for the good of all involved.

Until 2024, the enlightenment tools of Pluto (Scorpio) help you bring light to your career.

XI. FRIENDSHIPS

January 5, 2009–January 16, 2010 (Jupiter in Aquarius)

Exciting new friendships with foreigners or with people who travel a lot expand your horizons. You could become involved in humanitarian groups with high philosophical ideals, and as a result you may experience much joy and a sense of belonging to a greater social order.

During this period, the enlightenment tools of Jupiter (Sagittarius) help you bring light to your friendships.

January 26, 2009 (Solar Eclipse in Aquarius)
August 5, 2009 (Lunar Eclipse in Aquarius)

Changes in your friendships and associations with like-spirited people are heralded by these eclipses, leading to new goals and dreams. That which has shifted will become apparent within one month of these dates.

On these two dates, the enlightenment tools of Aquarius help you bring light to your friendships and dreams.

From the Present until April 19, 2010 (Chiron in Aquarius)
July 20, 2010–February 7, 2011 (Chiron in Aquarius)

During these two periods, as you are reforming your dreams and finding healing through friendships, you could be the agent of major changes in society.

During these times, the enlightenment tools of Aquarius help you bring light to your friendships.

From the Present until April 3, 2011 (Neptune in Aquarius)
August 4, 2011–February 2, 2012 (Neptune in Aquarius)

Your friendships open many new doors that are both spiritual and inspiring. Friends also artistically expand your horizons. You are drawn to like-spirited people and communities inspired by a common humanitarian ideal. Inasmuch as you are attentive to remaining realistic, during these periods you have the chance to fulfill your objectives and realize your long-term dreams.

During these few years, the enlightenment tools of Neptune (Pisces) help you bring light to your long-term dreams and your friendships.

XII. Subconscious

Since December 31, 2003 until May 26, 2010 (Uranus in Pisces)
August 13, 2010–March 10, 2011 (Uranus in Pisces)

Major breakthroughs in your subconscious and powerful dreams that may have a premonitory quality enable you to access knowledge that was previously buried. Freedom from karmic debts occurs suddenly.

Until March 2011, the enlightenment tools of Uranus (Aquarius) help you bring light to your subconscious.

January 17, 2010–June 5, 2010 (Jupiter in Pisces)
September 8, 2010–January 21, 2011 (Jupiter in Pisces)

These are the best times for a spiritual retreat. You're likely to experience a tremendous expansion of consciousness. As you access clearer visions, you are given powerful insights into the past, the present, and the future. At these times, your generosity of spirit is likely to involve wanting to help those who are in charitable institutions, hospitals, or even jails. Much spiritual wealth will be acquired from those endeavors. You could be inspired by music and attracted to shamanistic work.

During these months, the enlightenment tools of Jupiter (Sagittarius) help you bring light to your subconscious.

April 20, 2010–July 19, 2010 (Chiron in Pisces)
February 8, 2011–February 2019 (Chiron in Pisces)

There is a strong need for mystical fusion, and a wish to stay away from noise by accessing deeply transformative psychic powers.

During this time, the enlightenment tools of Pisces help you bring light to your soul.

April 4, 2011–August 3, 2011 (Neptune in Pisces)
February 3, 2012–January 27, 2026 (Neptune in Pisces)

You may have an enhanced sensitivity to discordance in the outer world. You need the solace of silence and solitude to restore your spirit. Meditation is greatly appealing to you now. Sitting by the ocean watching the waves or staring at a flower could be highly enjoyable activities. Your soul demands beauty and harmony. Artistically oriented Aries and Aries Rising are likely to create their best works. You may feel guided by an invisible hand during both your dreams and your waking hours. Subtle shifts are occurring in your subconscious that you may not even be able to define until several years from now.

During these periods, the enlightenment tools of Neptune (Pisces) help you bring light to your subconscious.

I. PERSONAL APPEARANCE

June 4, 2011–June 10, 2012 (Jupiter in Taurus)

This is a year when trust, hope, optimism, and adventurousness infuse your expression of yourself. As you follow a very ethical path, you feel a complete spiritual renewal. Many new doors open. You attract much luck and many exciting opportunities.

Between June 2011 and June 2012, the enlightenment tools of Jupiter (Sagittarius) help you bring light to your personal appearance.

II. MONEY

December 21, 2010 (Lunar Eclipse in Gemini)
June 1, 2011 (Solar Eclipse in Gemini)
December 10, 2011 (Lunar Eclipse in Gemini)
May 20, 2012 (Solar Eclipse in Gemini)
November 28, 2012 (Lunar Eclipse in Gemini)

Around these dates, shifts occur in how you make money and what security means to you. It is important that you review your values so that you're clear on what is important to you and what isn't. What has changed will be visible within a month of these eclipse dates.

During all these eclipses, the enlightenment tools of Mercury (Gemini) help you bring light to your finances.

June 11, 2012–June 26, 2013 (Jupiter in Gemini)

This is an amazing time of financial prosperity, especially if you are in the publishing or traveling business, a writer, a conference speaker, a university teacher, or a lawyer. But for money to flow effortlessly, your values need to be spotlessly ethical. Funds are available for traveling, writing, and furthering your education. As you are lavish with your

THE MAYAN
CALENDAR AND
THE SIGNS

273

abundance, making generous gifts and supporting those in need of your help, you attract more prosperity.

From June 2012 to June 2013, the enlightenment tools of Jupiter (Sagittarius) help you bring light to your finances.

III. Communication

July 21, 2009 (Solar Eclipse in Cancer)
December 31, 2009 (Lunar Eclipse in Cancer)
July 11, 2010 (Solar Eclipse in Cancer)
July 1, 2011 (Solar Eclipse in Cancer)

The more you listen to your feelings and intuition, the deeper the shifts in your daily environment. A brother, sister, or neighbor could require nurturing or protection. At these times, the way you communicate needs to be more connected to your emotions. It is within one month of these four dates that you will be able to really assess that which has changed.

Around these dates, the enlightenment tools of Cancer and the Moon help you bring light to your mental endeavors.

IV. Home

February 9, 2009 (Lunar Eclipse in Leo)

You are asked to make transformations in your home. You could either move or redecorate your house or apartment. You may want to make it a deeper expression of your heart—a haven of peace with a touch of glamour. You may have to take care of a parent, helping him or her to expand his or her vision. It is within a month of this date that you will truly know what has changed.

In February 2009, the enlightenment tools of Leo help you bring light to your home.

V. Creativity, Romance, and Children

From the Present until October 29, 2009 (Saturn in Virgo)
April 7, 2010–July 20, 2010 (Saturn in Virgo)

This transit makes you more aware of your uniqueness. Artists are particularly favored by this transit. The ability to diligently and meticulously work long hours leads to very marketable works. Hobbies and pleasures take a serious overtone. During these times, romance is not an impulsive involvement but is entered with the goal of building a long-term relationship. You receive a chance to explore inner obstacles to deeper intimacy, such as fears of commitment or emotional inhibitions. Your relationships with children are also imbued with discipline. You wish to help them develop solid skills so they can make their mark in the world.

> *During these two periods, the enlightenment tools of Saturn (Capricorn) help you bring light to your creativity, romance, and relationship with children.*

VI. Health, Pets, and Work

October 29, 2009–April 6, 2010 (Saturn in Libra)
July 21, 2010–October 4, 2012 (Saturn in Libra)

You are required to pay serious attention to the needs of your body. Do not overlook signs of trouble. This is the perfect period to adopt a healthy lifestyle with good, organic nutrition, drinking high-quality water, and starting to exercise regularly in a way that is in harmony with your energy. You may even find yourself attracted to studying the healing arts to become a practitioner. Work in general requires more focus and organizational skills. Through a concentrated effort, you are likely to accomplish much in a very short amount of time. Your relationship with coworkers may not be as warm, but it is professional and efficient. A small pet may be a source of responsibility, teaching you patience, love, and courage while grounding you in reality.

During these three years, the enlightenment tools of Saturn (Capricorn) help you bring light to your health.

VII. Marriage

October 5, 2012–September 18, 2015 (Saturn in Scorpio)
November 13, 2012 (Solar Eclipse in Scorpio)

In 2012, and until 2015, you reach a turning point in a committed relationship. Within one month of the November 13 eclipse, you will know whether this connection is meant to last or if it has served its purpose. If it does withstand this transit, you have the assurance that it will remain in your life for a very long time. The relationship may not inspire fireworks, but it is definitely grounded in reality, solid, and mature. This is someone you can grow old with, who is loyal, enriches your basic nature, and is supportive of your growth. The stability and integrity you feel in this relationship give you a sense of protection and peace. It is important, however, that you do not project upon another your own fears of a deeper involvement, which could make you feel restricted in an otherwise very positive relationship. This is your chance to examine closely what may be blocking you from experiencing a truer intimacy and to shift those inner obstacles.

Between October 2012 and September 2015, the enlightenment tools of Saturn (Capricorn) and Scorpio help you bring light to your marriage and close enlightenment tools.

VIII. Sexuality, Joint Finances, and Transformation

June 15, 2011 (Lunar Eclipse in Sagittarius)
November 25, 2011 (Solar Eclipse in Sagittarius)
June 4, 2012 (Lunar Eclipse in Sagittarius)

Within one month of these three dates, you will find that a great shift has occurred in finances shared with another. Even if at first it doesn't seem so, it is for the better. A chance to clear a debt, money coming from a legacy, insurance, or taxes presents itself. An increase in your partner's income could also open new options that weren't previously available. Whatever the source of your new flow of income, time is freed. You have now the energy to explore the afterlife and the concept of reincarnation as well as to study more esoteric knowledge.

On these dates, the enlightenment tools of Jupiter and Sagittarius help you transform your sexuality and joint finances.

IX. Long-Distance Travel, Philosophy, and Religion

July 7, 2009 (Lunar Eclipse in Capricorn)
January 15, 2010 (Solar Eclipse in Capricorn)
June 26, 2010 (Lunar Eclipse in Capricorn)
January 4, 2011 (Solar Eclipse in Capricorn)

On these eclipses, the repercussions of which will unravel for a whole month, travel is undertaken for serious reasons—both to gain a broader perspective on the world and to understand your own purpose more clearly. You also have a need to study, not for the sake of just acquiring knowledge but to consolidate the philosophical meaning you give to existence. Your connection to your higher self deepens. Learning, teaching, lecturing, and writing are all favored at this time.

On these dates, the enlightenment tools of Capricorn help you bring light to your travels, philosophy, and religion.

Since January 19, 2007 until January 4, 2009 (Jupiter in Capricorn)

The first week of January ends a period of two years that brought travels that expanded your understanding of the world in which you live. You may want to investigate foreign cultures and you will gain much from contacts with foreigners or fellow travelers. Those in the publishing industry are likely to have either written or promoted spiritual and ethical works. These would elevate your consciousness while inspiring expanding audiences. You are likely to seek higher education and enroll in a program that helps you connect more clearly with your higher mind.

During that period, the enlightenment tools of Jupiter (Sagittarius) help you bring light to your travels.

Since November 28, 2008 until November 21, 2024 (Pluto in Capricorn)

Long-distance travel brings profound, even borderline dangerous experiences that are likely to forever change your relationship to God. You could meet sages or people of vast spiritual wisdom. Contact with them helps you rebuild your connection to your higher self. You could discover yourself to have the gift of prophecy. Your opinions on religion and philosophy are likely to become black and white. During the years to come, any writing or public speaking you do could contribute to a complete revolution of the educational and legal systems.

Until 2024, the enlightenment tools of Pluto (Scorpio) help you bring light to your long-distance travels.

X. Career

January 5, 2009–January 16, 2010 (Jupiter in Aquarius)

Inasmuch as you maintain strict integrity, great professional opportunities further all your ambitions, leading to an expanded social status and increased recognition. Your deeper legal or political involvement makes a huge difference in the ethics of society.

During this year, the enlightenment tools of Jupiter (Sagittarius) help you bring light to your career.

January 26, 2009 (Solar Eclipse in Aquarius)
August 5, 2009 (Lunar Eclipse in Aquarius)

Within one month of these dates, changes in your career will be apparent. Either a new opportunity is presented to you or you will create your own.

On these two dates, the enlightenment tools of Aquarius help you bring light to your career.

From the Present until April 19, 2010 (Chiron in Aquarius)
July 20, 2010–February 7, 2011 (Chiron in Aquarius)

During these months, you could feel the need to heal something in your career or regarding your place in society. In a wish to have a meaningful job that helps others transmute pain you may also want to learn the healing arts.

Until February 2011, the enlightenment tools of Aquarius help you bring light to your career.

From November 28, 1998 until April 3, 2011 (Neptune in Aquarius)
August 4, 2011–February 2, 2012 (Neptune in Aquarius)

Your career could become very glamorous and filled with unusual excitement. You feel inspired by what you do and you bring inspiration to others. There is a spiritual and sacrificial (in the etymological sense of "making sacred") dimension to your work. If you are an artist, especially if you're involved in music, dance, or the making of images (painting, film, photography), fame could await you at this time. You exude a charisma that attracts others to you. During these times, the elusive, mystical quality you radiate enables you to live your ideals and serve a higher purpose.

Until April 2011 and between August 2011 and February 2012, the enlightenment tools of Neptune (Pisces) help you bring light to your career.

XI. Friendships

From the Present Until May 26, 2010 (Uranus in Pisces)
August 13, 2010–March 10, 2011 (Uranus in Pisces)

You're likely to experience separations from acquaintances with whom you don't share much anymore. Sudden new, exciting encounters occur with highly original or otherwise unusual people. Involvement in groups or associations focusing on "strange" topics (UFOs, metaphysical studies, scientific research of extrasensory phenomena) is very appealing and leads to powerful insights into the origins of humanity and of your own personal past. The compartmentalization of time in past, present, and future dissolves, giving access to higher, mind-blowing truths.

Until May 2010 and between August 2010 and March 2011, the enlightenment tools of Uranus (Aquarius) help you bring light to your friendships.

January 17, 2010–June 5, 2010 (Jupiter in Pisces)
September 8, 2010–January 21, 2011 (Jupiter in Pisces)

Traveling with friends expands your cultural and spiritual horizons. Involvement in humanitarian groups with positive, international people is greatly beneficial. Happiness comes through meaningful social gatherings, such as book clubs, yoga retreats, or time spent with associations fighting for a worthwhile cause. Long-term dreams are fulfilled during these periods.

Between January 2010 and June 2010, and September 2010 until January 2011, the enlightenment tools of Jupiter (Sagittarius) help you bring light to your friendships.

April 20, 2010–July 19, 2010 (Chiron in Pisces)
February 8, 2011–February 2019 (Chiron in Pisces)

You could become a role model for one of your friends, gently guiding that person to a higher path. Rejection from another could lead to very deep insights into your own nature. You could also become involved in a healing center, either as a patient or as a therapist.

Between April 2010 and July 2010, and between February 2011 and February 2019, the enlightenment tools of Pisces help you bring light to your friendships.

April 4, 2011–August 3, 2011 (Neptune in Pisces)
February 3, 2012–January 27, 2026 (Neptune in Pisces)

During these periods, spiritual friendships become the norm rather than the exception. The inspiring people you befriend at this time are connected to higher spheres of consciousness. You are likely to merge with their ideals and together work for the betterment of humanity. Subtle shifts are occurring in your long-term hopes and goals that you may not be able to define until much later.

> *Between April 2011 and August 2011, and between February 2012 and January 2026, the enlightenment tools of Neptune (Pisces) will help you bring light to your friendships.*

XII. SUBCONSCIOUS

June 6, 2010–September 7, 2010 (Jupiter in Aries)
January 22, 2011–June 4, 2011 (Jupiter in Aries)

During these two periods, deep insights into the meaning of time give you a greater understanding of life. The compassion that you develop makes you want to in turn extend a helping hand to those less fortunate than yourself—those who may be isolated from society (in charitable institutions, hospitals, or even jail). Healing is likely to flow through you, bringing much solace to those in need of spiritual inspiration.

May 27, 2010–August 13, 2010 (Uranus in Aries)
March 11, 2011–March 6, 2019 (Uranus in Aries)

Sudden breakthroughs in consciousness could occur in meditation, during your nighttime dreams, or when in isolation and silence. The veil between your reality and other dimensions breaks open, revealing aspects of your psyche of which you were not previously aware. Problems find unusual solutions. You are inspired to create works exposing the intricate dynamics underlying our lives.

During these times, the enlightenment tools of Jupiter (Sagittarius) and Uranus (Aquarius) help you bring light to your subconscious.

2009–2012 FOR GEMINI AND/OR GEMINI RISING

I. PERSONAL APPEARANCE

December 21, 2010 (Lunar Eclipse in Gemini)
June 1, 2011 (Solar Eclipse in Gemini)
December 10, 2011 (Lunar Eclipse in Gemini)
May 20, 2012 (Solar Eclipse in Gemini)
November 28, 2012 (Lunar Eclipse in Gemini)

On all these dates, you are likely to reinvent yourself, each time slightly differently. You feel the need to become all that you can be. The changes in the image you have of yourself and that you project to others will be visible within a month of these eclipse dates.

During all these eclipse dates, the enlightenment tools of Mercury (Gemini) help you bring light to your personal appearance.

June 11, 2012–June 26, 2013 (Jupiter in Gemini)

You impress others very positively at this time with the enthusiasm, exuberance, and faith you exude. You make others want to open doors for you. The more in line you are with your own integrity, the more beneficial these opportunities will be. You don't wish to be restricted in any way. This is a time of expansion and discovery of what is possible for you in a spirit of adventurousness and playfulness.

From June 2012 to June 2013, the enlightenment tools of Jupiter (Sagittarius) help you bring light to your image of yourself and the image you project to others.

II. Money

July 21, 2009 (Solar Eclipse in Cancer)
December 31, 2009 (Lunar Eclipse in Cancer)
July 11, 2010 (Solar Eclipse in Cancer)
July 1, 2011 (Solar Eclipse in Cancer)

Within a month of these four dates, beneficial shifts occur in your finances, leading to more security and a feeling of stability. You may discover a new source of income or you may revamp your budget by getting rid of unnecessary expenses.

On those dates, the enlightenment tools of Cancer and the Moon help you bring light to your finances.

III. Communication

February 9, 2009 (Lunar Eclipse in Leo)

Your exchanges with others come from the heart. They are warmer and more comforting. You could be drawn to the theater or some other dramatic expression of thoughts and feelings. A letter, a book, a phone call, a short trip, a sibling, or a neighbor could shift your consciousness and introduce you to information of which you weren't previously aware. Be careful of what you say on this day, as it would be irreversible. Within a month from the eclipse date, you will know exactly what has changed.

In February 2009, the enlightenment tools of Leo help you bring light to the way you think, learn, and communicate.

IV. Home

Since September 3, 2007 until October 28, 2009 (Saturn in Virgo)
April 7, 2010–July 20, 2010 (Saturn in Virgo)

The foundation of your life, including those things you take for granted, needs to be reassessed. You could investigate your family tree to understand yourself better. You could also explore your own past lives, which are likely to shed much light on your present circumstances. You may want to move or at least redecorate your home. You need your house or apartment to be a place that is private, affording you space to think and create. This is the perfect time to go through your closets and drawers and get rid of the items you haven't used in more than six months. A reorganization could also be called for where your parents are concerned. You may need to assume responsibility for their living arrangements. It may also be important to relate to them in a way that enables you to know them better—not as your parents, but as friends.

During these two periods, the enlightenment tools of Saturn (Capricorn) help you bring light to your home.

V. Creativity, Romance, and Children

October 29, 2009–April 6, 2010 (Saturn in Libra)
July 21, 2010–October 4, 2012 (Saturn in Libra)

Pleasures and romantic involvements are more serious than usual. You could take a whole new look at someone to whom you were previously attracted. You seek more mature or substantial people. If you are an artist, you are most likely to create works that you can both exhibit and sell. They may not be the most original ever created, but they have a sound and solid quality that appeals to more conventional aesthetes. You want your children to have a solid basis and a good education that will help them find their place in a shifting society.

During these two periods, the enlightenment tools of Saturn (Capricorn) help you bring light to your creativity and romance, and to your relationship with children.

VI. Health, Pets, and Work

October 5, 2012–September 18, 2015 (Saturn in Scorpio)
November 13, 2012 (Solar Eclipse in Scorpio)

Between 2012 and 2015, with a high point on November 13, 2012, your body is undergoing tremendous changes. Do not ignore any warning signal. If listened to early enough, nothing will degenerate into a more serious illness. You could now have violent reactions to foods that are not appropriate. You could find yourself indifferent to dishes that were previously appealing, and you may suddenly feel attracted to nutrients that weren't part of your diet before. Your physical form is shifting at a cellular level, getting rid of what no longer serves your higher growth and readying itself for more light. A form of symbolic death could occur, allowing you to regenerate in the deepest way. Profound healing, either received or offered, is also likely to occur during this period in time. You could discover that you have a magnetism that allows you to physically feel and transmute ancient traumas in other people.

During these periods, the enlightenment tools of Saturn (Capricorn) and Scorpio help you bring light to your health.

VII. Marriage

June 15, 2011 (Lunar Eclipse in Sagittarius)
November 25, 2011 (Solar Eclipse in Sagittarius)
June 4, 2012 (Lunar Eclipse in Sagittarius)

Within one month of these three dates, you will know what has changed in your intimate relationship. A shaky relationship is likely to end on one of these dates. In a good relationship, positive feelings will be enhanced, leading to an even greater involvement. If single, you are likely to meet a serious romantic prospect—someone who is adventurous and loves his/her freedom as much as you do. You have much to share with this exciting person, who expands your consciousness in magical ways.

*On these dates, the enlightenment tools of Sagittarius and Jupiter help
you bring light to your intimate relationship.*

VIII. Sexuality, Joint Finances, and Transformation

July 7, 2009 (Lunar Eclipse in Capricorn)
January 15, 2010 (Solar Eclipse in Capricorn)
June 26, 2010 (Lunar Eclipse in Capricorn)
January 4, 2011 (Solar Eclipse in Capricorn)

On these eclipse dates, the repercussions of which will unravel for an
entire month, you may need to be very grounded regarding money
shared with a partner (either by marriage or by professional association). Anything connected to taxes, insurance, or inheritance presents
responsibilities at this time and should not be overlooked. Sexuality is
also deeper than usual and requires that you be more attentive to its
possible consequences.

*On these dates, the enlightenment tools of Capricorn help you bring light
to your joint finances and your sexuality.*

Since January 19, 2007 until January 4, 2009 (Jupiter in Capricorn)

The first week of January ends a period of two years that brought much
expansion in joint financial ventures. Money shared with others is likely
to have significantly grown. If these resources are not squandered—as
is always the risk when Jupiter is involved—further investments are indicated. An adventurous sexual affair could open many new doors in
your consciousness.

*During that period, the enlightenment tools of Jupiter (Sagittarius) help
you bring light to your joint finances.*

From the Present until November 21, 2024 (Pluto in Capricorn)

In the next decade, you are being tested on your positive use of power
for the highest good. Sexuality is highly transformative and enables you

to touch dimensions of yourself that you never even knew about. Joint finances, especially those linked to the corporate world or inheritance, could come with strings attached. It is essential that you do not allow manipulation to lower your own standards and that your integrity remains intact. A fascination with death, life after death, and reincarnation could inspire you to deep metaphysical researches. This period could feel like you are undergoing a symbolic death followed by a rebirth, as all that was outgrown in your life is stripped away, giving you the ability to establish your power on a whole new basis.

Until 2024, the enlightenment tools of Pluto (Scorpio) help you bring light to joint finances, sexuality, and transformation.

IX. Long-Distance Travel, Philosophy, and Religion

January 5, 2009–January 16, 2010 (Jupiter in Aquarius)

Your optimism and faith soar high during these twelve months. The meaning of life becomes a fascinating area of research. You are likely to enthusiastically promote a philosophy of life that embraces very positive and idealistic concepts. Long-distance traveling, publishing, lecturing, or higher education bring your spiritual understanding to yet another level of consciousness, filling you and all those who listen to you with joy. Your aspirations for the future are fueled by grand, adventurous, and daring dreams for the betterment of humanity.

The enlightenment tools of Jupiter (Sagittarius) help you bring light to your long-distance travels, as well as to all matters related to philosophy and religion.

January 26, 2009 (Solar Eclipse in Aquarius)
August 5, 2009 (Lunar Eclipse in Aquarius)

On these dates, a sudden trip, a conference, or a book could completely and suddenly shift your philosophy of life. Your connection to your own higher self could free much energy for the rest of your life. It is within one month of these dates that you will really know what has changed.

On these two dates, the enlightenment tools of Aquarius help you bring light to long-distance traveling, philosophy, and religion.

January 2006–April 19, 2010 (Chiron in Aquarius)
July 20, 2010–February 7, 2011 (Chiron in Aquarius)

During these months, an intuition could change your understanding of a specific experience. An abstract idea could inspire a very concrete project that helps others see what was previously invisible. You are likely to become a teacher, showing others the way out of darkness.

During this period, the enlightenment tools of Aquarius help you bring light to your long-distance travels, philosophy, and religion.

Since November 28, 1998 until April 3, 2011 (Neptune in Aquarius)
August 4, 2011–February 2, 2012 (Neptune in Aquarius)

Philosophical interests are imbued with mysticism. A strong desire for enlightenment guides your metaphysical search, leading to unusual insights. You could meet a sage in a foreign land and naturally experience alternate states of consciousness. A form of fusion with the divine could shift your perceptions.

During these periods, the enlightenment tools of Neptune (Pisces) help you bring light to long-distance traveling, philosophy, and religion.

X. CAREER

Since December 31, 2003 until May 26, 2010 (Uranus in Pisces)
August 13, 2010–March 10, 2011 (Uranus in Pisces)

There are likely to be sudden changes in your career, either instigated from the outside or caused by your need for something new. A monotonous job is abruptly left for an exciting new career associated with scientific research, working with and/or for people, electronics, or financing. It is likely to be innovative and progressive work, highly personal, and unusual in some way, leading to the possibility of overnight fame.

During these periods, the enlightenment tools of Uranus (Aquarius) help you bring light to your career.

January 17, 2010–June 5, 2010 (Jupiter in Pisces)
September 8, 2010–January 21, 2011 (Jupiter in Pisces)

Beneficial career advancements occur. Lucrative opportunities enable you to increase your social prestige and gain recognition and honors from your peers. You could find your calling at this time. If your work ethics are impeccable, any vocation related to the law, politics, travel, business, or higher education is particularly favored.

During these two periods, the enlightenment tools of Jupiter (Sagittarius) help you bring light into your career.

April 20, 2010–July 29, 2010 (Chiron in Pisces)
February 8, 2011–February 2019 (Chiron in Pisces)

These are important years to find your niche in this changing society. Your ambitions could require some sacrifices. Finding a balance between your professional achievements and your personal life is necessary, as is enlisting the support of your family. You could be inspired by mentors who are in a position to open valuable doors for you. Fame and fortune can be reached at this time. During these years, any involvement in the healing arts is greatly beneficial.

During these two periods, the enlightenment tools of Pisces help you bring light to your career.

April 4, 2011–August 3, 2011 (Neptune in Pisces)
February 3, 2012–January 27, 2026 (Neptune in Pisces)

These are years when it may feel more important to have an enjoyable lifestyle than to just make money. As you follow your heart and seek inner satisfaction in the pursuit of personal ideals, changes in career are likely to occur. Strange circumstances combined with the special charisma that you radiate could lead to public acclaim. You are seen to embody style and beauty. Your increased sensitivity and profound intuition at these times make you very fit for healing or artistic professions—particularly those related to fashion, film, photography, painting, music, and dance. You may also be involved in social work that brings you to places of retreat such as a hospital, a jail, or a monastery. The shifts that occur are so subtle and happen over such a long period of time that you may not be able to define them until much later.

During these two periods, the enlightenment tools of Neptune (Pisces) help you bring light to your career.

XI. FRIENDSHIPS

June 6, 2010–September 7, 2010 (Jupiter in Aries)
January 22, 2011–June 4, 2011 (Jupiter in Aries)

Many benefits and much happiness are derived through your friendships at this time. You could become involved in philanthropic or religious groups that expand your social circle, allowing you to meet positive, optimistic people from a wide array of backgrounds. Traveling with friends is favored.

During those two periods, the enlightenment tools of Jupiter (Sagittarius) help you bring light to your friendships.

May 27, 2010–August 13, 2010 (Uranus in Aries)
March 11, 2011–March 6, 2019 (Uranus in Aries)

During these periods, the whole of humanity is your playground. Your acute intuition leads to original ideas. You attract spontaneous, exciting new friendships that deviate from the traditional path. These intellectual and spiritual connections are likely to be catalysts of transformation. You are drawn to like-spirited people who are unusual, walk to the sound of their own drummer, and are involved in humanitarian or original scientific projects. To keep your interest, it is important that both your individuality and your freedom are respected.

During these times, the enlightenment tools of Uranus (Aquarius) help
you bring light to your friendships.

XII. SUBCONSCIOUS

June 4, 2011–June 10, 2012 (Jupiter in Taurus)

During this year, you are likely to feel a need for isolation. You wish to explore profound philosophical and spiritual concepts. This time of retreat fills you with a deeper sense of happiness. Your dreams expand your vision and put you in touch with the hidden recesses of your own subconscious. Your generosity of spirit leads to a greater appreciation of the magic of life.

Between June 2011 and June 2012, the enlightenment tools of Jupiter
(Sagittarius) help you bring light to your subconscious.

2009–2012 FOR CANCER AND/OR CANCER RISING

I. PERSONAL APPEARANCE

July 21, 2009 (Solar Eclipse in Cancer)
December 31, 2009 (Lunar Eclipse in Cancer)
July 11, 2010 (Solar Eclipse in Cancer)
July 1, 2011 (Solar Eclipse in Cancer)

Within a month of these four dates, you will know what has shifted in the image you have of yourself and how others perceive you. You are likely to transform your personal appearance, take better care of your health, and change your style. Your approach to life in general is more committed and serious.

On these dates, the enlightenment tools of Cancer and the Moon help
you bring light to your personal appearance.

II. Money

February 9, 2009 (Lunar Eclipse in Leo)

Your income is likely to greatly increase with this eclipse. You may also feel the need to reevaluate your priorities and adopt new values. Within one month of this date, you will know with more certainty what has changed in your financial situation.

In February 2009, the enlightenment tools of Leo help you bring light to your values and finances.

III. Communication

Since September 3, 2007 until October 28, 2009 (Saturn in Virgo)
April 7, 2010–July 20, 2010 (Saturn in Virgo)

During these two periods, you are likely to go back to school to acquire practical training that will empower your career and further your ambitions. Your mental discipline is very high at these times. Serious reading is preferred to superficial conversations. The focused attention and concentration you display are perfect for research and any study requiring long-term commitment. The way you express yourself is also more structured and maybe somewhat cautious, but definitely mature and substantial. Your relationships with siblings may incur responsibilities.

During these two periods, the enlightenment tools of Saturn (Capricorn) help you bring light to your communications.

IV. Home

October 29, 2009–April 6, 2010 (Saturn in Libra)
July 21, 2010–October 4, 2012 (Saturn in Libra)

Domestic affairs may require more responsibility on your part. You may need to restructure the living circumstances of a parent. You are likely to reorganize your own home by increasing its efficiency in alignment with your personal and career needs. You may also choose to relocate, which means getting rid of what no longer serves a purpose in your life. You may become actively involved in real estate, mining, and/or anything related to food or ecology.

During these two periods, the enlightenment tools of Saturn (Capricorn) help you bring light to your home.

V. Creativity, Romance, and Children

October 5, 2012–September 18, 2015 (Saturn in Scorpio)
November 13, 2012 (Solar Eclipse in Scorpio)

Between 2012 and 2015, your sense of your own uniqueness becomes much more solid. The way you express your creativity is particularly highlighted on November 13, 2012. You want others to see what you are creating and you could even make a career out of your art. You could become more aware of your responsibilities toward your children. You are likely to encourage their ambitions and help them strengthen the skills they need to fulfill them. Love relationships take a more serious tone. An intimate connection with someone who enriches you is likely to be cemented during this transit.

During this time, the enlightenment tools of Saturn (Capricorn) help you bring light to the areas of creativity, romance, and children.

VI. Health, Pets, and Work

June 15, 2011 (Lunar Eclipse in Sagittarius)
November 25, 2011 (Solar Eclipse in Sagittarius)
June 4, 2012 (Lunar Eclipse in Sagittarius)

Your health comes into greater focus during these eclipses. Your body is shifting at a cellular level. You may want to reassess your nutrition and get more actively involved in an exercise program. The way you approach your work is also likely to change. You may get involved in a different field. A pet may walk into your life or you may renew your relationship with an existing one. Within one month of these three dates, you will know exactly what has shifted in your health and work.

On these three dates, the enlightenment tools of Jupiter and Sagittarius help you bring light to your health.

VII. Marriage

Since January 19, 2007 until January 4, 2009 (Jupiter in Capricorn)

The first week of January ends a period of one year that brought much good fortune to your marriage. If you were single, you most certainly attracted marriage opportunities. You may have gotten involved with a foreigner and/or someone whose optimism and faith in life are contagious. During this time, extravagance, prosperity, and freedom are experienced in close partnerships. Your benevolence and insistence on seeing the best in others greatly increase your popularity.

During this period, the enlightenment tools of Jupiter (Sagittarius) help you bring light to your marriage.

July 7, 2009 (Lunar Eclipse in Capricorn)
January 15, 2010 (Solar Eclipse in Capricorn)
June 26, 2010 (Lunar Eclipse in Capricorn)
January 4, 2011 (Solar Eclipse in Capricorn)

Your relationship to marriage is likely to be transformed on these eclipse dates, either because you decide to commit to someone or because it becomes clear that a difficult relationship needs to end. The repercussions of these realizations will unravel for a whole month.

On these dates, the enlightenment tools of Capricorn help you bring light to your marriage.

Since November 28, 2008 until November 21, 2024 (Pluto in Capricorn)

Marriage is an area that will transform deeply. You are likely to be involved with someone who is highly charismatic, deep, and powerful. The sexual attraction to this person may be enigmatic yet extremely compelling. A sense of destiny accompanies this connection. The profound feelings it awakens within you bring to light relationship issues of which you weren't aware or that you thought you had already overcome. The intensity of this link completely shifts your attitude toward marriage and intimacy. An existing relationship reaches new depths and leads to a greater commitment.

> *Until 2024, the enlightenment tools of Pluto (Scorpio) help you bring light to your marriage.*

VIII. SEXUALITY, JOINT FINANCES, AND TRANSFORMATION

January 5, 2009–January 16, 2010 (Jupiter in Aquarius)

Psychic experiences completely transform your understanding of the deeper underlying principles of life. In the search for answers to profound questions, you reach serenity and inner freedom. Sexuality brings self-transformation. Deep insights lead you beyond what has been traditionally taught by tantric traditions.

> *Between January 2009 and January 2010, the enlightenment tools of Jupiter (Sagittarius) help you bring light to your sexuality.*

January 26, 2009 (Solar Eclipse in Aquarius)
August 5, 2009 (Lunar Eclipse in Aquarius)

Changes are occurring in joint resources. You are likely to either receive an advance inheritance, a tax refund, or money from insurance. Deeper insights could transform the way you see life, death, and life after death. Within one month of these dates, the transformations that have occurred both in yourself and in your joint finances will be more apparent.

On these two dates, the enlightenment tools of Aquarius help you bring light to your sexuality and joint resources.

Since January 2006 until April 19, 2010 (Chiron in Aquarius)
July 20, 2010–February 7, 2011 (Chiron in Aquarius)

During these two periods, you have the opportunity to develop healing skills. You are also accessing a wisdom that gives you greater insight into the spiritual dimensions of life, death, the afterlife, and sexuality. You could even develop the gift of prophecy and perform miracles.

During these two periods, the enlightenment tools of Aquarius help you bring light to joint resources and sexuality.

Since November 28, 1998 until April 3, 2011 (Neptune in Aquarius)
August 4, 2011–February 2, 2012 (Neptune in Aquarius)

These years mark a powerful sensitivity to higher planes of consciousness. You could witness unusual psychic phenomena. Your own clairvoyant abilities or talents as a medium are developing. Something about joint finances seems to mysteriously give you the money you need when you need it. Whether it is through your partner's income, taxes, insurance money, or an inheritance, you could feel it is really coming from a divine source.

During these two periods, the enlightenment tools of Neptune (Pisces) help you bring light to joint resources and sexuality.

IX. LONG-DISTANCE TRAVEL, PHILOSOPHY, AND RELIGION

Since December 31, 2003 until May 26, 2010 (Uranus in Pisces)
August 13, 2010–March 10, 2011 (Uranus in Pisces)

Unexpected trips to a foreign country or higher education bring unusual experiences that shift your philosophical outlook. As you immerse yourself in a new culture, you could start drawing information seemingly out of thin air. Your beliefs leave the beaten path, projecting you into a bright and exciting unknown. Under this transit, a humanitarian reform of society feels very attractive and you are likely to commit to manifesting it with unorthodox new friends.

During these two periods, the enlightenment tools of Uranus (Aquarius) help you bring light to your long-distance trips and philosophy of life.

January 17, 2010–June 5, 2010 (Jupiter in Pisces)
September 8, 2010–January 21, 2011 (Jupiter in Pisces)

During these periods, travels to faraway lands are exhilarating and adventurous. You are not just visiting another locality, but immersing yourself in the culture, learning about the customs, trying to speak a foreign language. As you become one with others, distant memories emerge, leading to a shift in consciousness.

During these two periods, the enlightenment tools of Jupiter (Sagittarius) help you bring light to your long-distance trips and philosophy of life.

April 20, 2010–July 19, 2010 (Chiron in Pisces)
February 8, 2011–February 2019 (Chiron in Pisces)

Your wish to embrace the most varied and exciting life experiences leads to visionary insights and innovative thinking. There is no limit to how much you can now stretch your consciousness. During these years, your dreams, fueled by powerful intuitions, enable you to teach complex knowledge with great clarity.

During these two periods, the enlightenment tools of Pisces help you bring light to your long-distance trips and philosophy of life.

April 4, 2011–August 3, 2011 (Neptune in Pisces)
February 3, 2012–January 27, 2026 (Neptune in Pisces)

Subtle shifts are occurring that you may not be able to define until much later. The portal to your higher consciousness is opening wide, enabling you to channel otherworldly information. You could have mystical experiences in foreign lands. Evolved people have a special wisdom to personally share with you. You will come to realize that it was yours all along.

During these two periods, the enlightenment tools of Neptune (Pisces) help you bring light to your long-distance trips and philosophy of life.

X. Career

June 6, 2010–September 7, 2010 (Jupiter in Aries)
January 22, 2011–June 4, 2011 (Jupiter in Aries)

This is a year of great opportunities in your career. Advancements occur, propositions flow, and there is a sense of great freedom. Inasmuch as you remain perfectly ethical, the sky is the limit to what you can now accomplish. Recognition and honors are offered to you. Opportunities open in foreign countries. Anything in your career related to teaching, real estate, philosophy, travel, the law, publishing, acting, politics, or religion is greatly favored.

During those two periods, the enlightenment tools of Jupiter (Sagittarius) help you bring light to your career.

May 27, 2010–August 13, 2010 (Uranus in Aries)
March 11, 2011–March 6, 2019 (Uranus in Aries)

If you have been feeling out of place, now is the time to break free and begin an unusual career that will place you in close contact with people. You could be working with energy, crystals, or highly advanced computers able to map human consciousness. Your work is original, interesting, and very much in tune with the growing evolution of society.

During those two periods, the enlightenment tools of Uranus (Aquarius) help you bring light to your career.

XI. Friendships

June 4, 2011–June 10, 2012 (Jupiter in Taurus)

You are attracting positive friends who are either foreigners or well traveled. Together, you could create a form of community where all live in harmony, enriching each other and expanding each other's skills.

Between June 2011 and June 2012, the enlightenment tools of Jupiter (Sagittarius) help you bring light to your friendships.

XII. Subconscious

December 21, 2010 (Lunar Eclipse in Gemini)
June 1, 2011 (Solar Eclipse in Gemini)
December 10, 2011 (Lunar Eclipse in Gemini)
May 20, 2012 (Solar Eclipse in Gemini)
November 28, 2012 (Lunar Eclipse in Gemini)

It is important that you now commit to opening your heart. As you do, incredible new insights that were previously buried in your subconscious will flow through you. By clearly feeling your connection to all that is, your life takes on a whole new meaning. What has changed will be visible within a month of these eclipse dates.

During all these eclipses, the enlightenment tools of Mercury (Gemini) help you bring light to your subconscious.

June 11, 2012–June 26, 2013 (Jupiter in Gemini)

Your generosity of spirit and your compassion make you want to help those less fortunate than yourself. You could be involved in charitable institutions or hospitals. You are also drawn to probing deeper into the meaning of existence. Your soul needs much beauty, silence, and solitude at this time. Your most profound thoughts occur in retreat, leading you to spontaneous shamanistic journeys. As you expand your awareness, you also shift external reality both for yourself and for others.

From June 2012 to June 2013, the enlightenment tools of Jupiter (Sagittarius) help you bring light to your subconscious.

2009–2012 FOR LEO AND/OR LEO RISING

I. PERSONAL APPEARANCE

February 9, 2009 (Lunar Eclipse in Leo)

This is the day to recreate your personal appearance. You need to decide how you wish to define yourself, what you stand for, what is important to you, and what image you want to project. Within a month of this date, you will truly know how your impact on others has changed.

In February 2009, the enlightenment tools of Leo help you bring light to your personal appearance.

II. MONEY

Since September 3, 2007 until October 28, 2009 (Saturn in Virgo)
April 7, 2010–July 20, 2010 (Saturn in Virgo)

These are times to structure your finances and redefine your personal values. The money you enjoy is a result of your own work, and it's also accompanied by a sense of greater responsibility. Your values are mature and the manner in which you use your personal resources is focused and efficient. Intent on building more security, you are likely to develop new skills based on a keen business sense. As you plan for the future, your investments are solid and realistic.

During these two periods, the enlightenment tools of Saturn (Capricorn) help you bring light to your finances.

III. Communication

October 29, 2009–April 6, 2010 (Saturn in Libra)
July 21, 2010–October 4, 2012 (Saturn in Libra)

You could become aware of gaps in your knowledge. This makes you want to study in-depth a topic requiring both concentration and long-term efforts. The way you express yourself is serious and grounded. You are likely to prefer solitude to senseless chatter and you may seek the company of mature people you admire and from whom you can learn. This is a wonderful time to structure your intellectual skills and make a valuable impact on your daily environment. People listen to you, sensing that what you have to say is the result of wisdom backed by solid research. Your personal authority is palpable, inspiring much respect. Writing is favored by this transit, as are teaching and lecturing.

During these two periods, the enlightenment tools of Saturn (Capricorn) help you bring light to your communications.

IV. Home

October 5, 2012–September 18, 2015 (Saturn in Scorpio)
November 13, 2012 (Solar Eclipse in Scorpio)

Between October 2012 and September 2015 you are reassessing your foundations. Your home could be in need of repair, redecoration, or simply reorganization. You may also have outlived your present location and find a need to move. It is a time to establish a solid basis that gives you both peace and security. This is the perfect transit to go through your closets and recycle what you haven't used in more than six months. You may also need to reevaluate the concepts you take for granted. This could lead you to a personal archaeological dig. As you study your family tree and unearth past incarnations, you are able to recognize and let go of outmoded reactions. You could become responsible for a parent whom you need to honor and learn to know better.

Between October 2012 and September 2015, the enlightenment tools of Saturn (Capricorn) and Scorpio help you bring light to your home.

V. Creativity, Romance, and Children

June 15, 2011 (Lunar Eclipse in Sagittarius)
November 25, 2011 (Solar Eclipse in Sagittarius)
June 4, 2012 (Lunar Eclipse in Sagittarius)

On these dates, there is a shift in your relationship with children, how you express your uniqueness, and what you find pleasurable. You could be drawn to art classes, from which you create beautiful works that give you much pride. A love affair could be particularly romantic, with a touch of glamour and adventurousness. Warm feelings are awakened in your heart, which is wide open at these times. Within one month of these three dates, you will know exactly what has changed.

On these dates, the enlightenment tools of Jupiter and Sagittarius help you bring light to your creativity, romance, and relationship with children.

VI. Health, Pets, and Work

July 7, 2009 (Lunar Eclipse in Capricorn)
January 15, 2010 (Solar Eclipse in Capricorn)
June 26, 2010 (Lunar Eclipse in Capricorn)
January 4, 2011 (Solar Eclipse in Capricorn)

Your work, health, and relationships with pets are highlighted by these eclipses. Their repercussions will unravel for a whole month. You are likely to completely reorganize the way you work, restructure your nutrition, and adopt an exercise program that is in harmony with the true needs of your body. A pet could become a teacher, helping you heal at deep levels.

On these dates, the enlightenment tools of Capricorn help you bring light to your health, work, and relationship with pets.

Since January 19, 2007 until January 4, 2009 (Jupiter in Capricorn)

The first week of January ends a period of two years that brought much ease in your employment. You were probably offered greater opportunities for advancement, more travel for your work, and the ability to integrate philosophical and spiritual principles in service to others. This could possibly have been through volunteer work that expanded both your own horizons and those of the people you were involved with. Faith healing could have come into focus either because you benefitted from it or you have discovered that you had that gift.

During this period, the enlightenment tools of Jupiter (Sagittarius) help you bring light to your health, work, and relationship with pets.

Since November 28, 2008 until November 21, 2024 (Pluto in Capricorn)

Your body is undergoing deep transformations at a cellular level. You could be driven to make radical changes in your diet and to dramatically transform the way you dress. During these years, your healing powers are extremely strong. You have the gift of perceiving what hasn't yet declared itself and transmuting it on an energetic level. Where no one thought there would be any hope, you have the ability to perform miracles both on yourself and on others. The power of your spirit is strong enough to help you withstand pain. At work, you are driven by an almost compulsive need to serve. This could lead to an involvement with some advanced technologies that delve deeply into human physiology and awareness.

Until 2024, the enlightenment tools of Pluto (Scorpio) help you bring light to your health and work.

VII. Marriage

January 5, 2009–January 16, 2010 (Jupiter in Aquarius)

In an intimate relationship, common visions bring a beautiful sense of expansion. Your ideals regarding marriage make you bring this institution to a whole different level. Your partner mirrors back to you the best that you see in him/her. If you see him/her with love, he/she will mirror that love back to you. Your faith and optimism are contagious. You and your partner feel like companions walking together on the great adventure of life. Your sharing is both playful and philosophical. Your intimacy encourages each person's freedom to be him/herself. Your enthusiastic desire to connect with people animated by similar ideals could lead to personal fame.

> *During this year, the enlightenment tools of Jupiter (Sagittarius) help you bring light to the sphere of marriage, whether you are attached or not.*

January 26, 2009 (Solar Eclipse in Aquarius)
August 5, 2009 (Lunar Eclipse in Aquarius)

Close relationships are highlighted by these eclipses. If you are still single, you could meet an unusually free spirit with a touch of enchantment who reveals aspects of yourself of which you weren't aware. This is not a relationship that you can lean on but one that strengthens your independence. If you are already married, these eclipses make your commitment more real and comfortable. Close business partnerships are also likely to undergo a shift. People you work with or who no longer share a common vision leave. Others, who are more in line with your goals, come on board and support your efforts. Within one month of these dates, what has changed will become apparent.

> *On these two dates, the enlightenment tools of Aquarius help you bring light to your marriage and close partnerships.*

Since January 2006 until April 19, 2010 (Chiron in Aquarius)
July 20, 2010–February 7, 2011 (Chiron in Aquarius)

During these months, you become aware of relationship patterns that were hindering you. In an intimate relationship, the more generously you share your love, the faster you heal past wounds. If your career involves connecting with audiences, your popularity soars at these times. You relate to people in a magical way that is totally personal in its impersonality. You could also become someone's mentor or meet a great teacher.

During these two periods, the enlightenment tools of Aquarius help you bring light to your marriage.

Since November 28, 1998 until April 3, 2011 (Neptune in Aquarius)
August 4, 2011–February 2, 2012 (Neptune in Aquarius)

Your attunement to the spiritual connection between people could make a marriage with the wrong person extremely difficult. Telepathically tapping into the thoughts of your married partner is not unusual at this time. In a good intimate relationship, you may come to feel as one with your special mate. An ethereal magic infuses that connection with an otherworldly beauty. If that soul link is not forced but is very real, the ease and harmony that naturally flow are very blessed indeed.

During these two periods, the enlightenment tools of Neptune (Pisces) help you bring light to your marriage.

VIII. Sexuality, Joint Finances, and Transformation

Since December 31, 2003 until May 26, 2010 (Uranus in Pisces)
August 13, 2010–March 10, 2011 (Uranus in Pisces)

A vibrant interest in the underlying principles of life, death, and sexuality is deeply freeing. Unusual and unexpected psychic experiences could completely shatter your beliefs and change your perception of reality in such a way as to project you into the unknown. In the light of these exciting new discoveries, your dreams change. Joint money comes unexpectedly through a sudden business opportunity or inheritance.

During these two periods, the enlightenment tools of Uranus (Aquarius) help you bring light to your joint finances and sexuality.

January 17, 2010–June 5, 2010 (Jupiter in Pisces)
September 8, 2010–January 21, 2011 (Jupiter in Pisces)

The investigation of life's and death's mysteries leads to a profound expansion of consciousness. Clairvoyance is usually developed during this transit, as are medium skills. Money from a donation, an inheritance, taxes, or insurance offers you more comfort and frees energy to pursue metaphysical researches.

During these two periods, the enlightenment tools of Jupiter (Sagittarius) help you bring light to joint resources and sexuality.

April 20, 2010–July 19, 2010 (Chiron in Pisces)
February 8, 2011–February 2018 (Chiron in Pisces)

Your sensitivity to deep emotional undercurrents enables you to gain intense insights into the mysteries of life and death. Your healing powers are developing. You are able to transmute inner wounds both in yourself and in others.

During these two periods, the enlightenment tools of Pisces help you bring light to joint resources and sexuality.

April 4, 2011–August 3, 2011 (Neptune in Pisces)
February 3, 2012–January 27, 2026 (Neptune in Pisces)

Joint resources could be nebulous, yet money seems to come to you as you need it. Your awareness of higher planes of consciousness is so intense that your sense of being a separate entity dissolves. You may feel a oneness with all that is. Sexuality takes on an almost transcendent tone. Lovemaking is no longer a one-body, one-chakra encounter, but a multibody, multichakra energetic fusion. You are able to reach heights of ecstasy that project you into a meditative state. The physical becomes the vehicle for the metaphysical. Because these shifts occur over many years, you may not be able to define what has changed until much later.

During these two periods, the enlightenment tools of Neptune (Pisces) help you bring light to your joint resources and sexuality.

IX. Long-Distance Travel, Philosophy, and Religion

June 6, 2010–September 7, 2010 (Jupiter in Aries)
January 22, 2011–June 4, 2011 (Jupiter in Aries)

Long-distance travel brings many blessings and enrichments. Contact with foreigners and other cultures greatly expands your consciousness. You are able to relate the meaning of your personal existence to the grander scheme of things. You could feel inspired to write, lecture, or create an organization that helps others connect more clearly to their higher selves. As a role model of absolute integrity, you are likely to support legal reforms and fight for worthy social causes.

During these two periods, the enlightenment tools of Jupiter (Sagittarius) help you bring light to your long-distance travels and philosophy of life.

May 27, 2010–August 13, 2010 (Uranus in Aries)
March 11, 2011–March 6, 2019 (Uranus in Aries)

Trips are embarked upon on the spur of the moment. Even if you are going very far, take only a few items with you. Many exciting adventures await you in that locality. To freely embrace the experience, you need to be as unencumbered as possible. You could adopt the lifestyle of the culture you are in as your own, and as a result feel a freedom that you have never known. Unusual encounters with conscious people—those who have already reached enlightenment—help you understand how to develop your own mastery.

During these two periods, the enlightenment tools of Uranus (Aquarius) help you bring light to your long-distance travels and philosophy of life.

X. CAREER

June 4, 2011–June 10, 2012 (Jupiter in Taurus)

Being at the right place at the right time, you attract lucrative professional opportunities effortlessly. Luck accompanies your every step, opening greater and wider horizons to you, many of which are connected to other countries. Acting, politics, the law, teaching, and publishing are all enhanced by this transit. You find yourself wanting to give back to society as a result of the success you are enjoying. Your awareness of what money and generosity of spirit can change is profound.

Between June 2011 and June 2012, the enlightenment tools of Jupiter (Sagittarius) help you bring light to your career.

XI. FRIENDSHIPS

December 21, 2010 (Lunar Eclipse in Gemini)
June 1, 2011 (Solar Eclipse in Gemini)
December 10, 2011 (Lunar Eclipse in Gemini)
May 20, 2012 (Solar Eclipse in Gemini)
November 28, 2012 (Lunar Eclipse in Gemini)

Great changes are happening in the area of friendships. Mere acquaintances dissolve, while exciting, varied, interesting, mentally stimulating, and fun new relationships develop. The exchanges you have with those people enliven your spirit, remind you of your visions, and provide you with the tools necessary to manifest your goals. What has shifted will be evident within a month of each of these five eclipse dates.

During all these eclipses, the enlightenment tools of Mercury (Gemini) help you bring light to your friendships and long-term goals.

June 11, 2012–June 26, 2013 (Jupiter in Gemini)

You enjoy beneficial friendships with people from many countries and varied philosophical outlooks. They support the manifestation of your long-term dreams. During this year, you are likely to feel very comfortable in group settings and even to seek community living based on barter. Your friends are positive, enthusiastic, happy people with a broad vision and the faith to make everything come true.

From June 2012 to June 2013, the enlightenment tools of Jupiter (Sagittarius) help you bring light to your friendships.

XII. Subconscious

July 21, 2009 (Solar Eclipse in Cancer)
December 31, 2009 (Lunar Eclipse in Cancer)
July 11, 2010 (Solar Eclipse in Cancer)
July 1, 2011 (Solar Eclipse in Cancer)

Vivid dreams, powerful visions, and clear insights are shifting your awareness of who you really are. Do not fight a need for silence and solitude. They fulfill your soul's requirement for regeneration. You may need to sleep a lot during these times. Your spirit needs to freely float in search of the deeper meaning behind experience. You emerge from these eclipses renewed, with a stronger sense of your inner resources. A spiritual retreat greatly enhances your capacity to communicate directly with your subconscious. You may not be aware of what has changed until about one month following each of these four dates.

On these dates, the enlightenment tools of Cancer and the Moon help you bring light to your subconscious.

2009–2012 for Virgo and/or Virgo Rising

I. Personal Appearance

From the Present until October 28, 2009 (Saturn in Virgo)
April 7, 2010–July 20, 2010 (Saturn in Virgo)

You are completely rebuilding your image of yourself and the impact you have on your environment. These are times of great seriousness, practicality, and focus. You are leaving behind the structures that no longer serve your higher purpose. As you establish solid foundations for a specific project that will increase your social status and bring you more prosperity, you need more silence and solitude to concentrate. Much work is necessary to accomplish these new goals. At these times, your dignity, conscientiousness, responsibility, and self-reliance inspire much respect.

During these two periods, the enlightenment tools of Saturn (Capricorn) help you bring light to your personal appearance and the way you make an impact on your environment.

II. Money

October 29, 2009–April 6, 2010 (Saturn in Libra)
July 21, 2010–October 4, 2012 (Saturn in Libra)

During these three years, you are restructuring your values and personal assets. The financial benefits that stem from your practical work, self-sufficiency, and discipline may be slow in materializing, but they will be both stable and substantial. You are truly understanding what wealth means to you and how you can acquire more prosperity. The more responsible and generous you are in the handling of your resources, the more abundance will flow to you.

During these two periods, the enlightenment tools of Saturn (Capricorn) help you bring light to your finances.

III. Communication

October 5, 2012–September 18, 2015 (Saturn in Scorpio)
November 13, 2012 (Solar Eclipse in Scorpio)

Between 2012 and 2015, the way you communicate becomes very structured. Brothers and sisters, neighbors and cousins could become a source of responsibility. As they ask you to help them, this forces you to deeply examine what binds you to them. Your words have a powerful impact on others. Feeling that what you are sharing has its roots in profound personal experiences, they listen to what you have to say. People you respect and who have minds you admire inspire you to spend more time alone, studying matters of importance. You could emerge as a teacher—one whose ageless wisdom encompasses many cultures and civilizations. On November 13, 2012, this new role will be cemented.

Between October 2012 and September 2015, the enlightenment tools of Saturn (Capricorn) and Scorpio help you bring light to your communications.

IV. Home

June 15, 2011 (Lunar Eclipse in Sagittarius)
November 25, 2011 (Solar Eclipse in Sagittarius)
June 4, 2012 (Lunar Eclipse in Sagittarius)

On these dates, changes occur in your home. You could be drawn to a completely new locality, or you may repair and redecorate your current home. A relationship with a parent could change. Within one month of these three dates, you will know exactly what has shifted.

On these dates, the enlightenment tools of Jupiter and Sagittarius help you bring light to your domestic circumstances.

V. Creativity, Romance, and Children

July 7, 2009 (Lunar Eclipse in Capricorn)
January 15, 2010 (Solar Eclipse in Capricorn)
June 26, 2010 (Lunar Eclipse in Capricorn)
January 4, 2011 (Solar Eclipse in Capricorn)

On these dates, a deeper and more playful involvement is likely to occur in your relationship with children. Hobbies, romance, and creativity are also impacted. These repercussions will unravel for an entire month.

During this month, the enlightenment tools of Capricorn help you bring light to your creativity, romance, hobbies, and relationship with children.

Since January 19, 2007 until January 4, 2009 (Jupiter in Capricorn)

The first week of January ends a period of one year that most likely brought a new romance. In this relationship, you are able to share philosophical insights and enjoy playful and fun relationships with children whose education you expanded. It is a time when you hunger for living life to the fullest and experience all the pleasures that make you more vibrant and happier. Financial speculations lead to many beneficial and lucrative opportunities. As your personal expression is full of joy, your creativity is greatly enhanced, leading to works that both reflect your spiritual understanding and elevate the consciousness of those who seek your art.

During this period, the enlightenment tools of Jupiter (Sagittarius) help you bring light to your creativity.

Since November 28, 2008 until November 21, 2024 (Pluto in Capricorn)

In the next decade, your whole perception of love, pleasure, creativity, and your relationship with children is dramatically changing. It could feel like a symbolic death of what you understood before, leading to a complete regeneration. Love is intense and passionate. Accompanied by a feeling of destiny, it is a deep catalyst for transformation. If you are artistically inclined, your creations express sacredness and the deep mystery of life. There is something magical and compelling in your work that profoundly affects your audiences. The children around you have very unusual talents and special psychic gifts. Their power is striking. They are clear and ageless. They perceive things that defy intellectual understanding. They see through the lies and the hypocrisy of the society we are leaving behind. Through them, you are given a chance to relive your own childhood at a much higher level of consciousness. The more grateful you are, the more uplifting your life will be.

Until 2024, the enlightenment tools of Pluto (Scorpio) help you bring light to your creativity and love affairs, as well as your relationships with children.

VI. Health, Pets, and Work

January 5, 2009–January 16, 2010 (Jupiter in Aquarius)

More than usual, you are likely to be a nutrition and health crusader. As you embrace this change as an enthusiastic advocate of organic foods and holistic health, the conditions of your body greatly improve. You are attracted to yoga and other harmonious forms of exercise. You could discover you have skills for faith and distance healing. A need to serve those less fortunate than yourself is greatly appealing to you. The conditions at work and your relationships with coworkers become freer and more positive.

Between January 2009 and January 2010, the enlightenment tools of Jupiter help you bring light to your work and health.

January 26, 2009 (Solar Eclipse in Aquarius)
August 5, 2009 (Lunar Eclipse in Aquarius)

An inner new birth at a cellular level is awaiting you. At first it could feel like you're going through a form of symbolic death. All the old residues are being released in the form of flus, aches, and tensions. These two eclipses also affect your work, which could undergo a complete reorganization. Within one month of these dates, you will have clarity as to what has changed in your body.

On these two dates, the enlightenment tools of Aquarius help you bring light to your work and health.

Since January 2006 until April 19, 2010 (Chiron in Aquarius)
July 20, 2010–February 7, 2011 (Chiron in Aquarius)

During these months, you are deeply exploring what it means to have a body and how to take good care of it. Your capacity to transmute pain in others develops in spectacular ways. You are likely to utilize the properties of plants, use essential oils, and integrate the power of sound and music in your healings. The otherworldly visions you receive at this time are so clear that they can be applied in a very practical manner. Crafts can also be deeply healing to you and others. As you expect the best in yourself and see the highest in others, miracles occur.

During these two periods, the enlightenment tools of Aquarius help you bring light to your work and health.

Since November 28, 1998 until April 3, 2011 (Neptune in Aquarius)
August 4, 2011–February 2, 2012 (Neptune in Aquarius)

Your body is tuned to higher frequencies. This makes it extremely vulnerable to denser energies, such as pollution, negativity, or irradiated foods. The signals your body sends could be confusing. To heal, it is important that you choose lighter, vegetarian food and rely on alternative medicine such as homeopathy, acupuncture, acupressure, reflexology, or the Bach flower remedies. Color, sound, and crystals are also very powerful ways of returning to balance at this time. During these years, dance, yoga, tai chi, and meditation can also be extremely valuable practices. You are likely to develop very subtle healing energies. Your union with the energies of the universe enables you to channel divine light.

During these two periods, the enlightenment tools of Neptune (Pisces) help you bring light to your health.

VII. Marriage

Since December 31, 2003 until May 26, 2010 (Uranus in Pisces)
August 13, 2010–March 10, 2011 (Uranus in Pisces)

Relationships that have served their purpose and no longer are conducive to higher growth will not pass the test of this transit. You are attracted to dynamic, exciting relationships. They open new doors and introduce you to different friends and interests. If you are single, the person you could be drawn to is likely to be highly unusual, possibly even eccentric, and very freedom-loving. An existing marriage will survive only if it is flexible enough to welcome changes. You need to strike a delicate balance between intimacy and freedom. Too much freedom and you could wonder if you even have a relationship. Too much intimacy and you may feel suffocated. Unusual living arrangements with a love partner are appealing. You could decide to get legally married and yet live in different apartments. Or you may choose to live together but each of you may have a separate room and personal phone line. As you remain an individual within your marriage, you are not tempted to lean on another to complete you. You each become a fully standing pillar, but with a connection through which life can flow.

During these two periods, the enlightenment tools of Uranus (Aquarius) help you bring light to your marriage.

January 17, 2010–June 5, 2010 (Jupiter in Pisces)
September 8, 2010, and January 21, 2011 (Jupiter in Pisces)

Your approach to a deeply committed relationship is enthusiastic and filled with idealistic concepts. As you insist on seeing the best in your significant other, you bring out his/her most positive qualities. In turn, he/she boosts your own self-confidence. Marriage relationships are greatly favored by these transits. If you are still single, you probably won't remain so for very long. Within this period, you are likely to attract either a foreigner or someone with international experience. This learned person has a broad outlook on life and expands your own understanding. Together you are likely to feel like two pilgrims on the same journey to greater meaning and wider horizons. You are also likely to experience increased popularity during these times and possibly come in contact with a greater audience, supportive of who you are and the joy you express.

During these two periods, the enlightenment tools of Jupiter (Sagittarius) help you bring light into your marriage.

April 20, 2010–July 19, 2010 (Chiron in Pisces)
February 8, 2011–February 2019 (Chiron in Pisces)

In your marriage and in close relationships, you strive to create considerable beauty, peace, and harmony. You express unconditional love. You can see your intimate partner as a mentor or spiritual healer. All he/she is doing is mirroring you back to yourself.

During these two periods, the enlightenment tools of Pisces help you bring light to your marriage and close relations.

April 4, 2011–August 3, 2011 (Neptune in Pisces)
February 3, 2012–January 27, 2026 (Neptune in Pisces)

Your relationship to your marriage partner becomes extremely telepathic. You are likely to uncover your soul connection with that person, or, if you are still single, meet your spirit partner. The person you are likely to attract is deeply intuitive and spiritual, maybe also artistic, and certainly unusual in many respects. There is something very enchanted in that relationship. It touches deep vibrational cords in you that echo ancient times—in past incarnations—when you were together. The memories that flood back enable you to retrieve forgotten aspects of your truth and you become more balanced, open in your heart, and, as a result, whole. During these periods, your understanding that we are all one is acute and is reflected in the way you relate to others—with compassion and unconditional love. The shifts that are occurring are so subtle that you may not be able to define what occurred until much later.

During these two periods, the enlightenment tools of Neptune (Pisces) help you bring light to your marriage.

VIII. Sexuality, Joint Finances, and Transformation

June 6, 2010–September 7, 2010 (Jupiter in Aries)
January 22, 2011–June 4, 2011 (Jupiter in Aries)

Your psychic abilities develop greatly during these periods. An ancient wisdom emerges from deep within you, flooding you with serenity. Even in the darkest of darkness, you are able to see the light. Sexuality is likely to be a very special area of transformation. You transcend limitations you didn't know you had. Money shared with others—a business or marriage partner, coming from insurance, taxes, or an inheritance—greatly increases during these times. It offers you a sense of freedom and a chance to travel.

During these two periods, the enlightenment tools of Jupiter (Sagittarius) help you bring light to joint finances and sexuality.

May 27, 2010–August 13, 2010 (Uranus in Aries)
March 11, 2011–March 6, 2019 (Uranus in Aries)

Sudden and unusual shifts in joint finances such as with inheritances or tax-related money create the death of existing conditions and lead to a completely new understanding of the deeper meaning of life. Unexpected psychic phenomena are likely to occur. They are striking enough to break something open in your psyche. Powerful memories from past lives—which are directly relevant to what you are going through now—are reawakened. An unusual sexual relationship could transform your understanding of how your body mirrors your spirit. You are likely to become highly sensitive to the energy exchanges with this person. By being almost scientifically removed from your own experience, you could derive valuable insight into the true nature of sexuality and your own psyche.

During those two periods, the enlightenment tools of Jupiter (Sagittarius) and Uranus (Aquarius) help you bring light to your joint finances and sexuality.

IX. Long-Distance Travel, Philosophy, and Religion

June 4, 2011–June 10, 2012 (Jupiter in Taurus)

Your philosophy of life is positive and expansive. You are drawn to intellectual and spiritual journeys as well as long-distance travels, all of which open you to new ideas. Lecturing, publishing, and university-level education are highly favored by this transit. Your enthusiastic visions for the future inspire many to follow your lead and create a world of joy, openness, and integrity.

Between June 2011 and June 2012, the enlightenment tools of Jupiter (Sagittarius) help you bring light to your long-distance travels, as well as matters related to philosophy and religion.

X. Career

December 21, 2010 (Lunar Eclipse in Gemini)
June 1, 2011 (Solar Eclipse in Gemini)
December 10, 2011 (Lunar Eclipse in Gemini)
May 20, 2012 (Solar Eclipse in Gemini)
November 28, 2012 (Lunar Eclipse in Gemini)

During these dates, exciting new opportunities are unraveling in your career. You are likely to develop new skills and expand in new directions. Your place in society becomes clearer. What has changed will be visible within a month of these eclipse dates.

During all these eclipses, the enlightenment tools of Mercury (Gemini) help you bring light to your career.

June 11, 2012–June 26, 2013 (Jupiter in Gemini)

You are offered many beneficial opportunities in your career. You become a shining member of society who is looked up to by others for guidance and faith. The general recognition and even prestige you are likely to experience at this time necessitate even greater integrity on your part. You must be impeccable in the way you approach business.

From June 2012 to June 2013, the enlightenment tools of Jupiter (Sagittarius) help you bring light to your career.

XI. FRIENDSHIPS

July 21, 2009 (Solar Eclipse in Cancer)
December 31, 2009 (Lunar Eclipse in Cancer)
July 11, 2010 (Solar Eclipse in Cancer)
July 1, 2011 (Solar Eclipse in Cancer)

You experience a surge of creative impulses. Many new, fascinating people are drawn into your life. They open new realms of experience and provide you with more opportunities to share your gifts. Within a month of these four dates, you will know which changes have occurred in your friendships and in your long-term dreams.

On these days, the enlightenment tools of Cancer and the Moon help you bring light to your friendships and long-term dreams.

XII. SUBCONSCIOUS

February 9, 2009 (Lunar Eclipse in Leo)

You are likely to feel a freedom you have never experienced before. Your heart opens to the divine. Within a month of this date, the shift that has occurred in your subconscious will become very real to you.

In February 2009, the enlightenment tools of Leo help you bring light to your subconscious.

2009–2012 FOR LIBRA AND/OR LIBRA RISING

I. PERSONAL APPEARANCE

October 29, 2009–April 6, 2010 (Saturn in Libra)
July 21, 2010–October 4, 2012 (Saturn in Libra)

The image you project is more serious and self-contained. Your reserve and natural authority inspire respect. You are redefining your relationship with your body. A nutritional and exercise program formatted to your needs helps you feel fit and good. You are determining what works in your life and what you have outgrown. This is a time of responsibilities leading to great personal growth.

During these two periods, the enlightenment tools of Saturn (Capricorn) help you bring light to your personal appearance.

II. MONEY

October 5, 2012–September 18, 2015 (Saturn in Scorpio)
November 13, 2012 (Solar Eclipse in Scorpio)

It is important that you reassess your values. Your monetary situation needs to be structured and solid. As you become clear regarding how much you earn and spend, you can make plans for a long-term investment or save money for an important purchase. Your financial wisdom and responsibility are likely to enable you to build wealth that will be enjoyed for many years to come.

Between October 2012 and September 2015, the enlightenment tools of Saturn (Capricorn) and Scorpio help you bring light to your finances.

III. Communication

June 15, 2011 (Lunar Eclipse in Sagittarius)
November 25, 2011 (Solar Eclipse in Sagittarius)
June 4, 2012 (Lunar Eclipse in Sagittarius)

Your interest in deep exchanges with others grows at these times. You seek meaningful conversations and are drawn to serious reading. You could explore a topic you have always been attracted to but never had the time or opportunity to study. This could lead you back to school. Earning a degree that gives you solid credentials seems important. Teaching and writing are both likely activities for you. The people you attract in your daily environment are people you can respect, admire, and learn from. Your mental growth opens exciting new perspectives in your life. Within one month of these three dates, you will know for sure what has changed in your mental approach to life.

On these dates, the enlightenment tools of Jupiter and Sagittarius help you bring light to the way you express yourself and in your relationships with brothers and sisters.

IV. Home

Since January 19, 2007, until January 4, 2009 (Jupiter in Capricorn)

The first week of January ends a period of two years that brought a sense of comfort and security in your domestic circumstances. You could invest in real estate, move, or redecorate your home, which most likely is a place allowing much freedom of movement. It's a place where like-spirited people are able to gather to share their philosophy of life. Your relationship with your parents could be an area of much luck and prosperity at this time.

During this period, the enlightenment tools of Jupiter (Sagittarius) help you bring light to your home.

July 7, 2009 (Lunar Eclipse in Capricorn)
January 15, 2010 (Solar Eclipse in Capricorn)
June 26, 2010 (Lunar Eclipse in Capricorn)
January 4, 2011 (Solar Eclipse in Capricorn)

On these dates, the repercussions of which will unravel for an entire month, you need to reevaluate your domestic circumstances and establish your life on a solid foundation. An opportunity to move could present itself. At the very least, you feel the need to repair, redecorate, or refurnish your home to make it a better reflection of who you have become and what you want to manifest further in your life. A parent could require a deeper involvement on your part. You are likely to research your roots and possibly even dig into your past lives to clear some recurring patterns on your path.

On these dates, the enlightenment tools of Capricorn help you bring light to your home.

November 28, 2008–November 21, 2024 (Pluto in Capricorn)

Profound changes are occurring in your domestic circumstances. Financial, social, or political issues could force you to move. Deep transformations occur within your consciousness, helping you transmute patterns you have experienced lifetime after lifetime. You are able to quickly recognize and neutralize the manipulations, power struggles, or negativity that may occur in your relationship to your parents. You could be attracted to a location near a lake and possibly to a power vortex that is slightly isolated and mysterious. This transit helps you understand what security really is.

Until 2024, the enlightenment tools of Pluto (Scorpio) help you bring light to your domestic circumstances.

V. CREATIVITY, ROMANCE, AND CHILDREN

January 5, 2009–January 16, 2010 (Jupiter in Aquarius)

This year brings much luck to you. Your optimism and joy are contagious. If you are single, your faith and enthusiasm attract a like-spirited romantic partner who either travels a lot, lives in another state, or is a foreigner. Something in that relationship is particularly exciting. Your connection with this person on a sexual and heart level has the potential to bloom into the spiritual realms. This person, on the same journey of evolution as you, shares similar visions. In an existing relationship, romance is renewed and you could enjoy many nights out talking about your beliefs and discovering each other all over again. Your creativity is also greatly enhanced. The spiritual and humanitarian dimensions reflected in your works affect your audience's philosophical outlook. Money is likely to flow abundantly from the art you manifest at this time. Children find you a lot of fun. As you are attentive to encourage their honesty and fearlessness, the time spent in their company is happy and playful.

During this time, the enlightenment tools of Jupiter (Sagittarius) help you bring light to your creativity, romance, hobbies, and relationships to children.

January 26, 2009 (Solar Eclipse in Aquarius)
August 5, 2009 (Lunar Eclipse in Aquarius)

Imbued with emotions, your creativity is childlike and playful. You are reaching out to humanity and connecting with greater and more varied audiences. A new romance could come your way with someone who is unusual, quite free-spirited, and particularly mentally stimulating. As you learn more about this person, you discover much about yourself and are forced to become more self-reliant. The children around you are independent and could reveal some unusual gifts. Very sociable, they appreciate your friendship and the fact that you respect their uniqueness. Within one month of these dates, the changes that have occurred in all these areas will be clearer.

On these two dates, the enlightenment tools of Aquarius help you bring light to your creativity, romance, and relationships to children.

Since January 2006 until April 19, 2010 (Chiron in Aquarius)
July 20, 2010–February 7, 2011 (Chiron in Aquarius)

During these two periods, don't just admire other people's creativity, but value your own. Tremendous healing can flow through the art you manifest at this time. A painting you create could be a portal to other dimensions through which healing flows to the viewer. There is something particularly special in the way you assert your uniqueness. The recognition of your own wound enables you to tap into everyone's suffering and shift that old consciousness. The children around you could turn out to be powerful healers. You could become romantically attracted to someone with an unusual gift. This person has much magnetism in his/her hands and has a deep understanding of the properties of sound and plants. Realize that this person's unusual talents mirror your own.

During these two periods, the enlightenment tools of Aquarius help you bring light to your creativity, romance, and relationships to children.

Since November 28, 1998 until April 3, 2011 (Neptune in Aquarius)
August 4, 2011–February 2, 2012 (Neptune in Aquarius)

During this year, your inspiration is deeply spiritual. A mystical element permeates all your creations. Your sense of your own uniqueness is subtly shifting as you access higher planes of consciousness. You could find yourself attracted to a wise being. Something elusive permeates that connection, which is surrounded by unusual circumstances. Possibly romantic and inspiring, it brings you to a deep understanding of what love really is. This sacred relationship could feel more ethereal than material. There is magic, beauty, and an otherworldliness in that link. A child could adopt you. Although difficult to explain rationally, your soul link is clear to both of you. Music, solitude, and beauty deeply stir your emotions, leading to spontaneous states of meditation.

During these two periods, the enlightenment tools of Neptune (Pisces) help you bring light to your creativity, romance, and relationships to children.

VI. HEALTH, PETS, AND WORK

Since December 31, 2003 until May 26, 2010 (Uranus in Pisces)
August 13, 2010–March 10, 2011 (Uranus in Pisces)

Maintaining a routine could be extremely difficult during these periods. Constant disruptions seem to break the flow of what you had planned, testing your nervous balance. But if you are flexible enough to go with those sudden and unexpected changes, you will realize that the new direction they are leading you into frees you from what may have been limiting your work. Attraction to an uncommon occupation using vibrations, computers, and electricity for healing opens new realms of experimentation. At this time, your body is sensitive to magnetic fields. Cellular phones should not be carried on your person and microwaved food should definitely be banned. Your preferred form of exercise uses modern technology combining traditional, holistic movements. Pilates could be very beneficial.

During these two periods, the enlightenment tools of Uranus (Aquarius) help you bring light to your health and work.

January 17, 2010–June 5, 2010 (Jupiter in Pisces)
September 8, 2010–January 21, 2011 (Jupiter in Pisces)

If you do not fall prey to overindulgence, your health flourishes. Your positive attitude has the capacity to transmute any ailment. Faith healing is also a great possibility—either experienced or offered to another. Conditions at work are expansive. Many new doors open. Your relationships with coworkers are positive. A pet could be a great teacher and bring much joy into your life. Athletic activities are also favored with the ability to surpass previous records by training both your mind and your body.

During these two periods, the enlightenment tools of Jupiter (Sagittarius) help you bring light to your health, work, and relationship to pets.

April 20, 2010–July 19, 2010 (Chiron in Pisces)
February 8, 2011–February 2019 (Chiron in Pisces)

Your sensitivity to other people's suffering and your capacity to see the best in yourself and in others bring out magic even in those who feel separated from their own light. Craft-creating could be very soothing. As your own healing talents develop, you are led to exploring holistic cures.

During these two periods, the enlightenment tools of Pisces help you bring light to your health.

April 4, 2011–August 3, 2011 (Neptune in Pisces)
February 3, 2012–January 27, 2026 (Neptune in Pisces)

During these periods, your body is shifting at a cellular level. Its sensitivity to environmental conditions is so finely tuned that if you listen to its natural wisdom, you will be guided toward the optimal foods for your well-being. As your body is getting ready to integrate more and more light, what is denser is being gradually removed. This could cause some discomfort, which is best treated holistically (homeopathy, acupuncture, reflexology, massage, flower essences, acupressure). It is likely that you will want to wear organic fibers and practice a form of exercise in harmony with your natural energies, such as tai chi or yoga. You could also be drawn to work in the healing arts, including color, sound, crystals, and flower essences. The shifts that are occurring in your work and body are so subtle that you may not be able to define them until much later.

During these months, the enlightenment tools of Neptune (Pisces) help you bring light to your health.

VII. Marriage

June 6, 2010–September 7, 2010 (Jupiter in Aries)
January 22, 2011–June 4, 2011 (Jupiter in Aries)

Marriage brings much happiness either because you renew your vows with an existing partner or because you meet a foreigner or someone who is well traveled. This person's faith in life, enthusiasm, and infectious open-mindedness stimulates your own. This relationship goes well beyond a simple romantic attraction. There is much to be gained from this connection. It expands your understanding of the evolutionary journey marriage is, both philosophically and spiritually.

During these two periods, the enlightenment tools of Jupiter (Sagittarius) help you bring light to your marriage.

May 27, 2010–August 13, 2010 (Uranus in Aries)
March 11, 2011–March 6, 2019 (Uranus in Aries)

A meaningful relationship requires that you balance intimacy and freedom. This could lead to an unusual form of marriage. You could live together but each maintain your own bedroom and telephone line, or you may choose to marry but live in separate apartments. It is important that you maintain a sense of your own identity and that you do not sacrifice friendships or interests that are important to you. The freer you feel, the more committed you will be. It is only between two beings, each complete in his or her own right, that living love can flow. You are creating a rewarding new relationship paradigm, one that elevates each person through togetherness while respecting each other's uniqueness.

During those two periods, the enlightenment tools of Uranus (Aquarius) help you bring light to your marriage.

VIII. Sexuality, Joint Finances, and Transformation

June 4, 2011–June 10, 2012 (Jupiter in Taurus)

Positive circumstances surround joint finances, either because you benefit from an inheritance, enter a positive business association, receive the financial support you need from a bank, or your marriage partner has more money at his/her disposal to share with you. Psychic experiences are particularly transformative at this time. Through knowledge acquired in past incarnations, you are given profound insights into the mysteries of life, death, and the afterlife. Your clairvoyance could awaken at this time, connecting you with Earth spirits and bringing true healing to your soul. As you explore the more philosophical and spiritual aspects of physical intimacy, sexuality becomes also an area of deep adventurousness.

Between June 2011 and June 2012, the enlightenment tools of Jupiter (Sagittarius) help you bring light to your joint resources and sexuality.

IX. Long-Distance Travel, Philosophy, and Religion

December 21, 2010 (Lunar Eclipse in Gemini)
June 1, 2011 (Solar Eclipse in Gemini)
December 10, 2011 (Lunar Eclipse in Gemini)
May 20, 2012 (Solar Eclipse in Gemini)
November 28, 2012 (Lunar Eclipse in Gemini)

Travel brings transformation. As you immerse yourself in another culture, your philosophy of life transforms. You could meet wise beings mirroring your own depths. Your connection to your higher self becomes clearer. Writing and teaching are attractive. You are exposed to new concepts that expand your mental and spiritual horizons. Be spiritually innovative and adventurous. It's highly encouraged that you break free from any limits that may have held you back in a more traditional frame of reference. What has changed will be visible within a month of these eclipse dates.

During all these eclipse dates, the enlightenment tools of Mercury (Gemini) help you bring light to your long-distance trips, philosophy of life, and religion.

June 11, 2012–June 26, 2013 (Jupiter in Gemini)

During this year, long-distance travel is particularly beneficial. You are likely to immerse yourself in another culture and meet foreigners, international travelers, or philosophers who open you to higher realms of consciousness and help you connect deeper to your true self. Writing, teaching, and pursuing higher education expand your relationship to the divine.

From June 2012 to June 2013, the enlightenment tools of Jupiter (Sagittarius) help you bring light to your long-distance trips and philosophy of life.

X. Career

July 21, 2009 (Solar Eclipse in Cancer)
December 31, 2009 (Lunar Eclipse in Cancer)
July 11, 2010 (Solar Eclipse in Cancer)
July 1, 2011 (Solar Eclipse in Cancer)

Career opportunities give you a chance to embark on a whole new professional adventure. Even if your position in society had been enjoyable until now, some readjustments bring you closer to the fulfillment of your long-term ambitions. You could be given more responsibilities. If your profession involves contact with the public, your popularity now expands. Within one month of these four dates, you will know exactly what has changed.

On these dates, the enlightenment tools of Cancer and the Moon help you bring light to your career.

XI. Friendships

February 9, 2009 (Lunar Eclipse in Leo)

Solid relationships that have proven themselves throughout the years are unlikely to be affected by this eclipse. Mere acquaintances could dissolve, allowing new connections to be established with glamorous, powerful, generous, and possibly wealthy people. Their warmth and sunny dispositions are inspiring you to explore your own long-term dreams and goals. Within a month of this date, you will know exactly what has changed in your friendships.

In February 2009, the enlightenment tools of Leo help you bring light to your friendships.

XII. Subconscious

Since September 3, 2007 until October 28, 2009 (Saturn in Virgo)
April 7, 2010–July 20, 2010 (Saturn in Virgo)

Isolation may feel very soothing. These are beautiful times to go within and spend time on your own, reassessing the manner in which you have reached your goals. As you are ending one phase of your life and about to begin another, solitude and silence enable you to reinvent yourself. A spiritual retreat may feel very appealing to you. As you become conscious of previously hidden aspects of your psyche, shamanistic work is particularly beneficial. You can now erase outgrown programs and reach this state of ultimate peace, the starting point of unlimited possibilities.

During these two periods, the enlightenment tools of Saturn (Capricorn) help you bring light to your subconscious.

I. PERSONAL APPEARANCE

October 5, 2012–September 18, 2015 (Saturn in Scorpio)
November 13, 2012 (Solar Eclipse in Scorpio)

The image you project is one of authority. The seriousness of your personal appearance inspires respect in others—you could dress more formally with a preference for earthy colors. You are focused, efficient, and more reserved. The restructuring of your approach to life also includes a more healthy attitude toward diet and exercise. You could lose weight much more easily than usual.

Between October 2012 and September 2015, the enlightenment tools of Saturn (Capricorn) and Scorpio help you bring light to your personal appearance.

II. MONEY

June 15, 2011 (Lunar Eclipse in Sagittarius)
November 25, 2011 (Solar Eclipse in Sagittarius)
June 4, 2012 (Lunar Eclipse in Sagittarius)

Your financial situation changes for the better. A new source of income could arise. What made you feel safe is transforming. It is important that you reassess what you value. Within one month of these three dates, you will know exactly what has changed in your relationship to money.

On these dates, the enlightenment tools of Jupiter and Sagittarius help you bring light to your finances.

III. COMMUNICATION

Since January 19, 2007 until January 4, 2009 (Jupiter in Capricorn)

The first week of January ends a period of two years that brought tremendous mental expansions. You could meet philosophers, religious

THE MAYAN
CALENDAR AND
THE SIGNS

331

people, foreigners, or international travelers who show you different ways of thinking while exposing you to diverse cultures and other languages. Reading and studying feel like adventures into the unknown, opening many exciting new doors. Teaching and writing are enhanced by this transit. Short trips help reinvent your daily routine.

During this period, the enlightenment tools of Jupiter (Sagittarius) help you bring light to your communications.

July 7, 2009 (Lunar Eclipse in Capricorn)
January 15, 2010 (Solar Eclipse in Capricorn)
June 26, 2010 (Lunar Eclipse in Capricorn)
January 4, 2011 (Solar Eclipse in Capricorn)

On these dates, the repercussions of which will unravel for a whole month, the way you think, express your ideas, and learn are shifting. You may be tempted to go back to school to earn a degree and interact with people who have minds you respect. The new study you get involved with fills gaps in your education. Serious reading, lecturing, writing, and teaching are favored at this time. You are also able to develop a deeper connection with your brothers, sisters, cousins, and/or neighbors.

On these dates, the enlightenment tools of Capricorn help you bring light to your communications.

Since November 28, 2008 until November 21, 2024 (Pluto in Capricorn)

In the next decade your opinions are intense. Black and white, they leave no room for gray zones. You are courageous and direct in the way you express your ideas. Your knowingness comes from within. Your insights are sharp and clear, and the impact of your words on others is profound. Your ability to X-ray any situation and person could leave people feeling a little naked. Your opinions are valued by those who are not afraid of facing the truth. A mystical element permeates your verbal and written exchanges. It destroys old mental concepts and gives birth to new concepts. Your relationships with siblings and neighbors are passionate and transformative. In your daily environment, you attract powerful people who mirror your own charisma. Your magic is tangible and operates miracles on those who are strong enough to listen. With an eagle stare, you free them from bondages they might not have even suspected.

Until 2024, the enlightenment tools of Pluto (Scorpio) help you bring light to your mental exchanges with others.

IV. Home

January 5, 2009–January 16, 2010 (Jupiter in Aquarius)

A need to live more spaciously leads to either a reorganization of your home (adding a guesthouse or redecorating) or a complete relocation. You are likely to choose a place with a view and enough room to make you feel comfortable and happy. Your relationship with a parent expands your horizons, revealing aspects of yourself of which you weren't aware. A past life regression could completely shift ideas you took for granted without having given them much thought. A complete renewal of consciousness solidifies the foundation of your life.

During this period, the enlightenment tools of Jupiter (Sagittarius) help you bring light to your domestic circumstances.

January 26, 2009 (Solar Eclipse in Aquarius)
August 5, 2009 (Lunar Eclipse in Aquarius)

You could either relocate or reorganize your home. You need to be in a place where you can interact with many exciting and free-spirited people. Coming from varied horizons, they introduce you to different groups and new activities. As you examine all the values you take for granted, this is a great time to reassess your relationship with your parents and remember your childhood. You could also discover something in your past lives or your family tree that helps you better understand the foundation of your own life. Within one month of these dates, the changes that will have occurred in your domestic circumstances will be clear.

On these two dates, the enlightenment tools of Aquarius help you bring light to your domestic circumstances.

Since January 2006 until April 19, 2010 (Chiron in Aquarius)
July 20, 2010–February 7, 2011 (Chiron in Aquarius)

During these periods, you perceive the whole of humanity as being your extended family. Your need to nurture others is deeply soothing. As you help others, your own soul gets healed.

During these two periods, the enlightenment tools of Aquarius help you bring light to your domestic circumstances.

Since November 28, 1998 until April 3, 2011 (Neptune in Aquarius)
August 4, 2011–February 2, 2012 (Neptune in Aquarius)

During these years, you are likely to turn your home into a sanctuary—a place of spiritual retreat, peace, and harmony. You could simplify the decoration to a strict minimum and surround yourself with only objects of great beauty and spiritual meaning. Subtle psychic experiences could occur in your house or apartment, making you feel very dreamy. Out of respect for the magic of the energies created, you may wish to invite no one to your private space. You could also decide to completely dissolve having a home so that you can find your own truth, separate from the security of having a stable roof over your head. You also discover your deeper soul connections with family members, particularly your parents.

During these two periods, the enlightenment tools of Neptune (Pisces) help you bring light to your domestic circumstances.

V. CREATIVITY, ROMANCE, AND CHILDREN

Since December 31, 2007 until May 26, 2010 (Uranus in Pisces)
August 13, 2010–March 10, 2011 (Uranus in Pisces)

The art you create at this time embraces paradoxes and exposes bizarre aspects of society. As it shocks, it also awakens consciousness, and your audience realizes we have been blind, accepting that which is not in alignment with nature's laws. Romance is unusual and occurs in the most unexpected manner. You could be attracted to someone who is from a completely different background than yours and with whom there is a significant age difference (usually someone younger). Children are free-spirited and rebellious. They show definite signs of genius and don't fit at all into the normal schooling system, which is too slow and limiting for their fast understanding. They readily grasp the connection between seemingly unrelated concepts and could display unusual mental skills such as a capacity for quantum reading.

> *During these two periods, the enlightenment tools of Uranus (Aquarius) help you bring light to your creativity, romance, and relationships with children.*

January 17, 2010–June 5, 2010 (Jupiter in Pisces)
September 8, 2010–January 21, 2011 (Jupiter in Pisces)

You assert yourself with fearlessness, confidence, greater optimism, and joy. Feeling that you have nothing to hide or lose, you are very true to yourself. In turn, your integrity and honesty help improve your romantic relationships and your connections with children. Because others feel how real you are, they are given license to be themselves. Your creativity flows effortlessly. Art created at this time is glamorous and adventurous with a philosophical dimension, expanding the mental and spiritual horizons of the viewer. Your works could be particularly lucrative. Professional artists could be offered exhibits or overseas contracts. If you are still single, a romance with a foreigner or international traveler is likely to happen. This person is warm, positive, and philosophical, probably with a university degree and an encyclopedic mind. While generous, fun, and adventurous, this is not someone you can lean on. The more independent, spontaneous, and open-minded you are, the more exciting and freeing this relationship will prove to be.

During these two periods, the enlightenment tools of Jupiter (Sagittarius) help you bring light to your romances, creativity, hobbies, and relationships with children.

April 20, 2010–July 19, 2010 (Chiron in Pisces)
February 8, 2011–February 2019 (Chiron in Pisces)

If you are single, there is the possibility of a new romance with a spiritual mentor, awakening you to your own gifts with sound, plants, and crystals. As you excitedly commit to your own creativity, without any attachment or traditional expectations, your playfulness stirs other people's emotions, bringing the best out of them. The children around you are likely to reveal special healing gifts. Through their sensitivity to suffering as well as your own, a deep healing occurs.

During these two periods, the enlightenment tools of Pisces help you bring light to your creativity, romance, and relationship with children.

April 4, 2011–August 3, 2011 (Neptune in Pisces)
February 3, 2012–January 27, 2006 (Neptune in Pisces)

If you are in any way artistically inclined, you experience creation at its purest. Inspiration is imbued with a mystical quality. It flows from the divine. The expression of your uniqueness is subtly changing, reconnecting you to your truth. The children around you are spiritually advanced and artistically gifted. Because they are psychically clear, the purity of their innocence enables them to see through illusions, retrieving the beauty of every situation. Through unusual circumstances, you could also become romantically involved with a mystical artist who brings enchantment to life and helps you experience unconditional love. The shifts that are occurring are so subtle that you may not be able to define them until much later.

During these two periods, the enlightenment tools of Neptune (Pisces) help you bring light to your creativity and relationships with children.

VI. Health, Pets, and Work

June 6, 2010–September 7, 2010 (Jupiter in Aries)
January 22, 2011–June 4, 2011 (Jupiter in Aries)

If you don't fall prey to excesses of any sort, your health is excellent. The power of your mind aligns with your body's vitality to expand your athletic skills. Team sports lead to victory. Your relationships with co-workers are beneficial. So is your connection to a small being. This pet brings much joy into your life while acting as a benevolent yet wise teacher. If you are careful not to scatter your energies in too many directions at once, work opportunities are rewarding.

During this period, the enlightenment tools of Jupiter (Sagittarius) help you bring light to your work and health, and relationship with pets.

May 27, 2010–August 14, 2010 (Uranus in Aries)
March 11, 2011–March 6, 2019 (Uranus in Aries)

Any boredom or routine experienced in your work is likely to be disrupted during these periods. Sudden changes of work enable you to better express your uniqueness. Technology, science, electronics, or unusual therapies are attractive to you now. Therapies using vibration and positive magnetic fields are very effective with the shifts your body is going through. Healing also comes from extraterrestrial sources. A reconnection of more strands of your DNA is now quite possible. You could, during your sleep, be introduced to a brilliant invention that you are able to materialize during your waking hours.

During these two periods, the enlightenment tools of Uranus (Aquarius) help you bring light to your health.

VII. Marriage

June 4, 2011–June 10, 2012 (Jupiter in Taurus)

Marriage is extremely beneficial during this year. If you are already committed, this transit brings a tremendous expansion of consciousness with your partner and helps you discover dimensions of your interconnection that go well beyond a romantic and sexual attraction. Companions on the same spiritual journey led by a common vision, you could find much joy in traveling together and exploring new horizons. If you are still single, you are likely to establish a new relationship with either a foreigner or an international traveler, someone whose mind and knowledge are fascinating. This person is also warm, positive, and expansive, usually quite sexual, adventurous, and playful, yet with a philosophical depth that is particularly enticing. You have much to learn from this person who renews your faith in life.

Between June 2011 and June 2012, the enlightenment tools of Jupiter (Sagittarius) help you bring light to your marriage.

VIII. Sexuality, Joint Finances, and Transformation

December 21, 2010 (Lunar Eclipse in Gemini)
June 1, 2011 (Solar Eclipse in Gemini)
December 10, 2011 (Lunar Eclipse in Gemini)
May 20, 2012 (Solar Eclipse in Gemini)
November 28, 2012 (Lunar Eclipse in Gemini)

A new understanding of sexuality is likely to emerge during these dates. You become interested in Kundalini yoga or the study of tantric practices. These eclipses enable you to retrieve wisdoms acquired in past lives' initiations. As you access deeper knowledge, your perceptions also become more psychic and attuned to the mysteries of life, death, and transformation. Joint resources could become more diversified. What has changed will be visible within a month of these eclipse dates.

During all these eclipses, the enlightenment tools of Mercury (Gemini) help you bring light to your joint resources.

June 11, 2012–June 26, 2013 (Jupiter in Gemini)

Abundant financial help comes to you effortlessly. Whether through a positive business association, your marriage partner, insurance, a tax return, or a bank, you can count on being supported in your endeavors. Your clairvoyance develops dramatically, giving you insights into the mysteries of life, death, and the afterlife. Through a deep understanding of complex emotional patterns, profound healing occurs.

From June 2012 to June 2013, the enlightenment tools of Jupiter (Sagittarius) help you bring light to joint finances and sexuality.

IX. Long-Distance Travel, Philosophy, and Religion

July 21, 2009 (Solar Eclipse in Cancer)
December 31, 2009 (Lunar Eclipse in Cancer)
July 11, 2010 (Solar Eclipse in Cancer)
July 1, 2011 (Solar Eclipse in Cancer)

A long-distance trip could completely change your understanding of life and your connection to your higher self. A literal or symbolic spiritual journey could lead you into the unknown, where a wise being is awaiting you. You have much to learn from that encounter and from contact with a foreign culture. Conference speaking, attending a lecture, studying a philosophy book, encountering a religion that connects you with your own heart, publishing, and writing are all beneficial activities during these eclipses. A departure from your normal routine brings an exciting new friendship. Within a month of these four dates, you will know exactly what has changed.

On these dates, the enlightenment tools of Cancer and the Moon help you bring light to long-distance travel, philosophy, and religion.

X. Career

February 9, 2009 (Lunar Eclipse in Leo)

If you are a public figure or if you're aspiring to become one, this transit brings increased popularity. There is definitely more glamour in the way you relate to audiences. A career that you didn't have your heart totally into is likely to dissolve, allowing you to redefine your professional path and start a new vocation that makes your soul soar. The playfulness and childlike approach to your social ambitions attract much support along the way. Within a month of this date, much will have changed for the better in your career and long-term goals.

In February 2009, the enlightenment tools of Leo help you bring light to your career.

XI. Friendships

Since September 3, 2007 until October 28, 2009 (Saturn in Virgo)
April 7, 2010–July 20, 2010 (Saturn in Virgo)

You may enjoy fewer friendships, but they are more authentic. The people you wish to spend time with are those you respect and admire for having proven themselves through thick and thin. You are also restructuring your long-term dreams and goals. You could become the leader of some group activity or of an association with a humanitarian purpose. Joining forces with like-spirited people brings a vision for the betterment of mankind into manifestation.

During these two periods, the enlightenment tools of Saturn (Capricorn) help you bring light to your friendships.

XII. Subconscious

October 29, 2009–April 6, 2010 (Saturn in Libra)
July 21, 2010–October 4, 2012 (Saturn in Libra)

Your subconscious has many messages for you. Keeping a pad and paper next to your bed or starting a dream journal is a good idea. The exploration of the symbols coming up in dreamtime lead to a personal journey into the unknown. A spiritual retreat unearths things within you that were previously hidden. Time spent in silence and isolation is highly beneficial. Going deeper within yourself helps you figure out what works in your life and what no longer does. This marks the end of one dimension of your life and the beginning of a whole new version of your truth.

During these two periods, the enlightenment tools of Saturn (Capricorn) help you bring light to your subconscious.

2009–2012 for Sagittarius and/or Sagittarius Rising

I. Personal Appearance

June 15, 2011 (Lunar Eclipse in Sagittarius)
November 25, 2011 (Solar Eclipse in Sagittarius)
June 4, 2012 (Lunar Eclipse in Sagittarius)

You are likely to completely reinvent your personal appearance: change your style, get a new haircut, have a makeover. As you are more focused on your goals, your general approach to life becomes more adventurous, optimistic, and vibrant. Within one month of these three dates, you will know exactly what has changed in your image of yourself and the impact you make on others.

On these dates, the enlightenment tools of Jupiter and Sagittarius help you bring light to your personal appearance.

II. Money

Since January 19, 2007 until January 4, 2009 (Jupiter in Capricorn)

The first week of January ends a period of two years that brought much financial abundance. You established lucrative business partnerships, invested your money wisely, and put your resources to good use, reaping many positive results. You most possibly contributed to charitable causes and the good fortune you shared with others comes back to you a thousandfold. The feeling that life is abundant on every level accompanied this easy and expansive transit.

> *During this period, the enlightenment tools of Jupiter (Sagittarius) help you bring light to your finances.*

July 7, 2009 (Lunar Eclipse in Capricorn)
January 15, 2010 (Solar Eclipse in Capricorn)
June 26, 2010 (Lunar Eclipse in Capricorn)
January 4, 2011 (Solar Eclipse in Capricorn)

Whether it is the development of a new source of income or the restructuring of your existing resources, changes are occurring in your finances. This is an excellent day to know exactly how much money you have at your disposal, establish a solid budget, and save in investments for the future. What is set in motion today will become clearer within a month.

> *On these dates, the enlightenment tools of Capricorn help you bring light to your finances.*

Since November 28, 2008 until November 21, 2024 (Pluto in Capricorn)

Your relationship with money is shifting. If you have been too materialistic, your financial resources will be taken away until you transform your values. Once you truly understand what money means to you, what you can do with it for yourself and for other people, you will be in a position to start attracting huge amounts of wealth. However, for that to happen, you must absolutely have pure intentions. This innocence can only be achieved by realizing that money is really an energy that cannot be possessed or held on to, but needs to flow freely.

Until 2024, the enlightenment tools of Pluto (Scorpio) help you bring light to your finances.

III. Communication

January 5, 2009–January 16, 2010 (Jupiter in Aquarius)

In your community, you are known to be the defender of worthy causes. Your mind is open and your attitude is positive and generous. Your daily environment brings many opportunities for growth and expansion that help you go beyond previous limitations and discover many exciting ideas. Your relationships with your siblings and neighbors are beneficial, both philosophically and financially. Traveling, teaching, writing, and learning trigger exciting new insights.

During this period, the enlightenment tools of Jupiter (Sagittarius) help you bring light to your communications.

January 26, 2009 (Solar Eclipse in Aquarius)
August 5, 2009 (Lunar Eclipse in Aquarius)

Learning, teaching, and short-distance travels are enhanced by these two eclipses, bringing beneficial shifts to your consciousness. A class providing positive, practical information enhances your existing skills and bridges gaps in your knowledge. Unusual people who open you to a new level of understanding are attracted to your environment. Relationships with siblings and neighbors shift, revealing your true connection to them. Within one month of these dates, the changes that have occurred in your communications and immediate environment will be clear.

On these two dates, the enlightenment tools of Aquarius help you bring light to your communications.

Since January 2006 until April 19, 2010 (Chiron in Aquarius)
July 20, 2010–February 7, 2011 (Chiron in Aquarius)

Healing, learning, and communication enrich each other. You could be asked to write about health or you may feel the need to develop a specific skill to enhance your healing abilities. The mastery you acquire enables you to elevate the consciousness of the people you regularly meet to yet another level.

During these two periods, the enlightenment tools of Aquarius help you bring light to your communications.

Since November 28, 2008 until April 3, 2011 (Neptune in Aquarius)
August 4, 2011–February 2, 2012 (Neptune in Aquarius)

During these periods, you express yourself in a highly spiritualized manner. Channeling, telepathy, and clairaudience are greatly enhanced. Your heightened sensitivity to vibration could enable you to hear what people are thinking. Yoga, meditation, spending time by the ocean, and listening to music are all very soothing to your soul. You could develop artistic abilities, take an interest in photography or film, or start painting, composing music, writing poems, acting, or dancing. The people you encounter in your daily environment have a strong mystical dimension. Your relationships with siblings and neighbors are infused with a sense of otherworldliness.

During these two periods, the enlightenment tools of Neptune (Pisces) help you bring light to your communications.

IV. Home

Since December 31, 2007 until May 26, 2010 (Uranus in Pisces)
August 13, 2010–March 10, 2011 (Uranus in Pisces)

Whatever you took for granted, binding you to old ways of being and thinking, is shaken by this transit. Breakthroughs in consciousness free you from inherited conditionings that held you from your divine truth. The whole basis on which your life was established now shifts. A move at these times is not simply a change of residence but a break from the past, giving you a chance to completely recreate your personal foundation.

During these two periods, the enlightenment tools of Uranus (Aquarius) help you bring light to your domestic circumstances.

January 17, 2010–June 5, 2010 (Jupiter in Pisces)
September 8, 2010–January 21, 2011 (Jupiter in Pisces)

The foundation of your life is healthy and secure. You feel settled, comfortable, and happy within yourself. Acquiring land, building an extension to your house, redecorating your living quarters, or simply inviting your friends over for dinners, around which you share deep insights, bring a sense of expansion. Your parents' influence is beneficial both spiritually and financially. You feel at peace with them and they, in turn, enrich your understanding of your own childhood.

During these two periods, the enlightenment tools of Jupiter (Sagittarius) help you bring light into your domestic circumstances.

April 20, 2010–July 19, 2010 (Chiron in Pisces)
February 8, 2011–February 2019 (Chiron in Pisces)

The development of your healing abilities increases your sensitivity to others. As you tap into what you as an individual share with the whole of humanity, you discover your true spiritual roots. The way you understand how we each belong to the greater whole brings enlightenment to many.

During these two periods, the enlightenment tools of Pisces help you bring light to your domestic circumstances.

April 4, 2011–August 3, 2011 (Neptune in Pisces)
February 3, 2012–January 27, 2026 (Neptune in Pisces)

You either see your home as a sanctuary, a place of spiritual retreat filled with peace, magic, and beauty, or your awareness that the whole Earth is your home makes it difficult to settle in just one specific location. As layers and layers of who you have been in past lives come to the surface, your true roots and spiritual ancestry become much clearer. Your psychic abilities expand. The shifts that are occurring are so subtle and over such a long period of time that you may not be able to define what has changed until much later.

During these two periods, the enlightenment tools of Neptune (Pisces) help you bring light to your domestic circumstances.

V. Creativity, Romance, and Children

June 6, 2010–September 7, 2010 (Jupiter in Aries)
January 22, 2011–June 4, 2011 (Jupiter in Aries)

Your creative intelligence is at its height. Any work of art you manifest at this time has a philosophical dimension and, on a material level, could provide you with a great source of income. You could also become romantically involved with a foreigner or someone who travels a lot, whose zest for life and generosity enrich you on many levels. Way beyond candlelit dinners, the connection with this person reaches into mutually shared spiritual realms. Your fearlessness in revealing your truth puts others at ease. Your self-confidence is at an all-time high. Your relationships with children are positive and adventurous. As you support their sense of integrity, you also teach them the courage to be themselves.

The enlightenment tools of Jupiter (Sagittarius) help you bring light to your creativity, romance, and relationships with children.

May 27, 2010–August 13, 2010 (Uranus in Aries)
March 11, 2011–March 6, 2019 (Uranus in Aries)

Unusual forms of self-expression feel attractive to you. Your social life expands considerably during these times, exposing you to a patchwork of very different personalities walking to the beat of their own drummer and coming from unusual backgrounds. A romantic interest could develop with one or several of them, possibly short-lived but very freeing. Children are particularly independent at these times, even acting rebelliously. They also show signs of genius and their intuition could be so sharp that they come up with sudden answers to your questions with a clarity that stuns you.

During these two periods, the enlightenment tools of Uranus (Aquarius) help you bring light to your creativity, romance, and relationships with children.

VI. Health, Pets, and Work

June 4, 2011–June 10, 2012 (Jupiter in Taurus)

Your work could involve travel, the law, publishing, higher education, or religion. Your optimistic and positive attitude attracts many beneficial opportunities for growth and expansion, and enlists the support and help of colleagues who want you to succeed. In a wish to share your good fortune with those less privileged, you may feel attracted to volunteer work. Provided that you do not fall prey to any excess, your health flourishes under this transit.

Between June 2011 and June 2012, the enlightenment tools of Jupiter (Sagittarius) help you bring light to your health.

VII. Marriage

December 21, 2010 (Lunar Eclipse in Gemini)
June 1, 2011 (Solar Eclipse in Gemini)
December 10, 2011 (Lunar Eclipse in Gemini)
May 20, 2012 (Solar Eclipse in Gemini)
November 28, 2012 (Lunar Eclipse in Gemini)

A good relationship grows stronger and a challenging one may come to an end. If you are single, you are likely to meet a romantic interest who is youthful, witty, and with varied interests. As you recognize inner blocks to intimacy, you are able to resolve outgrown relationship patterns. Finding what vision or common goal you share with the person in your life is important at these times. What has really changed in the area of intimate relationships becomes visible within a month of these eclipse dates.

> *On all these eclipses, the enlightenment tools of Mercury (Gemini) help you bring light to your marriage.*

June 11, 2012–June 26, 2013 (Jupiter in Gemini)

You experience expansion, growth, and freedom in a committed relationship. Your marriage partner is likely to be a jovial person, well established, positive, and open-minded. If you are single, the opportunity to meet such a person is very likely at this time. You share a spiritual and philosophical bond with this person—who could come from a vastly different horizon than yours—either because of his/her level of education, or because he/she is from a foreign culture or is widely traveled. As if you were two pilgrims walking toward the same spiritual destination, your journey together is an adventure. The exchange of your most cherished values and ideas is enriching to each other. The playfulness of your bond isn't denied by the philosophical depths you also share.

> *From June 2012 to June 2013, the enlightenment tools of Jupiter (Sagittarius) help you bring light to your marriage.*

VIII. Sexuality, Joint Finances, and Transformation

July 21, 2009 (Solar Eclipse in Cancer)
December 31, 2009 (Lunar Eclipse in Cancer)
July 11, 2010 (Solar Eclipse in Cancer)
July 1, 2011 (Solar Eclipse in Cancer)

You could receive a tax refund, money from insurance, or your marriage partner could come into financial abundance that he/she shares with you. Knowledge from a past life emerges, giving you deeper insights into the mysteries of life, death, the afterlife, and sexuality. It is also important that you understand and use your power positively. Within a month of these four dates, you will know exactly what has changed in your joint finances, sexuality, and understanding of deeper aspects of your psyche.

> *On these dates, the enlightenment tools of Cancer and the Moon help you bring light to your joint finances and sexuality.*

IX. Long-Distance Travel, Philosophy, and Religion

February 9, 2009 (Lunar Eclipse in Leo)

A desire to further your education, write a book, study philosophy, teach, or travel is highlighted by this eclipse. Immersion in a foreign country could completely transform your understanding of life. You are likely to encounter a wise being through whom your connection to your own higher self becomes clearer. Within a month of this date, the changes that have occurred in your philosophy of life and understanding of religion will be very clear.

> *In February 2009, the enlightenment tools of Leo help you bring light to your long-distance travels and philosophy of life.*

X. Career

Since September 3, 2007 until October 28, 2009 (Saturn in Virgo)
April 7, 2010–July 20, 2010 (Saturn in Virgo)

You become extremely visible in your chosen career. Your successes and the means you use to attain them are out in the open for all to see and benefit. You are now in a position to affect many people. As you guide others toward the light, it is important that you are focused and clear on your role as a leader, with a great sense of integrity and responsibility. Added work, maturity, and efficiency are necessary.

During these two periods, the enlightenment tools of Saturn (Capricorn) help you bring light to your career.

XI. Friendships

October 29, 2009–April 6, 2010 (Saturn in Libra)
July 21, 2010–October 4, 2012 (Saturn in Libra)

You feel responsible for your friends. You further define your shared goals for the future and provide them with much support. As you distance yourself from mere acquaintances, your true friendships with people you respect and admire are solid and serious. Having stuck by your side in good and hard times, they deserve your full loyalty. Groups are attractive to you only if they serve a practical purpose.

During these two periods, the enlightenment tools of Saturn (Capricorn) help you bring light to your friendships.

XII. Subconscious

October 5, 2012–September 18, 2015 (Saturn in Scorpio)
November 13, 2012 (Solar Eclipse in Scorpio)

A retreat in silence and solitude enables you to transmute any remaining karma. In this chosen isolation you reexamine your whole journey, tie loose ends, and thus peacefully complete a life cycle. The powerful insights retrieved lead you to wisdom and peace.

During this time, the enlightenment tools of Saturn (Capricorn) and Scorpio help you bring light to your subconscious.

2009–2012 FOR CAPRICORN AND/OR CAPRICORN RISING

I. PERSONAL APPEARANCE

Since September 3, 2007 until January 4, 2009 (Jupiter in Capricorn)

The first week of January ends a one-year period that greatly increased your self-confidence and expanded your spiritual understanding of yourself. Your optimism, faith, and general happiness attracted many beneficial people and positive opportunities. You were more open to transforming that which needed to evolve within you. With greater personal honesty and joy, you were able to make those changes smoothly. Your horizons expanded enormously, revealing unknown gifts that were yours to enjoy all along.

During this period, the enlightenment tools of Jupiter (Sagittarius) help you bring light to your personal appearance.

July 7, 2009 (Lunar Eclipse in Capricorn)
January 15, 2010 (Solar Eclipse in Capricorn)
June 26, 2010 (Lunar Eclipse in Capricorn)
January 4, 2011 (Solar Eclipse in Capricorn)

On these dates, the repercussions of which will unravel for an entire month, you are completely recreating your personal appearance to reflect inner changes. Clothing, makeup, and hair could become more formal. You are more focused and efficient, grounded in your personal power and confident. You are intensely geared toward the manifestation of your ambitions, and people sense your natural authority. The image you project inspires respect and admiration.

On these dates, the enlightenment tools of Capricorn help you bring light to your personal appearance.

From the Present until November 21, 2024 (Pluto in Capricorn)

A complete regeneration of your style and personal appearance are at hand. Circumstances test your courage and strength of character, forcing a previous false sense of identity to crumble. As you really understand who you are spiritually, the image you rebuild is closer to your real truth and more vibrant. Your impact on others gradually gains power and authority. Possible spiritual experiences are likely to further your awareness of yourself and awaken intense psychic abilities. You are drawing to you people who hope that some of your magic will rub off on them.

Until 2024, the enlightenment tools of Pluto (Scorpio) help you bring light to your personal appearance.

II. Money

January 5, 2009–January 16, 2010 (Jupiter in Aquarius)

Ethical professional dealings bring great financial rewards. Money flows effortlessly during this transit. You are able to afford travel, higher education, and luxuries. Contributions to charitable causes are beneficial. The more generous you are with your wealth, the more solid and enduring it becomes. You are a living example that life is abundant and scarcity is but an illusion.

During this period, the enlightenment tools of Jupiter (Sagittarius) help you bring light to your finances.

January 26, 2009 (Solar Eclipse in Aquarius)
August 5, 2009 (Lunar Eclipse in Aquarius)

An unexpected new source of income could be offered to you in an unusual way. Your values need reexamining. Ask yourself if your focus on material and spiritual realities is in balance. This is a good time to re-structure your resources and decide which expenditures are important and which are not. Within one month of these dates, the changes that have occurred in your finances will be clearer to you.

On these two dates, the enlightenment tools of Aquarius help you bring light to your finances.

Since January 2006 until April 19, 2010 (Chiron in Aquarius)
July 20, 2010–February 7, 2011 (Chiron in Aquarius)

An innate talent supports your uniqueness while proving quite lucra-tive. The sense of freedom you derive from exploring and sharing that special gift is exhilarating. If faced with what at first seems like a finan-cial drawback, remain very philosophical and confident. That challenge will prove to be a blessing. An adjustment in what you value materially heals your relationship with money forever.

During this period, the enlightenment tools of Aquarius help you bring light to your finances.

Since November 28, 1998 until April 3, 2011 (Neptune in Aquarius)
August 4, 2011–February 2, 2012 (Neptune in Aquarius)

During these periods, your attachment to material possessions de-creases in subtle ways. Belongings are seen as useful, but they're not as necessary to your well-being as spiritual values. You may donate many clothes and objects to a charitable cause. At these times, meditating or taking a stroll on the beach seems much more pleasurable than aggres-sively pursuing ambitions in a closed office. In order to free yourself from the pressure of always earning more money, you are likely to downsize. The gratitude you feel for the minimum you have enhances your happiness, your inner peace, and your joy. You could also turn art into a lucrative profession and decide to paint or compose for a living.

During these two periods, the enlightenment tools of Neptune (Pisces) help you bring light to your finances.

III. Communication

Since December 31, 2007 until May 26, 2010 (Uranus in Pisces)
August 13, 2010–March 10, 2011 (Uranus in Pisces)

Your ability to connect elements that don't seem related leads to brilliant new insights. Your mental flexibility creates breakthroughs in your consciousness. Not one to respect the status quo, you say things as you see them and you're not afraid to make waves. The way you express your thoughts is unusual, even slightly disturbing. You are the great awakener, shaking people out of their sleeping zone with strange but valid observations. Unorthodox studies are appealing at this time. Your capacity to embrace paradoxes opens uncharted intellectual territories.

During these two periods, the enlightenment tools of Uranus (Aquarius) help you bring light to your communications.

January 17, 2010–June 5, 2010 (Jupiter in Pisces)
September 8, 2010–January 21, 2011 (Jupiter in Pisces)

Your understanding and tolerance are greatly enhanced. Wanting to see the best in others, you choose to focus on the silver lining of every dark cloud. Your optimism and generosity of spirit are infectious. Beneficial encounters in your daily environment expand your mental horizons. They stimulate you to read more, take a class, or travel to exciting new places. Writing and teaching are also very beneficial during these times. Your relationships with siblings and neighbors are positive and pleasant. They could even bring financial benefits.

During two periods, the enlightenment tools of Jupiter (Sagittarius) help you bring light into your communications.

April 20, 2010–July 19, 2010 (Chiron in Pisces)
February 8, 2011–February 2019 (Chiron in Pisces)

You could develop an interest in a specialized field related to health and healing. As your expertise grows, you develop the power to transmute limited/limiting conditions in your daily environment.

During these two periods, the enlightenment tools of Pisces help you bring light to your communications.

April 4, 2011–August 3, 2011 (Neptune in Pisces)
February 3, 2012–January 27, 2026 (Neptune in Pisces)

Your interest in art and esoteric matters greatly increases. Channeling, clairvoyance, or telepathy offer you subtle information. Your enhanced imagination and need for beauty, peace, and harmony also draw you to music, poetry, photography, film, meditation, dance, and yoga. You may feel soothed by the sound of the waves of the ocean. You become more aware of your soul connection to brothers, sisters, cousins, and/or neighbors. The shifts that are occurring are so subtle and over such a long period of time that you may not be able to define the inner changes until much later.

During these two periods, the enlightenment tools of Neptune (Pisces) help you bring light to your communications.

IV. Home

June 6, 2010–September 7, 2010 (Jupiter in Aries)
January 22, 2011–June 4, 2011 (Jupiter in Aries)

Much expansion occurs in your home, either because you are acquiring real estate, redecorating your house or apartment, or gathering with philosophically inclined friends with whom you rethink the world. You feel at peace and secure. Your relationship with your parents is positive and brings much abundance on both a spiritual and financial level. You are encouraged to fearlessly look at yourself. Your happiness infuses you with confidence. Your desire to become a better human being is honest and inspiring.

During these two periods, the enlightenment tools of Jupiter (Sagittarius) help you bring light to your domestic circumstances.

May 27, 2010–August 13, 2010 (Uranus in Aries)
March 11, 2011–March 6, 2019 (Uranus in Aries)

Breaks with past conditioning and outgrown circumstances occur at these times. These upheavals, which shake your very foundations, liberate you from what no longer serves your growth. Sudden and unexpected insights from your past (this lifetime or others) make you more aware of your innate psychic gifts. The home you are likely to choose could be unusual in some way. For example, it may use solar energy. It respects your freedom of movement. Your friends enjoy gathering at your place. Lively philosophical and spiritual discussions broaden your horizons.

During these two periods, the enlightenment tools of Uranus (Aquarius) help you bring light to your domestic circumstances.

V. CREATIVITY, ROMANCE, AND CHILDREN

June 4, 2011–June 10, 2012 (Jupiter in Taurus)

You feel happy and expansive. A romantic involvement with someone whose background is vastly different from yours brings much enrichment to you. This person is warm, open-minded, generous, positive, and adventurous. His/her deep intellectual and spiritual dimensions favorably increase your awareness of the world around you, making you fall in love with life all over again. Any work of art you produce has a far-reaching impact on your viewers, leading to both philosophical and financial abundance. Your relationships with children are positive and mutually beneficial. Sharing athletic activities with them or just talking and listening is fun and interesting.

Between June 2011 and June 2012, the enlightenment tools of Jupiter (Sagittarius) help you bring light to your creativity, romance, and relationships with children.

VI. Health, Pets, and Work

December 21, 2010 (Lunar Eclipse in Gemini)
June 1, 2011 (Solar Eclipse in Gemini)
December 10, 2011 (Lunar Eclipse in Gemini)
May 20, 2012 (Solar Eclipse in Gemini)
November 28, 2012 (Lunar Eclipse in Gemini)

During these five dates, your health comes into focus. It is important that you reevaluate your diet and exercise regimen. Choosing to eat fruits of various colors and vegetables and breathing deeply are essential to your well-being. The more fresh air you get, the better you feel. What has changed will be visible within a month of these eclipse dates.

During all these eclipses, the enlightenment tools of Mercury (Gemini) help you bring light to your health, work and relationships with pets.

June 11, 2012–June 26, 2013 (Jupiter in Gemini)

Your health is excellent. Outdoor athletic activities that increase your vitality and physical strength are appealing. You attract many beneficial opportunities at work and you are supported by coworkers who cheer for your success. A happier, more positive, playful, and serene attitude eases the way you deal with your responsibilities. You could be asked to travel for work. Publishing, the law, religion, and philosophy expand your mental horizons. Volunteering activities seem like a worthwhile way of sharing your luck with those less fortunate than yourself.

From June 2012 to June 2013, the enlightenment tools of Jupiter (Sagittarius) help you bring light to your health, work, and relationships with pets.

VII. Marriage

July 21, 2009 (Solar Eclipse in Cancer)
December 31, 2009 (Lunar Eclipse in Cancer)
July 11, 2010 (Solar Eclipse in Cancer)
July 1, 2011 (Solar Eclipse in Cancer)

Shifts occur in your intimate relationship. A good marriage is solidified by these eclipses, while a difficult one could dissolve. If you are single, you could meet someone significant on one of these dates. A sense of familiarity and a soul connection infuse that meeting. Within a month of these four dates, you will know with clarity what has changed in your marriage.

On these dates, the enlightenment tools of Cancer and the Moon help you bring light to your marriage.

VIII. Sexuality, Joint Finances, and Transformation

February 9, 2009 (Lunar Eclipse in Leo)

Money from your marriage partner, taxes, insurance, or an inheritance could transform the resources you have at your disposal. Deep esoteric insights change your perception of life, death, and the afterlife. Ancient knowledge resurfaces from your subconscious. If you haven't been involved in a sexual relationship for a while, this time could bring a lover who profoundly transforms your attitude toward sexual intimacy. Issues surrounding the constructive use of power are also highlighted by this eclipse. Within a month of this date, you will know exactly what has changed in your joint finances.

In February 2009, the enlightenment tools of the Sun and Leo help you bring light to your joint finances and sexuality.

IX. Long-Distance Travel, Philosophy, and Religion

Since September 3, 2007 until October 28, 2009 (Saturn in Virgo)
April 7, 2010–July 20, 2010 (Saturn in Virgo)

This is a time of serious study. You may want to get a university degree and/or spend time abroad, immersing yourself in a foreign culture and learning more about your place in the world. Teaching, writing nonfiction, publishing, philosophy, religion, and the law are all highlighted. You are grounded enough to channel spiritual information you can share with others in a practical manner.

During these two periods, the enlightenment tools of Saturn (Capricorn) and Scorpio help you bring light to your long-distance travels and philosophy of life.

X. Career

October 29, 2009–April 6, 2010 (Saturn in Libra)
July 21, 2010–October 4, 2012 (Saturn in Libra)

Your career requires much discipline, organization, and responsibility. Your social status is enhanced. Ultimate integrity is required to fulfill your personal and professional ambitions. The visibility of your actions places you in a leadership role. Through balance and justice, you inspire many people.

During these two periods, the enlightenment tools of Saturn (Capricorn) help you bring light to your career.

XI. Friendships

October 5, 2012–September 18, 2015 (Saturn in Scorpio)
November 13, 2012 (Solar Eclipse in Scorpio)

Mere acquaintances are likely to fall by the wayside. The people who have supported you through the ups and downs of life remain. Your friends are fewer but more solid. You respect and admire them. They have climbed the social ladder before you and are giving meaning to their lives. You could be given responsibility for a group that needs to be restructured. Your ambitions are backed by hard work. Your long-term dreams are realistic and grounded.

During these times, the enlightenment tools of Saturn (Capricorn) help you bring light to your friendships.

XII. Subconscious

June 15, 2011 (Lunar Eclipse in Sagittarius)
November 25, 2011 (Solar Eclipse in Sagittarius)
June 4, 2012 (Lunar Eclipse in Sagittarius)

You may feel the need for a spiritual retreat. Silence and solitude help you focus on your soul and see with clarity what you have accomplished until now and how you have done it. Premonitory dreams are likely. A wish to explore your psyche further could lead to shamanistic studies or the exploration of symbols and archetypes. These are times when you are confronted with your karma and are given a chance to transmute it. Within one month of these three dates, you will know exactly what has shifted in your subconscious.

On these dates, the enlightenment tools of Jupiter and Sagittarius help you bring light to your subconscious.

2009–2012 for Aquarius and/or Aquarius Rising

I. Personal Appearance

January 5, 2009–January 16, 2010 (Jupiter in Aquarius)

Your self-image and the impact you make on other people are confident, healthy, and happy. Your optimism attracts many new opportunities, enhancing every area of your life. Your level of integrity is at an all-time high and you are unlikely to preach something you are not fully living.

Your faith in the essential goodness of life and people makes you focus on the silver lining of every cloud, thus creating even more positive manifestations. Your love of life is contagious. You embody your spirituality in adventurous ways. Through your finest human qualities, your divinity shines.

Between January 2009 and January 2010, the enlightenment tools of Jupiter (Sagittarius) help you bring light to your personal appearance.

January 26, 2009 (Solar Eclipse in Aquarius)
August 5, 2009 (Lunar Eclipse in Aquarius)

From your hair to your shoes, you want to change everything in your personal appearance to match your inner truth. As your self-image shifts, so does the impact you are making on other people. The more independent you are, the more you become a role model. Your uniqueness gives others permission to be themselves. Within one month of these dates, you will be clear on what has changed in your personal appearance.

On these two dates, the enlightenment tools of Aquarius help you bring light to your personal appearance.

Since January 2006 until April 19, 2010 (Chiron in Aquarius)
July 20, 2010–February 7, 2011 (Chiron in Aquarius)

Your personal magnetism and healing abilities become stronger. Many are attracted to you, seeing you as a spiritual mentor. You are drawn to light and crystals. Drawing from positive extraterrestrial energies helps you access high-frequency vibrations. As you transmute ancient inner wounds, you heal all the people who share that same program.

During these two periods, the enlightenment tools of Aquarius help you bring light to your personal appearance.

Since November 28, 1998 until April 3, 2011 (Neptune in Aquarius)
August 4, 2011–February 2, 2012 (Neptune in Aquarius)

Your compassion and sensitivity to your environment greatly increase. If you are a woman, more mysterious clothes or makeup attract you. If you are a man, your charisma becomes more subtle. Your self-image and the impact you make on others integrate higher frequencies. Your ability to energetically feel what people are thinking could make it difficult to place clear boundaries between yourself and others. Spending time by the ocean or listening to music with waves in the background help regenerate your spirit and discern what is yours and what isn't. As the veil separating you from infinity thins and your mind spontaneously drifts into beautiful visions, you need more sleep. You may not quite realize what has changed in you until much later.

During these two periods, the enlightenment tools of Neptune (Pisces) help you bring light to your personal appearance.

II. Money

Since December 31, 2003 until May 26, 2010 (Uranus in Pisces)
August 13, 2010–March 10, 2011 (Uranus in Pisces)

The way in which you were used to making a living could abruptly end, forcing you to find exciting, unusual sources of income that are much more in alignment with your truth. Outgrown, traditional values need to be reassessed. Barter could open interesting new possibilities. After reexamining your real needs, you could decide that dramatically downsizing will make you happier. No more a slave to materiality, you are very present, can travel and express your uniqueness. As your focus on things lessens, your freedom, peace, and joy increase.

During these two periods, the enlightenment tools of Uranus (Aquarius) help you bring light to your finances.

January 17, 2010–June 5, 2010 (Jupiter in Pisces)
September 8, 2010–January 21, 2011 (Jupiter in Pisces)

Money flows effortlessly to you. The rewards from past work are visible, enabling you to make a long-distance trip or invest in your higher education. Money could come from spiritual work and/or anything related to the law, a university grant, publishing, or conference speaking. Your values are expanding. You could be attracted to opulence such as expensive furniture, grandiose artworks, or horses, and you may wish to only go to the finest hotels and restaurants. Those luxuries are allowed by the financial abundance that is now yours to enjoy.

During these times, the enlightenment tools of Jupiter (Sagittarius) help you bring light into your finances.

April 20, 2010–July 19, 2010 (Chiron in Pisces)
February 8, 2011–February 2019 (Chiron in Pisces)

It is important that you live what you preach and integrate what you value in your daily life. Your compassion enhances a gift you have. As you spiritualize the way you make money, your finances heal. Contentment with what you have increases your ability to tap into the abundance of life.

During these two periods, the enlightenment tools of Pisces help you bring light to your finances.

April 4, 2011–August 3, 2011 (Neptune in Pisces)
February 3, 2012–January 27, 2026 (Neptune in Pisces)

Your attitude toward money gradually changes during these years. Your values become increasingly more spiritual. As you trust that scarcity is an illusion and that money is an energy that needs to circulate, you attract what you need, just when you need it. You may create an income out of your healing gifts, "smell" money where no one else believes there is any income to be made, and become a master at turning what other people have discarded into beautiful objects. The shifts that are occurring are so subtle and over such a long period of time that you may not be able to define what has transformed in your finances until much later.

During these two periods, the enlightenment tools of Neptune (Pisces) help you bring light to your finances.

III. Communication

June 6, 2010–September 7, 2010 (Jupiter in Aries)
January 22, 2011–June 4, 2011 (Jupiter in Aries)

Your mental attitude is open, tolerant, and positive. The people you meet in your daily environment reflect those same qualities. They greatly expand your horizons either because of their education or their origins, which are very different from yours. Studies involving the law, philosophy, religion, or foreign languages are greatly favored at this time. You could travel more than usual. The foreigners you meet enrich your outlook. Your relationships with siblings and neighbors are positive and dynamic. Nothing is hidden and everything is expressed. Your honesty and your integrity are what attract people to you. Writing, teaching, conference speaking, and publishing are also favored.

During these two periods, the enlightenment tools of Jupiter (Sagittarius) help you bring light to your communications.

May 27, 2010–August 13, 2010 (Uranus in Aries)
March 11, 2011–March 6, 2019 (Uranus in Aries)

The ways you think and express yourself break away from traditional patterns. Your intuition is particularly developed and in a flash could provide you with answers to your questions. As your telepathy develops and you channel more information from other realms, breakthroughs in consciousness arise. Scientific insights, technology, computers, and unusual methods of communication are all particularly attractive to you now. You could invent a device that connects people in a revolutionary way by picking up vibrations. With your capacity to function at the speed of light comes a certain level of impatience. Sustaining long hours of work could feel tedious.

During these two periods, the enlightenment tools of Uranus (Aquarius) help you bring light to your communications.

IV. Home

June 4, 2011–June 10, 2012 (Jupiter in Taurus)

Invest in land, get involved in farming, start your own vegetable garden, or at the very least sprout seeds and grow herbs in your kitchen. Your concern with protecting the Earth's resources could spark an interest in recycling. If you build an extension or redecorate your home, it will be with Earth-friendly materials, possibly using solar energy and chemical-free colors. Feeding your loved ones holistic, natural foods is also important, as is being generous. At this time, your family is particularly open. The opulence of your home makes people feel welcome and nurtured. The more you share your abundance, the more you receive.

Between June 2011 and June 2012, the enlightenment tools of Jupiter (Sagittarius) help you bring light to your domestic circumstances.

V. Creativity, Romance, and Children

December 21, 2010 (Lunar Eclipse in Gemini)
June 1, 2011 (Solar Eclipse in Gemini)
December 10, 2011 (Lunar Eclipse in Gemini)
May 20, 2012 (Solar Eclipse in Gemini)
November 28, 2012 (Lunar Eclipse in Gemini)

If you are artistically inclined, these are times of tremendous inspiration. You are likely to create interesting work using different mediums. Romance is also stimulated. You could meet a delightful person to talk to, from whom you have much to learn. There is a joy, a light, a playfulness, and an ease in that connection. You are totally present to the present. Your relationships with children are also flowing, sparking new interests. Creating crafts with them, reading, writing, watching movies, and playing deepen your bond. What has changed will be evident within a month of these dates.

During all these eclipses, the enlightenment tools of Mercury (Gemini) help you bring light to your creativity, romance, and relationships to children.

June 11, 2012–June 26, 2013 (Jupiter in Gemini)

A romance could tremendously expand your horizons. The person you could get involved with travels a lot, is intellectually stimulating, and/or introduces you to new friends and interests. Artistic creativity is playful and concentrates on the larger picture rather than on details. Your work proves quite lucrative. Financial investments bring luck. In your relationships with children, you stress the importance of honesty and integrity. Through a trip, a world atlas, or an encyclopedia, you expand their horizons by exposing children to other cultures.

From June 2012 to June 2013, the enlightenment tools of Jupiter (Sagittarius) help you bring light to your creativity, romance, and relationships with children.

VI. HEALTH

July 21, 2009 (Solar Eclipse in Cancer)
December 31, 2009 (Lunar Eclipse in Cancer)
July 11, 2010 (Solar Eclipse in Cancer)
July 1, 2011 (Solar Eclipse in Cancer)

Your body could develop unusual sensitivities to foods or the environment. It is important that you listen to its wisdom. Nurturing yourself, sleeping, and drinking enough water or natural juices are all therapeutic. Luxurious baths with music, flower petals, shells, and candlelight emotionally touch something beautiful in you. Whether it is a little fountain or the waves of the ocean, the sound of flowing water is soothing to your mind. You could develop an intuitive form of healing using water, pearls, and silver. The opportunity to work from home allows you to create a space that feels warm and comfortable. Within a month of these four dates, you will know exactly what has changed in your relationship to your body, in your work, and in your relationships with pets.

On these dates, the enlightenment tools of Cancer and the Moon help you bring light to your health.

VII. MARRIAGE

February 9, 2009 (Lunar Eclipse in Leo)

A great shift occurs in your marriage. A good relationship is strengthened by this eclipse, and a shaky one is likely to dissolve. If you have been single, this could be the time when you meet your significant other. A new relationship formed around this eclipse is warm and playful with a touch of glamour. You could be drawn to someone who is charismatic and generous, maybe even larger than life, who radiates love and joy. You are also likely to better understand what being in a committed relationship means to you and how to deepen that bond. Within a month of this date, you will know exactly what has changed.

In February 2009, the enlightenment tools of Leo help you bring light to your marriage.

VIII. SEXUALITY, JOINT FINANCES, AND TRANSFORMATION

Since September 3, 2007 until October 28, 2009 (Saturn in Virgo)
April 7, 2010–July 20, 2010 (Saturn in Virgo)

Joint finances bring added responsibilities and require both restructuring and grounding. You also become serious regarding death and the afterlife, and you're likely to research your past lives scientifically. A deeper understanding of immortality and how to prepare for that reality become of interest at this time. You are able to put your wisdom to practical use and integrate it in your daily life. You could also be drawn to studying the impact of sexuality on health. Tantric yoga is likely to be appealing, as are books that explain sexuality from an energetic and spiritual point of view. Unless physical intimacy can be shared with only one partner, celibacy is preferred, enabling you to contain your energies and grow stronger psychically.

During these two periods, the enlightenment tools of Saturn (Capricorn) help you bring light to your joint finances and sexuality.

IX. Long-Distance Travel, Philosophy, and Religion

October 29, 2009–April 6, 2010 (Saturn in Libra)
July 21, 2010–October 4, 2012 (Saturn in Libra)

Higher education is undertaken seriously. Traveling expands your understanding of the world and your philosophy of life. You could spend many months in a retreat in a foreign country. Isolated from your everyday routine, you are able to create a new spiritual foundation for your life. You are attracted to nonfictional topics that require structured research. Self-improvement is methodical. Teaching and public speaking based on academic knowledge and personal experiences strengthen your personal authority. The peace and harmony you seek help you reach balance.

During these two periods, the enlightenment tools of Saturn (Capricorn) help you bring light to your long-distance trips and philosophy of life.

X. Career

October 5, 2012–September 18, 2015 (Saturn in Scorpio)
November 13, 2012 (Solar Eclipse in Scorpio)

All the ambitions you worked long and hard for come to fruition. Your position in society is solid. Whatever you built in your career around

November 13 is visible and will be there for a long time. Your achievements attract the respect and admiration of peers who recognize your natural authority. Your contribution makes a difference while giving further meaning to your life.

Between October 2012 and September 2015, the enlightenment tools of Saturn (Capricorn) help you bring light to your career.

XI. FRIENDSHIPS

June 15, 2011 (Lunar Eclipse in Sagittarius)
November 25, 2011 (Solar Eclipse in Sagittarius)
June 4, 2012 (Lunar Eclipse in Sagittarius)

Solid friendships that have proven themselves through thick and thin remain. Acquaintances or relationships with people to whom you have been feeling less and less of a connection are likely to dissolve. New people walk into your life. They are dynamic, adventurous, positive, freedom-loving, educated, and well-traveled. Your long-term dreams are resurfacing and now have a chance to become reality. You could become part of a team inspired by a vision. Within one month of these three eclipses, you will know exactly what has changed.

On these dates, the enlightenment tools of Jupiter and Sagittarius help you bring light to your friendships.

XII. SUBCONSCIOUS

Since January 19, 2007 until January 4, 2009 (Jupiter in Capricorn)

The first week of January ends a period of two years that expanded your consciousness. You could have been involved in a serious spiritual practice (such as shamanism), had a dream that revealed aspects of your waking reality, started to meditate, and/or gotten insights from a friend whose wisdom awoke your own mastery. Your best ideas were developed in silence and solitude.

During this period, the enlightenment tools of Jupiter (Sagittarius) help you bring light to your subconscious.

July 7, 2009 (Lunar Eclipse in Capricorn)
January 15, 2010 (Solar Eclipse in Capricorn)
June 26, 2010 (Lunar Eclipse in Capricorn)
January 4, 2011 (Solar Eclipse in Capricorn)

On these dates, the repercussions of which will unravel for a whole month, major insights into your subconscious help reorganize your psyche. You seek isolation, silence, and solitude, wish to read or meditate, and may even go away on a retreat. The need to understand yourself at deeper levels could lead to shamanistic journeys or the exploration of your past lives.

On these dates, the enlightenment tools of Capricorn help you bring light to your subconscious.

Since November 28, 2008 until November 21, 2024 (Pluto in Capricorn)

As ancient behavioral patterns surface—the darkness of which could shock you—a complete regeneration of your subconscious occurs. You could have the impression of symbolically dying and being reborn. Vivid dreams, meeting your spirit guides, and/or encountering your power animal connect you with your magical powers. Through this intense inner process, you become aware that you can manifest whatever you envision with a pure heart.

Until 2024, the enlightenment tools of Pluto (Scorpio) help you bring light to your subconscious.

I. Personal Appearance

Since December 31, 2003 until May 26, 2010 (Uranus in Pisces)
August 13, 2010–March 10, 2011 (Uranus in Pisces)

You could surprise others—and maybe even yourself—by suddenly rebelling against all the boundaries that have limited you. As your consciousness expands, your style and your physical appearance change also. Your newfound freedom feels threatening only to those who fear the unknown. As you leave your own comfort zone, you become a powerful awakener and role model. Those who are flexible enough to welcome change are inspired by you.

During these two periods, the enlightenment tools of Uranus (Aquarius) help you bring light to your personal appearance.

January 17, 2010–June 5, 2010 (Jupiter in Pisces)
September 8, 2010–January 21, 2011 (Jupiter in Pisces)

You are optimistic, expansive, and in love with life. Your joy and belief in the goodness of life attract positive and helpful people who introduce you to many beneficial opportunities. Your high moral standards make you live what you preach. Your spiritual faith permeates and elevates your daily life.

During these two periods, the enlightenment tools of Jupiter (Sagittarius) help you bring light to your personal appearance.

April 20, 2010–July 19, 2010 (Chiron in Pisces)
February 8, 2011–February 2019 (Chiron in Pisces)

Your healing abilities emerge strongly. Old wounds transmute. A lightbearer, you help others free themselves from the bondage of limiting/limited conditionings.

THE MAYAN
CALENDAR AND
THE SIGNS

During these two periods, the enlightenment tools of Pisces help you bring light to your personal appearance.

April 4, 2011–August 3, 2011 (Neptune in Pisces)
February 3, 2012–January 27, 2026 (Neptune in Pisces)

Your old self-image gradually dissolves to allow your truth to emerge. This process parallels the connect-the-dots drawings done by children, which in the end reveal a hidden picture. You are more dreamy than usual, needing more sleep, expressing more compassion, and seeking the ocean to replenish your soul, whether it is by actually going to the beach or just listening to classical music with waves in the background. Dance, poetry, meditation, yoga, and tai chi are other activities that help you connect with the infinity of life. The shifts are so subtle that you may not be able to define them until much later.

During these two periods, the enlightenment tools of Neptune (Pisces) help you bring light to your personal appearance.

II. Money

June 6, 2010–September 7, 2010 (Jupiter in Aries)
January 22, 2011–June 4, 2011 (Jupiter in Aries)

The rewards for your past work flow effortlessly. Your confidence in your creative ideas creates diversified sources of income. The wealth you feel manifests in your external reality, offering you more freedom. With the faith that you will be further provided for, you are likely to invest your prosperity in a long-distance trip or study toward a university degree.

During these two periods, the enlightenment tools of Jupiter (Sagittarius) help you bring light to your finances.

May 27, 2010–August 13, 2010 (Uranus in Aries)
March 11, 2011–March 6, 2019 (Uranus in Aries)

An unexpected change in your income could force you to reassess what you value. Breaking away from the burden of things you don't necessarily need—downsizing—is the answer. There is neither frustration nor a sense of deprivation. The lighter and more detached you are from material possessions, the freer you feel. You could be drawn to unusual ways of making money, such as relying on barter or marketing a unique talent.

During these times, the enlightenment tools of Uranus (Aquarius) help you bring light to your finances.

III. Communication

June 4, 2011–June 10, 2012 (Jupiter in Taurus)

The people you encounter in your daily environment are positive and optimistic. Who they are and what motivates their actions interest you. You are also eager to learn the law, philosophy, religion, or a foreign language. Traveling, writing, public speaking, and teaching are also particularly beneficial. Your own faith in life is inspiring.

Between June 2011 and June 2012, the enlightenment tools of Jupiter (Sagittarius) help you bring light to your communications.

IV. Home

December 21, 2010 (Lunar Eclipse in Gemini)
June 1, 2011 (Solar Eclipse in Gemini)
December 10, 2011 (Lunar Eclipse in Gemini)
May 20, 2012 (Solar Eclipse in Gemini)
November 28, 2012 (Lunar Eclipse in Gemini)

Changes occur in your domestic circumstances, either because you transform your home by redecorating or adding an extension, or because you choose to relocate. The place you are drawn to allows much freedom of movement and enables you to expand your social life with intellectually stimulating people. Your relationship with a parent could change, either because you need to reorganize his/her life or because you are able to discuss things that were never openly expressed. What has changed will be visible within a month of these eclipse dates.

During all these eclipses, the enlightenment tools of Mercury (Gemini) help you bring light to your domestic circumstances.

June 11, 2012–June 26, 2013 (Jupiter in Gemini)

You need to feel much comfort, peace, and joy in your domestic circumstances. You could either invest in real estate or relocate and choose to be close to a like-spirited community. You could also expand your home by adding an extension or redecorating. A pied-à-terre in between trips, it is also a place where you generously entertain people with varied philosophical viewpoints who stimulate you intellectually. An involvement in a Greenpeace-like movement reconnects you to the Earth, our mother.

From June 2012 to June 2013, the enlightenment tools of Jupiter (Sagittarius) help you bring light to your domestic circumstances.

V. Creativity, Romance, and Children

July 21, 2009 (Solar Eclipse in Cancer)
December 31, 2009 (Lunar Eclipse in Cancer)
July 11, 2010 (Solar Eclipse in Cancer)
July 1, 2011 (Solar Eclipse in Cancer)

Your sensitivity is enhanced. As you draw on personal memories from your childhood and tap into your intuitive understanding of what connects people, your artistic creations awaken intimate emotional responses in others. A romance could develop with someone who feels familiar, even though you may only have just met that person. Your sense of belonging to each other makes it natural to share yourself. An existing love connection feels comfortable. Cooking at home, talking by the fireplace, and staring at the moonlight are valued moments of togetherness. Your relationships with children are warm and loving. Whether they are your own or not, they feel like family. This could be a time when you discover that you are expecting a baby, considering adoption, or are chosen by a child. Within a month of these four dates, you will know exactly what has shifted.

On these dates, the enlightenment tools of Cancer and the Moon help you bring light to your creativity, romance, hobbies, and relationships with children.

VI. Health, Pets, and Work

February 9, 2009 (Lunar Eclipse in Leo)

Your relationship to your body comes to the forefront during this eclipse. The changes in your physical structure require a reevaluation of your nutrition and exercise program. You are likely to be attracted to a diet that puts color back into your meals and to activities that involve much fresh air and sunlight. Activities such as dance and playful team sports shift your energy beautifully. Your healing gifts develop using light, crystals, and possibly gold. Your attitude at work is warm and positive, attracting the support of your colleagues. A new opportunity arises. Within a month of this date, you will know exactly what has changed.

In February 2009, the enlightenment tools of Leo help you bring light to your health.

VII. Marriage

Since September 3, 2007 until October 28, 2009 (Saturn in Virgo)
April 7, 2010–July 20, 2010 (Saturn in Virgo)

Marriage is tested at these times. You have to be very realistic with regard to what you have. After some restructuring, a good marriage will emerge stronger, while a shaky one is likely to dissolve. If you are single, this could change. You are likely to be attracted to a substantial and mature person you can both respect and admire. Intimacy brings responsibilities, but you now have the desire to build a solid, long-lasting romantic connection. Your partnerships with people with whom you share a common vision are serious and grounded in reality. You expect from those close to you the same level of hard work, commitment, and persistence you offer.

During these two periods, the enlightenment tools of Saturn (Capricorn) help you bring light to your marriage.

VIII. Sexuality, Joint Finances, and Transformation

October 29, 2009–April 6, 2010 (Saturn in Libra)
July 21, 2010–October 4, 2012 (Saturn in Libra)

A restructuring of joint resources occurs. Added responsibilities are connected to money shared with people you are close to (business or marriage partner). You are forced to clarify your long-term goals. You are likely to seriously investigate the meaning of death, the possibility of the afterlife, and how to attain immortality. Any esoteric research is grounded and solid. Your attitude toward sexuality is serious. You prefer to commit to intimacy with only one person. If no one is in your life, you have the wisdom and patience to quietly wait. A period of celibacy strengthens and elevates your personal energies to a higher frequency.

During these two periods, the enlightenment tools of Saturn (Capricorn) help you bring light to your joint finances and sexuality.

IX. Long-Distance Travel, Philosophy, and Religion

October 5, 2012–September 18, 2015 (Saturn in Scorpio)
November 13, 2012 (Solar Eclipse in Scorpio)

Your connection to your higher self becomes tangible. Higher education grounds your perceptions, offering you the tools you need to structure and share—through writing or public speaking—what you are channeling. Long-distance traveling is undertaken to study or to immerse yourself in a foreign culture you feel you have much to remember or learn from. Ancient knowledge that was for many centuries forgotten or obscured reemerges through your own wisdom.

Between October 2012 and September 2015, the enlightenment tools of Saturn (Capricorn) and Scorpio help you bring light to your long-distance travels and philosophy of life.

X. CAREER

June 15, 2011 (Lunar Eclipse in Sagittarius)
November 25, 2011 (Solar Eclipse in Sagittarius)
June 4, 2012 (Lunar Eclipse in Sagittarius)

Great shifts occur in your career. Financial abundance and a sense of freedom come with a promotion, opening exciting new horizons or the option of independently launching your own business. Within one month of these three dates, you will know with certainty what has changed.

On these dates, the enlightenment tools of Jupiter and Sagittarius help you bring light to your career.

XI. FRIENDSHIPS

Since January 19, 2007 until January 4, 2009 (Jupiter in Capricorn)

The first week of January ends a period of two years that expanded your social circle. You are most probably with a group of dynamic people concretizing a common vision. Your friends, who are either athletic, are from different cultures, or have a broad encyclopedic knowledge, are positive, open-minded, and enthusiastically involved in humanitarian endeavors. Many benefits come from these associations, which most likely help you reconnect with dreams you had forgotten about.

During this period, the enlightenment tools of Jupiter (Sagittarius) help you bring light to your friendships.

July 7, 2009 (Lunar Eclipse in Capricorn)
January 15, 2010 (Solar Eclipse in Capricorn)
June 26, 2010 (Lunar Eclipse in Capricorn)
January 4, 2011 (Solar Eclipse in Capricorn)

On these dates, the repercussions of which will unravel for an entire month, your friendships are changing. Your core support group is unlikely to be affected, but you could find that you are distancing yourself from those people whose integrity and ambitions you no longer respect. The new friends you seek are mature, responsible, and solid. The authority they radiate and the respect they inspire support your goals and enhance your clarity.

On these dates, the enlightenment tools of Capricorn help you bring light to your friendships.

Since November 28, 2008 until November 21, 2024 (Pluto in Capricorn)

Your life is changing fundamentally. What used to feel attractive no longer seems appealing. As your ideals shift, so does your social circle. Charismatic and metaphysical people become catalysts of your transformation. Their power mirrors your own. As you are stripped of dreams that no longer serve a higher purpose, an amazing new truth emerges, helping you formulate your real contribution to the reformation of humanity.

Until 2024, the enlightenment tools of Pluto (Scorpio) help you bring light to your friendships.

XII. Subconscious

January 5, 2009–January 16, 2010 (Jupiter in Aquarius)

Tolerance and compassion permeate your understanding of others. The exploration and deepening of your spirituality become all-important. A retreat in silence, solitude, and meditation expands your inner life. You feel one with all beings. You could discover a place of infinite wisdom and peace within yourself on your own, or you may meet someone who guides you to your light. That ordinary person has developed extraordinary skills that have the power of awakening yours. Volunteering in a charitable organization helps you reach out to those less privileged than yourself.

During this period, the enlightenment tools of Jupiter (Sagittarius) help you bring light to your subconscious.

January 26, 2009 (Solar Eclipse in Aquarius)
August 5, 2009 (Lunar Eclipse in Aquarius)

Powerful dreams offer insights into elusive situations. Through unexpected circumstances, a veil is removed, awakening your psychic abilities. Beings from spiritual realms, such as ascended masters or angels, impart inspiration and wisdom. You are able to connect with the archetypal roots shared by humanity as a whole. You can suddenly see with clarity certain patterns that you now have a chance of letting go forever. Within one month of these dates, you will know what has changed in your subconscious.

On these two dates, the enlightenment tools of Aquarius help you bring light to your subconscious.

Since January 2006 until May 2010 (Chiron in Aquarius)
August 2010–February 2011 (Chiron in Aquarius)

Through isolation either chosen or forced, a past life connection with plants and crystals reemerges. As you use those abilities, you gain profound insights into your own soul. Your yearning for a fusion with the divine is profound.

During these two periods, the enlightenment tools of Aquarius help you bring light to your subconscious.

Since November 28, 1998 until April 3, 2011 (Neptune in Aquarius)
August 4, 2011–February 2, 2012 (Neptune in Aquarius)

When you dream, meditate, and spend time in silence and solitude, subtle insights flood your consciousness. They connect you to the oneness of life. Your compassion is intensified, as is your ability to see the invisible and know the unknowable. The more you immerse yourself in the sacred space that leads humanity back to its divine origins, the more darkness is dispelled by your expanding light.

During these two periods, the enlightenment tools of Neptune (Pisces) help you bring light to your subconscious.

12

Practical Steps to Enlightenment

Reaching enlightenment should not be ascetic, tedious, and boring. Instead, it can be a fun journey that fills us with excitement, positive feelings, and peace. Our thoughts, our emotions, what is in our environment, the books we read, the music we listen to, the people we interact with, what we feed our bodies, the way we breathe and exercise are all of utmost importance. A simple awareness of our daily inner and outer realities will make a huge difference. With just a few shifts, our whole consciousness can turn around and effortlessly place us on the joyful road to enlightenment.

Lexigrams: Ascension/Enlightenment/Master

Lexigrams are a fun and profound way of discovering the secret meaning of words. Using *only* the letters in a word or name (any repeated letter is underlined as many times as it is repeated), try to discover all the words you can. Using *only* the words discovered, create as many meaningful sentences as possible. Even if their structure seems slightly strange, the hidden significance that will emerge will amaze you.

ASCENSION

A	S	C	E	N	I	O
ace	sane	cane	eon	nice	in	on
a	sin	case		nose	is	one
an	sonic	cone		nine	inn	ocean
as		canine		none	ice	
anise		coin		no		
				noise		

AS ONE (We shall understand that we are one, that which we do to another or see in another is really mirroring ourselves.)

NONE, NINE, ONE (From the void, we reach the ultimate diversity before reaching oneness.)

NO COIN (Money no longer will be a value.)

NO ACE (No privilege. As we reach the consciousness that we are one, no one is better or higher than another.)

NO SINS or SINS IN ICE (Sins are no longer even a concept.)

A SONIC OCEAN (As we become enlightened, we also become acutely aware of all the vibrations surrounding us.)

NO NOISE (It is much more difficult to reach peace of mind when surrounded by constant noise, distractions, and sounds that are not in alignment with our natural rhythms. True silence is the essence of enlightenment.)

MASTER

M	A	S	T	E	R
mat	at	star	tame	east	rest
met	a	sat	tear		rat
mare	as	set	team		ram
mate		same	term		rate
		stare			
		stem			

STARE AT A STAR (As we meditate, watching a star, we remember that we too are starseeds and that nothing we do on Earth is separated from the other universes.)

AS A TEAM (As we team up, and thus complement each other's gifts, we expand our highest potential.)

STAR MATE (We become masters as we remember the connection our soul has with other stars and their inhabitants. Although in seemingly different forms and dimensions, they nonetheless are one with us.)

AT REST (Only when we shall have reached inner peace and silence can we consider ourselves to be masters.)

ENLIGHTENMENT

E̲	N̲	L	I	G	H	T̲	M
eel	night	light	in	get	heel	title	mile
	net	line	it	gene	him	tile	might
	Nile	let		ghee		teen	met
		lit				tin	mine
		lime				them	meet
						thin	mint

LET THE LIGHT IN (Enlightenment occurs when we switch the light on and allow it to illuminate darkness that can no longer remain dark.)

GET IT! (We do not have a choice. As it is the caterpillar's destiny to turn into a butterfly, it also is ours to become enlightened.)

THE LIGHT GENE (Suggesting that enlightenment is in our DNA.)

IN LINE (With the laws of the universe, we become one with all that is.)

MET IN THE LIGHT (We know each other from before this incarnation.)

MEET HIM IN THE LIGHT (Become one with the divine.)

Enjoy! I'm sure you can come up with more words and sentences to enrich the meaning of those magical words.

PRACTICAL CHECKLIST FOR ENLIGHTENMENT
PHYSICALLY, MENTALLY, EMOTIONALLY, AND SPIRITUALLY

To ascend, we need to become more and more "of the light." We must raise our frequencies. Without leaving our home or buying anything new, there are very practical things we can do on a daily basis to ascend.

Right here, right now, with a minimal amount of effort, these steps can make all the difference in the world. The following checklist is by no means exhaustive, but should offer you a solid starting point. You will experience, almost immediately, clarity, joy, and peace.

1. PHYSICALLY

Avoid as much as possible:

- Drugs

- Alcohol

- Nicotine

- Caffeine

- Sugar/corn syrup

- Microwaved foods and drinks

- Processed foods

- Going to sleep after midnight

- Eating later than three hours before going to sleep

- Sunglasses (which lower our immune system and weaken our eyesight)

- Cosmetics containing parabens

- Fluoride and mercury

- Clutter

- Cellular phones when not absolutely necessary

- Watching television more than one hour a day

- Loud, discordant music

- Lack of exercise

- Lack of fresh air

- Tap water

The absolutely *yes* list:

- Exercise every day (swimming, tai chi, martial arts, walking, yoga), and outdoors as much as possible.

- Breathe deeply!

- Drink lots of pure, crystal quartz–charged water (allow crystals to soak for a few hours in the water you are going to drink).

- Eat mostly raw, fresh, organic fruits and vegetables, charged for at least 15 minutes on a purple plate (www.purpleplates.com).

- Eat several regular small meals a day.

- Eat the right combinations. (Our foods are divided in five major groups: fats, proteins, carbohydrates, vegetables, and fruits. Fruits should always be eaten alone. Proteins and carbohydrates should never be mixed at the same meal, but each should be served with vegetables. For example, fish and rice or meat and potatoes are very difficult to digest. Fish or meat should always be served with vegetables. Fats really only mix well with vegetables.)

- Fast one day a week (take in only water or pure, freshly juiced organic fruit).

- Once a week do a water enema (an empty, refillable pouch can be bought from any drugstore for about $10).

• Once a month do a colonic (google to find a location close to you).

• Fast for ten days at least twice a year. (Master cleanse: Squeeze the juice of one lemon in a tall glass, add one to two tablespoons of grade B maple syrup, a pinch of cayenne pepper, and fill with pure water. Drink six to eight glasses of this lemonade a day and nothing else for a minimum of five days. You can function in your daily life up to twenty days on this fast, but you absolutely need, at least the first days, to do a lukewarm water enema each day to rid your body of the toxins that will start being released. After that, as needed.)

• Amaroli. (Drinking our own urine. Although this may sound repulsive, it has been advocated by ayurvedic medicine for centuries and could save our lives in the case of a drought. The water of life contains many valuable minerals and reveals the state of our body. If your body is toxic, it will taste acidic. If you're in good health, it will have the wonderful taste of a light vegetable broth. See www.universal-tao.com.)

• Drink every day water with some apple cider vinegar (one to two tablespoons per glass).

• Eat fresh garlic and honey on a daily basis.

• Brush your skin regularly.

• Take warm showers ended by a cold shower.

• Experience acupuncture/homeopathy/naturopathy/Reiki/massage/Bach flower remedies/reflexology/Rolfing/Qigong.

• Meditate every day.

• Sleep at least nine hours every night in a television- and electronic-free bedroom.

• Dress in colors.

- Wear real gemstones (www.gemisphere.com or www.alexandracabri jewelry.com).

- Get a pet. (Cats are powerful healers and masters. Dogs teach us unconditional love and joy.)

2. MENTALLY/EMOTIONALLY/SPIRITUALLY

Avoid:

- Negative thoughts and words

- Criticism

- Judgment of self and others

- Procrastination

- Dishonesty

- Lack of commitment

- Not being grounded

- Lack of discriminating tastes

- Wishful thinking

- Fear

- Resentment

- Jealousy

- Victimization

- Indecisiveness

- Holding on to old wounds

- Selfishness

- Greed

- Being scattered

- Violence (also in movies)

- Pride

- Arrogance

- Being cowardly

- Financial debts

- Anger

- Excesses (sex, obsessions . . .)

- Insecurities

- Avoid all the concepts carried by the old consciousness:

    - *"You have to work hard to make a living."*

    - *"You can't have it all."*

    - *"It's a rat race."*

    - *"I don't have any money."*

    - *"Sickness and old age are unavoidable."*

    - *"Relationships suck."*

    - *"It's not my fault/problem."*

    - *"Poor me!"*

You get the idea!

But *do* be:

- Positive

- Kind

- Appreciative

- Grateful

- Honest

- Fair

- Happy

- Grounded

- Open-minded

- Playful

- Lighthearted

- Loyal

- Warm

- Generous

- Present to the present

- Loving

- Caring

- Considerate

- Creative

- Supportive of others

- Nurturing

- Healing

- Surrendering

- Loyal

- Sensitive

- Compassionate

- Responsible

- Forgiving

- Powerful

- Free

- Simple

- Balanced

- Adventurous

- Efficient

- Understanding

- Flexible

- Communicative

- Strong

- Welcoming

- Full of grace

Have:

- Trust (particularly in yourself)

- Faith

- Passion

- Respect

- Spontaneity

- Patience

- Integrity

- Inner peace

- Positive and exciting goals

- An inner vision

- Clarity

- Humor

- Inner confidence

- Joy

- Enthusiasm

- Positive expectations

And *do*:

- Simplify your life.

- Clear your closets.

- Give yourself times of complete solitude and silence.

- Listen to your inner voice.

- Follow your heart.

- Create lists of positive short- and long-term goals.

- Embrace all that you are, especially those parts that you feel may need improvement.

- Honor all of life.

- Use only positive words when you speak.

- Empower yourself and others.

- Think and feel only in terms of unlimited abundance and joy.

- Send love and blessings whenever you enter a public place (in line at the bank, at the post office, in a grocery store, etc.). People's moods will change for the better without them even knowing why.

- Take *full* responsibility for whatever disturbs you in other people by silently repeating to yourself, "I'm sorry. Please forgive me. I love you. Thank you." (www.hooponopono.org)

AROUND-THE-HOUSE CHECKLIST

IN YOUR KITCHEN

As much as possible avoid:

- Microwaves

- Processed foods

- Caffeinated drinks

- Sodas

- Cigarettes

- Alcohol

- Drugs

- Soy products (which negatively impact our thyroid)

- Meat

- Dairy products (meant for calves, not humans)

- Sugar

- Products containing corn syrup

- Paper towels (which increase deforestation)

- Teflon pots and pans (which release toxic fumes)

Clear clutter out of:

- Refrigerator

- Drawers

Do buy:

- Fresh, organic fruits and vegetables (particularly lemons, apples, bananas, avocados, and tomatoes)

- Grade B maple syrup and cayenne pepper

- Pure apple cider vinegar

- Cold-pressed olive oil

- Garlic

- Honey

- Bee pollen

- Seaweeds (nori, wakame, kombu, arame . . .)

- Himalayan crystal salt (www.americanbluegreen.com)

- Green tea

- Yerba maté herb tea

- Fresh apricot kernels

- Rice or almond milk

- Tahini or almond butter

- Ghee (clarified butter)

- Raw chocolate powder

- Cast iron, titanium, or glass cookware

- Bach flower remedies (www.bachflower.com)

- Intestinal formulas #1, #2, and Superfood (www.herbdoc.com)

- Laser-enhanced food supplements (www.gematria.com)

- Rainbow Whole Food Lightning (www.naturesplus.com)

- Sprouting jars and sprouting seeds (www.sprouting.com)

- Water filter (www.gematria.net)

- Purple plates to charge fruits, vegetables, and water with positive vibrations (www.purpleplates.com)

- Crystals

- Environment-friendly dishwashing and laundry liquid

- Pure castile soap (for fruit and hand washing as well as a general cleaner)

- Green plants

IN YOUR BEDROOM

As much as possible avoid:

- Electronic alarm clock

- Telephone (especially cellular and cordless)

- Television set

- Computer

- Nonspiritual books and images

• Mirrors (they attract lower vibrations; you can cover them with fabric when sleeping)

Clear clutter out of:

• Drawers

• Closets

Do get:

• Green plants

• Crystals

• Soothing, healing music

• A meditation cushion

• Peaceful, spiritual images

• An eye cushion

• Earplugs

• A water fountain

• A salt lamp

• Candles or crystals illuminated from underneath (at IKEA) or Christmas lights

• Incense

• Indian bells

• Tibetan or crystal singing bowl

- A comforter and curtains with a pure, bright color

- Terra Tachyon products (www.terratachyon.com)

IN YOUR LIVING ROOM

As much as possible avoid:

- Television set (when not in use, you can either put it away in a closet or cover its screen with a beautiful fabric)

- Loud, aggressive music

- Violent and negative films (thrillers, horror, pornography)

- Negative, violent books

- Tabloids and entertainment/celebrity magazines

- Newspapers

- Meaningless, unspiritual pictures

- Cellular phones (turn off when not in use)

- Phones with no "ringer off" function

Do get:

- Crystals

- Green plants

- Soothing, healing music (Mozart played for twenty-four hours non-stop has the same cleansing effect as sage)

- Incense (particularly a bunch of natural sage sprigs and/or a piece of Palo Santo holy wood)

- Positive, spiritual books

- Spiritual pictures

- A pet friend

- A salt lamp

- Candles or crystals illuminated from underneath

- Lots of natural sunlight and fresh air

- Cushions, curtains, couches, table mats, or runners with pure, bright colors

- Tachyons, particularly the Arrow of the Alchemist (www.terratachyon .com)

ON YOUR BALCONY / IN YOUR GARDEN

As much as possible avoid:

- Clutter

- Lack of beauty

Do get:

- Wind chimes

- A hummingbird feeder

- Nice plants

- Crystals

- Garden lights

IN YOUR BATHROOM

As much as possible avoid:

- Cosmetics, soaps, creams, or lotions containing parabens

- Chemical air fresheners

- Medication

- Fluoride toothpaste

Clear clutter:

- In drawers and cupboards

- Throw away any product that is more than six months old

Do get:

- A refillable enema pouch

- Crystals (to place in the water of your bath)

- Green plants

- Incense or natural air fresheners

- Essential oil burner

- Chakra sprays (www.holisticbodytherapy.com)

- Aura-Soma products (www.aura-soma.net)

- Homeopathic remedies

- Detox foot pads (www.feelgoodstore.com)

- Fluoride-free toothpaste

- Paraben-free body lotions (www.ManifestWellnessNow.com)

- Egyptian Magic healing cream (www.egyptianmagic.com)

- 100% natural skin care Simply Divine Botanicals (www.simplydivine botanicals.com)

- Paraben-free sunscreen (www.albabotanica.com)

- Pure castile soap (hand and body wash, shampoo)

- Dead Sea mineral bath salts

- Apple vinegar and/or essential oils to place in your bathwater

IN YOUR CAR

Avoid as much as possible:

- Plastic bottles

- Discordant music

Do get:

- Survival backpack (checklist found later in this chapter)

- A large supply of spring water in SIGG aluminum or dark blue glass bottles

- Eco-friendly reusable grocery bags

- A blanket

- A sleeping bag

- A map

- A pen and writing pad

- Uplifting, healing music

- Little crystals

- A beach mat

- An umbrella

- Walking shoes

- A fuel ionizer (www.purpleplates.com)

THE SURVIVAL BACKPACK

There is a saying that it's better to be safe than sorry. This is why you should have a survival backpack. You will realize that most of its contents are already in your home and that there isn't much you will need to buy. It's fun to put together and once it's created, you won't need to think about it anymore. It could be in your car at all times. It's the best insurance that you will never have to use.

- Large plastic sheets (picnic tablecloths)

- Duct tape and large, double-sided tape

- Scissors

- Army knife

- Rubber bands

- Bandages

- Cotton balls

- Rubbing alcohol

- Lighter

- Water-resistant matches

- Flashlight

- Warm clothes (one sweater, one pair of pants, one trenchcoat, warm socks, walking shoes, underwear, hat)

- One superabsorbent large towel

- Big pack of baby wipes

- Soap

- Toilet paper

- Toothbrush and toothpaste

- Deodorant

- Paraben-free sunscreen

- Egyptian Magic Skin Cream

- Water pouch

- Cup with lid

- Spoon

- Dried fruit

- Dried food for your pet

- Two little containers for your pet: one for food, one for water

In plastic sandwich bags (in case of a flood):

- Cash

- Credit cards

- Valid passport

- Insurance information

- Driver's license

- Vaccination papers for your pet

Books, Music, Card Decks, and Web Sites That Support Enlightenment

Philosophy

Krishnamurti, anything by him, but particularly:

- *The First and the Last Freedom*

- *Freedom from the Known*

- *Meditations*

Kahlil Gibran

- *The Prophet*

Pierre Teilhard de Chardin, anything by him, particularly:

- *The Future of Man*

Chris Griscom, anything by her, particularly:

- *Ecstasy Is a New Frequency*

Peace Pilgrim

- *Steps Toward Inner Peace*

A Course in Miracles (Foundation for Inner Peace)

The *I Ching* (the Chinese oracle *Book of Changes*)

Joe Vitale and Ihaleakala Hew Len

- *Zero Limits: The Secret Hawaiian System for Wealth, Health, Peace, and More*

Robert James

- *What Is This Thing Called Aloha?*

Ralph Blum

- *The Book of Runes*

John Randolph Price

- *The Abundance Book*

EXTRATERRESTRIALS/ANGEL CHANNELING

Doreen Virtue, anything by her, particularly:

- *How to Hear Your Angels*

- *Angels 101*

- *Chakra Clearing*

- *The Crystal Children*

Any of her card decks, particularly:

- *Magical Messages from the Fairies oracle cards*

- *Saints and Angels oracle cards*

- *Ascended Masters oracle cards*

- *Messages from Your Angels oracle cards*

- *Daily Guidance from Your Angels oracle cards*

Barbara Marciniak, anything by her, but particularly:

- *Bringers of the Dawn*

- *Earth: Pleiadian Keys to the Living Library*

David Miller

- *Connecting with the Arcturians*

Patricia Cori

- *The Cosmos of Soul: A Wake-up Call for Humanity*

Sanaya Roman, anything by her, particularly:

- *Personal Power Through Awareness*

- *Living with Joy*

- *Creating Money*

Any of her tapes, particularly:

- *Feeling Inner Peace*

- *Radiating Unconditional Love*

- *Taking a Quantum Leap*

ASTROLOGY

Linda Goodman, anything by her, particularly:

- *Linda Goodman's Sun Signs*

- *Linda Goodman's Love Signs*

Stephen Arroyo

- *Astrology, Karma & Transformation*

Marc Edmund Jones

- *The Sabian Symbols in Astrology*

THE MAYAN CALENDAR

Carl Johan Calleman

- *The Mayan Calendar and the Transformation of Consciousness*

Karen Majorowski

- *Daily Guide to the Mayan Sacred Calendar*

SPIRITUAL BIOGRAPHIES

Lynn V. Andrews, anything by her, starting with:

- *Medicine Woman*

Dan Millman, anything by him, starting with:

- *The Spiritual Warrior*
- *Sacred Journey of the Spiritual Warrior*

Fynn

- *Mister God, This Is Anna*

Marlo Morgan

- *Mutant Message Down Under*

Elizabeth Haich

- *Initiation*

Paramahansa Yogananda

- *Autobiography of a Yogi*

Wilfried Huchzermeyer

- *The Mother: A Short Biography*

Roland Vernon

- *Star in the East, Krishnamurti, the Invention of a Messiah*

Baird Spalding

- *Life and Teaching of the Masters of the Far East* (vols. I, II, and III)

RELATIONSHIPS

Richard Carlson

- *The Don't Sweat Guide for Couples*
- *Don't Sweat the Small Stuff in Love* (with Kristine Carlson)

Ralph Blum and Bronwyn Jones

- *Relationship Runes*

Krishnamurti

- *The Mirror of Relationship: Love, Sex and Chastity*

Pierre Teilhard de Chardin

- *On Love*
- *On Happiness*

Gerald Jampolsky

- *Love Is Letting Go of Fear*

Adam J. Jackson

- *The Ten Secrets of Abundant Love*

SEXUALITY

Nik Douglas and Penny Slinger

- *Sexual Secrets: The Alchemy of Ecstasy*

Translated by Sir Richard Burton and F. F. Arbuthnot

- *The Illustrated Kama Sutra: The Classic Eastern Love Texts*

Mantak Chia and William U. Wei

- *Sexual Reflexology*

Mantak Chia and Maneewan Chia

- *Healing Love Through the Tao: Cultivating Female Sexual Energy*

Mantak Chia and Douglas Abrams

- *The Multi-orgasmic Man*

CRYSTALS

Cassandra Eason

- *The Illustrated Directory of Healing Crystals*

Melody

- *Love Is in the Earth*

Judy Hall

- *The Crystal Bible: A Definitive Guide to Crystals*
- *Crystal Prescriptions*

Daya Sarai Chocron

- *Crystals and Gemstones: Balance Your Chakras and Your Life*

Michael Katz

- *Gemstone Energy Medicine: Healing Body, Mind and Spirit*
- *Wisdom of the Gemstone Guardians*

Martha Bochnik and Tommy Thompson

- *Holistic Wellness with Tachyons*

Pets

Kate Solisti-Mattelon

- *Conversations with Cat: An Uncommon Catalog of Feline Wisdom*
- *Conversations with Dog: An Uncommon Dogalog of Canine Wisdom*
- *Conversations with Horse: An Uncommon Dialog of Equine Wisdom*

Dawn Baumann Brunke

- *Animal Voices*

Spiritual Novels

Trina Paulus

- *Hope for the Flowers*

Dorothy Bryant

- *The Kin of Ata Are Waiting for You*

Hermann Hesse

- *Siddhartha*

Joan Brady

- *God on a Harley*

Susan Trott

- *The Holy Man*

Richard Bach

- *Jonathan Livingston Seagull*

- *The Bridge Across Forever*

- *One*

Astrid Lindgren

- *Pippi Longstocking*

John English

- *The Shift*

Health, Nutrition, and Beauty

Gabriel Cousens

- *Spiritual Nutrition and the Rainbow Diet*

Dick Gregory

- *Dick Gregory's Natural Diet for Folks Who Eat: Cooking with Mother Nature*

Arnold Ehret

- *Arnold Ehret's Mucusless Diet Healing System*

Dr. Peter J. D'Alamo and Catherine Whitney

- *Eat Right 4 Your Type*

William Dufty

- *Sugar Blues*

Patrick Quillin

- *Amazing Honey, Garlic & Vinegar*

Aromatherapy

Judith White

- *Home Spa*

Gill Farrer-Halls

- *The Aromatherapy Bible*

Judy Chapman

- *Aromatherapy: Recipes for Your Oil Burner*

Environment

Dr. Masaru Emoto

- *The Hidden Messages in Water*

- *Love Thyself: The Message from Water*

- *Water Crystal oracle cards*

Sun Bear

- *Black Dawn, Bright Day*

Web Sites

www.gematria.com (laser-enhanced food supplements)
www.gematria.net (water filter)
www.herbdoc.com (colon cleanse and general detox)
www.bachflower.com (the Bach flower remedies)
www.therawfoodsite.com (master cleanse)
www.healingdaily.com (food combining)
www.sprouting.com (sprouting in your kitchen)
www.americanbluegreen.com (healthy salt)
www.universal-tao.com (amaroli, urine therapy)

www.purpleplates.com (Tesla-inspired energy plates and fuel ionizer)
www.holisticbodytherapy.com (chakra sprays)
www.feelgoodstore.com (detox foot pads)
www.mytamiko.com (an entirely nonsurgical face-lift that works!)
www.manifestwellnessnow.com (paraben-free face and body products)
www.egyptianmagic.com (a phenomenal, natural healing skin cream)
www.gemisphere.com (the most powerful therapeutic gemstone necklaces)
www.terratachyon.com (more information on the beautiful, cosmic terra tachyon jewelry)
www.getyourmillionshere.com (to enhance abundance in your life)
www.whatsuponplanetearth.com (on the process of ascension)
www.mayanmajix.com (on the Mayan calendar)
www.simplydivinebotanicals.com (natural skin care)

MUSIC

David Bradstreet and Dan Gibson

- *Natural Stress Relief (Solitudes)*

Robert Haig Coxon, anything by him, but particularly:

- *Crystal Silence I, II, and III*

- *Crystal New Age Stories*

- *The Silent Path*

Wolfgang Amadeus Mozart, anything by him, particularly:

- Symphony no. 40; the *Jupiter* symphony

And any music or song with positive and joyous lyrics that makes you happy and lifts your spirit!

About the Author

Michelle Karén, M.A., D.F.Astrol.S., is French and Finnish. She was born in Helsinki on January 18 (Capricorn Sun, Leo Rising, and Virgo Moon). At the time of her birth, her father, a journalist, was translating horoscopes to supplement his family's income. Psychic and a medium as a child, Michelle realized astrology was her vocation when her father, upon returning from a trip to New York, brought her a copy of *Linda Goodman's Sun Signs*. She was fourteen.

Michelle studied linguistics and languages at Georgetown University for one year. At twenty-one, she obtained her master's degree in philosophy with honors at the University of Geneva, Switzerland, with a thesis titled "The Role of Archetypes in the Direction/Meaning of Human Existence in Carl Gustav Jung's Works."

Soon thereafter, she received her diploma from the Faculty of Astrological Studies in London, under the primary tutorship of Cordelia Mansall, D.F.Astrol.S. She then continued graduate studies in medieval horary astrology with Olivia Barclay and read extensively on her own while doing thousands of astrology readings in French and English.

Michelle also has a professional degree in yoga from the French yoga school École Française de Yoga du Sud-Est Méditerranée.

She studied acting for seven years at the Beverly Hills Playhouse, where the professional actors Jocelyn Jones, Allen Williams, Richard Lawson, Jeffrey Tambor, Gary Imhoff, and Robert Walden were her teachers. After performing in several feature films in Hollywood, Michelle continues her training at the Gene Bua Acting for Life Studio in Burbank, California. She also enjoys a modeling career and is the French voice of the Honda Canada navigation system, Bluetooth system, and Microsoft and Clarion auto PC, France. She has dubbed several films in

French and given her voice—among other roles—to William Hurt's girlfriend in *Rare Birds*.

A martial artist, Michelle initially was trained in Aikido, and is presently a member of the National Black Belt Club in Tae Kwon Do.

She also paints and volunteers with FreeArts, creating crafts with abused children.

For more than fifteen years, Michelle studied classical piano in the conservatories of Paris, Geneva, and at American University in Washington, D.C. She also worked privately with Russian concert pianist Alexis Golovine.

She is the author of eight books in French, Finnish, and English on astrology, living food nutrition, yoga, and spiritual novels, one of which won a literary prize in France in 1990. Her first book in English, *Aruna: An Initiation Tale,* was published in the United States in February 2006. Michelle wrote that story when she was twenty years old, following a vision she had.

Over the years, she has contributed to various newspapers and magazines in Europe and in the United States, and has written a monthly column for the *Sedona Journal*.

She has been the guest of many top radio and television shows in several countries. Sought internationally, she does readings in more than thirty countries. In March 2006, she was selected among world-famous practitioners to be the Exclusive Astrologer to the Stars at the Seventy-eighth Academy Awards in Hollywood.

Michelle has lived in Finland, England, France, Switzerland, Canada, and the United States. In 1995, she moved to Los Angeles, and shares her life with her very special Leo cat, Rafayel, whose name means "Only God Heals."

The uniqueness of Michelle's precise and in-depth readings, which employ astrology, tarot cards, numerology, and her psychic abilities, is that she doesn't just analyze the charts. She heals planetary energies, enabling significant life shifts to occur. She is reputed to be able to read people whom no one can read.

To find out more about Michelle Karén's work and/or contact her, you are most welcome to visit her Web site at www.michellekaren.com.

MICHELLE KARÉN'S PLANETARY REFERENCE GUIDE

	MONDAY	TUESDAY	WEDNESDAY	THURSDAY	FRIDAY	SATURDAY	SUNDAY
0–1 AM	Moon	Mars	Mercury	Jupiter	Venus	Saturn	The Sun
1–2 AM	Saturn	The Sun	The Moon	Mars	Mercury	Jupiter	Venus
2–3 AM	Jupiter	Venus	Saturn	The Sun	Moon	Mars	Mercury
3–4 AM	Mars	Mercury	Jupiter	Venus	Saturn	The Sun	Moon
4–5 AM	The Sun	Moon	Mars	Mercury	Jupiter	Venus	Saturn
5–6 AM	Venus	Saturn	The Sun	Moon	Mars	Mercury	Jupiter
6–7 AM	Mercury	Jupiter	Venus	Saturn	The Sun	Moon	Mars
7–8 AM	Moon	Mars	Mercury	Jupiter	Venus	Saturn	The Sun
8–9 AM	Saturn	The Sun	The Moon	Mars	Mercury	Jupiter	Venus
9–10 AM	Jupiter	Venus	Saturn	The Sun	Moon	Mars	Mercury
10–11 AM	Mars	Mercury	Jupiter	Venus	Saturn	The Sun	Moon
11–12 AM	The Sun	Moon	Mars	Mercury	Jupiter	Venus	Saturn
12–1 PM	Venus	Saturn	The Sun	Moon	Mars	Mercury	Jupiter
1–2 PM	Mercury	Jupiter	Venus	Saturn	The Sun	Moon	Mars
2–3 PM	Moon	Mars	Mercury	Jupiter	Venus	Saturn	The Sun
3–4 PM	Saturn	The Sun	The Moon	Mars	Mercury	Jupiter	Venus
4–5 PM	Jupiter	Venus	Saturn	The Sun	Moon	Mars	Mercury
5–6 PM	Mars	Mercury	Jupiter	Venus	Saturn	The Sun	Moon
6–7 PM	The Sun	Moon	Mars	Mercury	Jupiter	Venus	Saturn
7–8 PM	Venus	Saturn	The Sun	Moon	Mars	Mercury	Jupiter
8–9 PM	Mercury	Jupiter	Venus	Saturn	The Sun	Moon	Mars
9–10 PM	Moon	Mars	Mercury	Jupiter	Venus	Saturn	The Sun
10–11 PM	Saturn	The Sun	The Moon	Mars	Mercury	Jupiter	Venus
11–12 PM	Jupiter	Venus	Saturn	The Sun	Moon	Mars	Mercury

0. (Pluto): power, sexuality, and passion

1. (the Sun): independence and creativity

2. (the Moon): intuition and sensitivity

3. (Jupiter): traveling, luck, philosophical, or philanthropic endeavors

4. (Uranus): change, freedom, and rebellion

5. (Mercury): communication

6. (Venus): love

7. (Neptune): meditation, channeling, healing, music, art, and yoga

8. (Saturn): discipline, focus, and anything requiring hard work

9. (Mars): energy and courage

When meeting someone for the first time, add their age and yours at the time of the meeting, reduce to a simple digit and see what planet dominates your meeting and why you came together. You can also add your day and month of birth with their day and month of birth.

Schedule meetings that require feeling and imagination on Mondays (the Moon); energy on Tuesdays (Mars); communication on Wednesdays (Mercury); a broadening of horizons on Thursdays (Jupiter); romance, peace, or reconciliation on Fridays (Venus); discipline on Saturdays (Saturn); and creativity or play on Sundays (the Sun).

When someone calls or e-mails, note the time the message was sent and check which planet was dominant at that moment. It will give you an indication of the person's real intentions.